SPECTRUM®

Language Arts

Grade 8

Published by Spectrum®
an imprint of Carson Dellosa Education
Greensboro, NC

Spectrum®

An imprint of Carson Dellosa Education

Send all inquiries to:
Carson Dellosa Education
P.O. Box 35665
Greensboro, NC 27425

Printed in the USA
03-300207784

ISBN 978-1-4838-1212-0

Table of Contents Grade 8

Chapter 1 Grammar

Parts of Speech

Sentences

Chapter 2 Mechanics

Capitalization

Table of Contents, continued

NAME ______________________

Chapter 1 Grammar
Lesson 1.1 Common and Proper Nouns

Common nouns name people, places, things, and ideas.

People: driver, musician, brother, pediatrician, firefighter
Places: tunnel, courthouse, zoo, backyard, desert, bedroom
Things: desk, helicopter, dictionary, microphone, pine tree
Ideas: nervousness, environmentalism, justice, religion

Proper nouns name specific people, places, and things. Proper nouns are capitalized. For proper nouns that consist of more than one word, capitalize the first letter of each important word.

People: Aunt Lucy, General Eisenhower, Juan, Ms. Braga
Places: New Mexico, People's Republic of China, Lake Michigan
Things: Eiffel Tower, Baja Bill's Burritos, Declaration of Independence
Ideas: Hinduism, Marxism

Rewrite It

Rewrite each sentence below. Replace the common nouns shown in boldface with proper nouns.

1. I went to visit **my aunt** in **the city** last summer.

   ____

2. On **a certain day of the week**, we took a taxi to **the museum**, where the works of **an artist** were being exhibited.

   ____

3. We stopped at **the street where the museum was located** and paid our fare.

   ____

4. As we exited the cab, I spotted **the tallest building in the city**.

   ____

5. Inside the museum, I realized I had left my **smart phone** in the taxi!

   ____

6. We spoke with **the security guard**, and he was kind enough to call **the cab company**.

   ____

7. As we waited, I took a moment to admire a **specific religion's** tapestry.

   ____

8. At last, we were told **the cab driver** had my phone, but he was now in **a suburb of the city**.

   ____

9. We arranged to meet him at **a restaurant** later in the day, and I got my phone back.

   ____

NAME ______________________

Lesson 1.1 Common and Proper Nouns

Proof It

Correct the mistakes in the use of common and proper nouns using proofreading marks.

/ = lowercase letter
≡ = capitalize letter

1. The westide metropolitan library will host a Fundraising Event this Saturday.
2. The Major Religions of China are confucianism, taoism, and buddhism.
3. The Bill Of Rights are the first ten amendments of the United States constitution.
4. Elizabeth and her Cousin traveled to lake Ontario during june and july.
5. NASA Scientists are developing a robot that can explore mercury's surface.
6. Most of the arctic ocean is covered by Sea Ice during Winter.
7. Tony allen is a Nigerian Drummer who currently lives in Paris.
8. June 14 is national flag day.
9. Cane Toads in australia are an example of an Invasive Species.
10. On New Years eve each year, officer Markley visits his Nieces in New York city.
11. The Beauty Bouquet Flower Shop is at the Corner of Fourth street and Wilson boulevard.
12. The north sea is located between great Britain and the Nations of Scandinavia.
13. On fridays, my whole family gets together to play Cards and Board Games, like Monopoly and Scrabble.
14. Some of the Founding Fathers wrote about Freedom and the Pursuit of Happiness.
15. The statue of liberty and the Grand Canyon are well known United States Landmarks.

Try It

Write a paragraph about your favorite author or actor. Use at least six common and six proper nouns correctly.

____

____

____

____

____

____

____

____

NAME ______________________

Lesson 1.2 Collective and Abstract Nouns

Collective nouns are used to describe groups of specific animals, people, or things.

A group of birds is a *flock*.
A group of ships is a *fleet*.
A group of judges is a *panel*.

A collective noun refers to a single group, so it acts as a singular noun. When a collective noun is plural (refers to more than one group), it acts as a plural noun.

Incorrect: The *flock fly* south for the winter.
Correct: The *flock flies* south for the winter.
Correct: The *flocks fly* south for the winter.

Abstract nouns describe ideas rather than people, places, or things that can be perceived with the five senses.

pleasure   grumpiness   inability   contentment

Complete It

Circle the verb in each sentence that correctly completes the sentence.

1. Next week, the committee (decide, decides) whether to approve the new bike lane.
2. A swarm of bees (chase, chases) a foolish young cub that wanted their honey.
3. Bunches of grapes (rot, rots) inside a misplaced crate.
4. This pair of shoes (hurts, hurt) my feet and (needs, need) to be returned to the store.
5. My staff (enjoys, enjoy) our weekly outings to a nearby restaurant for lunch.

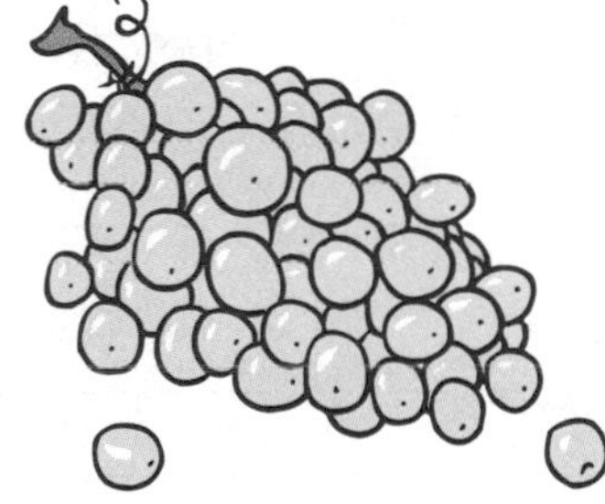

6. The huge bouquets of daisies (fill, fills) the room with a bright, fresh scent.
7. A team of oxen (wait, waits) inside the barn, ready to be hitched to the wagon.
8. A pack of wolves (startle, startles) the sheep.
9. The panel of judges (award, awards) blue ribbons to the top performers.
10. Whenever the National Anthem begins, the audiences (stand, stands) at attention.
11. The fleet of ships (leave, leaves) at dawn.
12. Swarms of flies (cloud, clouds) the air above the pig sty.

NAME ______________________

Lesson 1.2 Collective and Abstract Nouns

Identify It

Circle the abstract nouns in the sentences below.

1. My uncle is convinced that the key to happiness is eating good food.
2. Louis plans to major in agriculture at the University of Minnesota.
3. Early childhood is often a time of freedom and exploration.
4. Your mathematical capabilities never cease to amaze me.
5. Can intelligence be measured accurately by testing?
6. Sometimes the truth is harder to believe than the reality.
7. The process of learning how to program a computer may be daunting.
8. What type of shoes do I need to buy for ballet class?
9. Mr. Thompson's greatest pleasure is spending the afternoon reading.
10. As the students continued to misbehave, Ms. Yang's patience was tested.
11. Imagine my delight when Grandpa Hennessy finally arrived from Ireland.
12. Never ignore the opportunity to help someone who is in trouble.
13. Hiro's dedication was recognized with an award given at the banquet.
14. My fear of snakes kept me from attending the most recent field trip.
15. Yoko demonstrated her maturity by being the first to apologize.

Try It

Collective nouns for specific animals are often unusual. Use a dictionary or the Internet to look up the collective noun for each type of animal and use it in a sentence.

1. crows: ______________________
2. baboons: ______________________
3. vultures: ______________________
4. stingrays: ______________________
5. raccoons: ______________________
6. foxes: ______________________
7. emus: ______________________
8. eagles: ______________________

NAME ______________________________

Lesson 1.3 Plurals and Possessives

Although plural and possessive nouns often sound similar, they are spelled differently and have different meanings.

> Plural noun: The *novelists* gathered in Chicago for a conference.
> Singular possessive noun: The *novelist's* main character traveled to Chicago.
> Plural possessive noun: The *novelists'* meeting was postponed until next month.

Proof It

Use proofreaders' marks to correct the mistakes in plural and possessive nouns in the sentences below.

1. Deserts' cover about 20 percent of Earths surfaces.
2. Harsh conditions mean that deserts are home to animals with special adaptations.
3. Deserts inhabitant's include lizards, snakes, fennec foxes, and scorpions.
4. Our planets largest habitat is the marine biome.
5. Biomes relationships are vital to Earth's well-being.
6. Hippo's, rhino's, and lion's make their homes in grassland biomes.
7. The tundras extreme cold makes it a poor place for vegetation to flourish.
8. One reason that forest biomes' are important to Earth is tree's ability to absorb carbon dioxide.
9. Hot, semiarid, coastal, and cold are the four types of desert's.
10. Mosquitoes ability to live in a tundra biome surprises many people.
11. Tropical forest's, such as rain forests, produce plants that are not found anywhere else in the world.
12. A coral reefs many structures provide homes to countless sea creature's.
13. The worlds youngest biome is the Arctic tundra.
14. An invasive animals' behavior can eventually affect more than one biome.

NAME ______________________

Lesson 1.3 Plurals and Possessives

Rewrite It

Rewrite each phrase below to make it a plural, a singular possessive, or a plural possessive.

1. the backpacks belonging to the girls ______________________
2. the tail of the raccoon ______________________
3. the experiment belonging to the scientists ______________________
4. the baseball glove of Roberto ______________________
5. more than one sweater ______________________
6. the cat belonging to the Browns ______________________
7. the covers of the books ______________________
8. the painting of Charles ______________________
9. more than one strawberry ______________________
10. the moon belonging to the planet ______________________
11. the leaves of the trees ______________________
12. the buttons of the remote control ______________________

Try It

Write a sentence for each word in the box.

trains	train's	trains'	birds	bird's	birds'

1. ______________________
2. ______________________
3. ______________________
4. ______________________
5. ______________________
6. ______________________

Lesson 1.4 Appositives

An **appositive** is a noun or phrase that renames another noun in a sentence. The appositive offers more information about the noun.

Lucille, my great aunt in Texas, owns a small art gallery.
The phrase *my great aunt in Texas* is an appositive that renames *Lucille.*

When the appositive is nonessential, or not necessary to the sentence, it should have a comma before and after it. In the example above, you can remove the appositive, and the sentence still makes sense.

When the appositive is essential to the meaning of the sentence, do not set it off with commas. In the following sentence, removing the appositive *Jane Austen* would make the sentence much less clear.

The author *Jane Austen* wrote six novels.

Identify It
In each sentence below, underline the appositive. On the line, write **E** if it is essential and **NE** if it is nonessential.

1. China, one of the world's most populated countries, is one of Earth's oldest civilizations. ______
2. Beijing, China's capital city, is also known as Peking. ______
3. Mount Everest, Earth's tallest mountain, lies on the border of China and neighboring Nepal. ______
4. The bicycle, China's main form of transportation, is a speedy and energy-efficient way to travel. ______
5. China is home to the giant panda, an animal that survives primarily on bamboo. ______
6. China's neighbor Mongolia shares the Gobi Desert with China. ______
7. Students around the world are currently learning China's official language, Mandarin Chinese. ______
8. China, a country whose history is divided into dynasties, has a communist government today. ______
9. The Chinese, talented inventors, created things like paper, compasses, porcelain, and silk. ______
10. The Chinese leader Mao Tse-tung was instrumental in China's shift to a communist government. ______

Lesson 1.4 Appositives

Complete It

There is an appositive in each sentence below. On the line, write **E** if it is essential and **NE** if it is nonessential, and add commas where necessary.

1. Ian my brother's best friend is moving to California in the fall. ______
2. Families from all over the county will be attending the summer's best entertainment the Highland County Fair. ______
3. Russian my mother's first language is difficult to learn because it uses a different alphabet. ______
4. Some athletes increase the amount of complex carbohydrates or starches they consume before an event. ______
5. An undersea earthquake can cause tsunamis or massive waves. ______
6. The artist Claude Monet was especially known for his paintings of water lilies. ______
7. Alina whistled for Peter her new Jack Russell terrier and fed him his dinner. ______
8. Next weekend, we'll be going to my cousin Josh's bar mitzvah the Jewish ceremony in which a boy becomes a man. ______
9. The library does not have any available copies of Darren's favorite book, *Al Capone Does My Shirts*. ______
10. The dream that Quinn had since she was a little girl to meet tennis legend Venus Williams in person was finally coming true. ______
11. The British doctor Edward Jenner created the smallpox vaccine and saved many lives. ______
12. Each Halloween Mia loves to read the chilling stories of horror writer Edgar Allan Poe. ______

Try It

Write four sentences that contain appositives. Write **E** or **NE** after each to tell whether you used an essential or nonessential appositive.

1. ____
2. ____
3. ____
4. ____

NAME ______________________

Lesson 1.5 Personal Pronouns

A **pronoun** is a word used in place of a noun. A **subject pronoun** can be used as the subject of a sentence. It can be singular (*I, you, he, she, it*) or plural (*we, you, they*).

They canceled the meeting because of bad weather.

An **object pronoun** is the object of a verb or a preposition. It can also be singular (*me, you, him, her, it*) or plural (*us, you, them*).

Please give *him* my thanks for the lovely bouquet.

A **possessive pronoun** shows possession. Singular possessive pronouns are *my, your, his, her,* and *its,* and plural possessive pronouns are *our, your,* and *their.*

Your teeth should be brushed at least twice a day.

Some singular and plural possessive pronouns can stand alone: *mine, yours, his, hers, its, ours, theirs.*

The pickup truck was *ours.* Wilma donated *hers* to the church bazaar.

Complete It

Circle the pronouns that correctly complete the sentences.

1. (Mine, My) friend Kyoko ordered butterfly eggs for (our, ours) science experiment.
2. (They, Theirs) soon arrived, safely shipped inside (their, hers) sealed container.
3. (We, Ours) opened (it, hers) to find the eggs lying in rows on a leaf.
4. Kyoko lifted the leaf from (it, its) box and placed (it, its) inside an aquarium.
5. The aquarium was (her, hers), so (I, me) prepared the sugar water.
6. In just a couple of days, the caterpillars hatched and began wriggling (theirs, their) little bodies.
7. (We, Our) fed (theirs, them) every day, and before long, (them, they) had grown much bigger.
8. Kyoko called (me, mine) one day with exciting news: some of (they, them) had attached (theirs, their) bodies to twigs.
9. (My, Mine) mother used (her, hers) camera to record the process.
10. A caterpillar sheds (its, their) striped skin and hardens to form a chrysalis.
11. (You, Your) would be amazed by (them, its) beauty.
12. When (it, its) finally splits open, a butterfly emerges and spreads (it, its) wings.

NAME ______________________

Lesson 1.5 Personal Pronouns

Rewrite It

The sentences below contain errors in pronoun usage. Rewrite each sentence to correct the errors.

1. Mine Aunt Helga was married last week to hers best friend.

   ____

2. Frogs enlarge them vocal sacs to make sounds that will attract a mate.

   ____

3. Them shipped theirs automobile overseas so its would be waiting for they in England.

   ____

4. Henry painted yours portrait, framed it, and wrapped them as a gift.

   ____

5. The St. Louis Cardinals played they last home game yesterday.

   ____

6. Its is the largest hydroelectric dam anywhere near ours city.

   ____

7. Theirs dog stands on it front paws and, to mine amazement, takes a few steps.

   ____

8. The library stores thems down in the basement, so us needs to find the stairs.

   ____

9. I handed hims mine science textbook and told hims to open them to page 135.

   ____

10. Yours is on the top shelf, and mines is below it on the second shelf.

    ____

Try It

Write sentences containing each type of pronoun.

1. subject pronoun: ______________________

   ____

2. object pronoun: ______________________

   ____

3. possessive pronoun that comes before a noun: ______________________

   ____

4. possessive pronoun that stands alone: ______________________

   ____

NAME ______________________

Lesson 1.6 Intensive and Reflexive Pronouns

Intensive and **reflexive pronouns** are pronouns that end in *-self* or *-selves*. The way the pronoun is used determines whether it is intensive or reflexive.

Intensive pronouns usually appear right after the subject of a sentence. They emphasize the subject.

> You *yourself* will pull up the damaged sod and reseed the area.
> Johan *himself* stacked the boxes and cleaned out the garage.

Reflexive pronouns appear elsewhere in the sentence and refer back to the subject.

> I gave *myself* a pat on the back for completing the project.
> The monkeys played among *themselves* while we watched.

Identify It

Identify whether the boldface word in each sentence is an intensive or reflexive pronoun. Write **I** on the line if it is intensive, and write **R** if it is reflexive. Then, underline the noun the pronoun refers to.

1. ______ Mr. Henkins explained that the garden **itself** would sit on a hill above the pond.
2. ______ After purchasing their tickets at the box office window, Madeline and Sonja bought **themselves** some popcorn and bottled water at the concession stand.
3. ______ For safety reasons, a roofer should always attach **himself** by rope to a well secured hook on the rooftop.
4. ______ The rocking chairs **themselves** will be hand delivered by my brother and uncle.

5. ______ The raccoon fed **itself** midstream while balanced on a rock.
6. ______ Before speaking with the principal, I reminded **myself** to take a deep breath and remain calm.
7. ______ My family and I treat **ourselves** to a pizza once in a while.
8. ______ With the day's last light illuminating its peak, the mountain presented **itself** as a lone beacon in the approaching dark.
9. ______ At tonight's meeting, Laurie **herself** will explain why the bill did not pass.
10. ______ Please allow **yourself** plenty of time to complete the project.
11. ______ Sterling **himself** would have a hard time believing the mess we've made.
12. ______ The kittens saw **themselves** in the mirror and tried to play with their reflections.

NAME ______________________

Lesson 1.6 Intensive and Reflexive Pronouns

Complete It

Complete each sentence below with a reflexive or an intensive pronoun.

1. Kyle and Luiz ______________ worked all summer to build the two-story tree house.
2. Shawn scooped up a spoonful of jam and finished making ______________ a sandwich.
3. Please go downstairs and get the laundry ______________ .
4. I ______________ plan to spend the morning sanding and staining this chair.
5. Moments before the first bell rings, the students at Lincoln Jr. High gather ______________ at the front entrance.
6. The dishwasher ______________ will need to be installed by a plumber.
7. Deep inside the cave, a colony of bats can keep ______________ well hidden throughout the day.
8. Grandma Tang ______________ collects snow globes and salt shakers.
9. Last winter, my brother and I built ______________ an igloo and camped in it overnight.
10. Coach Lewis told his players, "You ______________ must dig down deep to find the strength to win!"
11. Genes ______________ are arranged on twisted strings of chemicals called DNA.
12. Hiroshi ______________ was born in Japan and raised as a Buddhist.
13. The MacGregor twins captured ______________ on video rapping together.
14. A cat can give ______________ a bath with its tongue.
15. On Wednesdays I have band practice, but I also practice guitar by ______________ for an hour each day.

Try It

Write a short paragraph describing your proudest accomplishment, including what others thought of it. Use at least two reflexive pronouns and two intensive pronouns in your paragraph.

____

____

____

____

____

____

NAME ______________________________

Lesson 1.7 Indefinite Pronouns

Indefinite pronouns are pronouns that do not refer to a specific noun.

another	anybody	anyone	anything	each	everybody	everyone
everything	nobody	no one	nothing	one	somebody	someone

Does *anybody* know where the post office is?
No one chooses the green balloon.
Someone left a note on the front door.

Most indefinite pronouns are singular, but the following are plural:

both few many others several

Many of my friends are going to the play on Saturday.
Both landed at the airfield on the west side of town.

Some indefinite pronouns, such as *all, any, most, none*, and *some*, are either singular or plural, depending on their meaning in the sentence.

Any eligible child is encouraged to take part in the contest.
Any of these children are eligible to take part in the contest.

Proof It

Use proofreading marks to correct any errors in verb usage. If the sentence is correct, place a checkmark on the line.

ℯ = deletes a word or letter
^ = inserts a word or letter

1. ______ Both of the children reads for about an hour before bed each night.
2. ______ None of the classes is going to the planetarium this semester.
3. ______ Despite the rain, everybody stays in line, each person equally determined to get a ticket to the show.
4. ______ Few of the trees in the orchard is producing apples at this point in the season.
5. ______ If someone phones about the gift, please don't say anything to my mother.
6. ______ Each of the horses are provided with a separate stall inside the barn.
7. ______ Most of the cupcakes is being saved for the party at school tomorrow.
8. ______ Everyone heading out to pan for gold in the stream need to bring along spare clothes.
9. ______ I can hear thunder in the distance, so please be sure all the windows is shut.
10. ______ Several of Zander's teammates are heading into the locker room.

Lesson 1.7 Indefinite Pronouns

Complete It

Complete each sentence by adding an indefinite pronoun. More than one indefinite pronoun may work, but be sure the pronoun you choose makes sense and agrees in number with the verb.

1. The game is rather simple, so ______________ can explain the rules quickly to a new player.
2. The lights are off, and the driveway is empty, so most likely ______________ is home.
3. ______________ of the people in my yoga class have attended for several years.
4. ______________ soldier who leaves the base without permission is considered AWOL.
5. Brandon can't decide between two different brands of cell phone, because ______________ provides an equal number of pros and cons.
6. At the top of the silo, ______________ chickadees take turns perching at the highest point.
7. ______________ of the fence is rotted and falling apart, so ______________ will need to make repairs.
8. ______________ who knows how to restring a violin will be eligible for the position as music teacher's assistant.
9. ______________ child I don't know is waving to my little sister.
10. ______________ about the new art studio is making Maurice excited for the school year to start.
11. Hannah dropped the box of dishes, but miraculously ______________ of the plates are broken.
12. Only a ______________ of the sled dogs are going to be chosen to take part in the Iditarod.

Try It

Write a persuasive paragraph convincing others to try your favorite food. Include at least five indefinite pronouns in your paragraph.

____

____

____

____

____

____

NAME ______________________

Lesson 1.8 Pronoun Shifts

A **pronoun shift** happens when a writer changes pronouns in the middle of a sentence or paragraph. This can confuse the reader.

In this example, the writer changes from *we* (first-person plural) to *you* (second-person singular):

Incorrect: If *we* want to learn to play hockey, *you* should sign up for the beginners' team at the rec center.

Correct: If *we* want to learn to play hockey, *we* should sign up for the beginners' team at the rec center.

In this example, there is no agreement between *weeds* (a plural noun) and *it* (third-person singular pronoun).

Incorrect: The *weeds* growing in the garden are a nuisance because *it* takes nutrients from the vegetable plants.

Correct: The *weeds* growing in the garden are a nuisance because *they* take nutrients from the vegetable plants.

Identify It

In the sentences below, underline each pronoun and the noun it refers to. If the sentence is correct, make a checkmark on the line. If a pronoun shift occurs, make an **X** on the line.

1. ______ Caroline doesn't want to try sushi, because you can get food poisoning from eating raw fish.
2. ______ If the students don't think the new policy is fair, he or she should tell the principal.
3. ______ Layla's parents are expecting their new refrigerator to be delivered this afternoon.
4. ______ After we arrived at the theater, we realized that you should come at least half an hour early to find a decent parking space.
5. ______ The doctor gave the intern a short lecture on the kind of behavior they expected.
6. ______ An artist must always keep experimenting with new ideas and techniques in their artwork.
7. ______ Kris and Antonio wanted to skateboard at the park after finishing our dinner.
8. ______ As long as you study, you should pass the exam with no problems.

NAME ______________________________

Lesson 1.8 Pronoun Shifts

Complete It

Circle the pronoun that correctly completes the sentence.

1. The grubs were destroying the garden, but Mom chose not to use pesticides to kill (it, them).
2. Maureen used fresh clams in the chowder because (its, they) have more flavor than canned ones.
3. Della's new assistant only began work a week ago, but (she, you) is a quick learner.
4. If a child wants to ride the roller coaster, (they, he or she) must be 48 inches tall.
5. The rocking chair is missing paint from (its, their) left armrest.
6. The photographer quickly kneeled as (you, he) attempted to capture an interesting view of the couple dancing.
7. The hospital board is meeting on Tuesday to approve (its, your) new budget for the year.
8. Although the dancers had performed eight nights in a row, (she, they) were still filled with enthusiasm and energy.
9. Most people choose to visit the amusement park on weekends, so I guess (they, we) don't mind crowds.
10. Roberto and Dani are planning to go to the van Gogh exhibit at the museum if (you, they) can still get tickets.
11. If a student is dissatisfied with a grade, (you, he or she) should talk to the teacher.
12. Dmitri's teammates cheered for him as (he, they) rounded the bases.

Try It

On the lines below, write a short description of a time you were a member of a team. Circle each pronoun you use, and proofread your paragraph to be sure there are no pronoun shifts.

____

____

____

____

____

____

____

____

NAME ______________________________

Review Chapter 1 Lessons 1–8

Review: Common and Proper Nouns, Collective and Abstract Nouns, Plurals and Possessives, Appositives

Identify the underlined word using the key in the box. Write your answer on the line following each underlined word.

a. common noun	**b.** proper noun	**c.** collective noun	**d.** abstract noun

1. It was hard to know how to handle my mother's sorrow ______ when Grandma Carol ______ passed away last February ______ .
2. Ella's visit to Latta Plantation ______ in North Carolina sparked some questions ______ about slavery ______ and the Civil War ______ .
3. A convoy ______ of army trucks passed us on the highway ______ , and I felt a sudden gratefulness ______ for the sacrifice ______ that American soldiers make.
4. Aziz stared in delight ______ at the flock ______ of seagulls and quickly snapped a series ______ of photographs ______ with his new camera.

In the sentences below, circle singular possessives, underline plurals, and underline plural possessives twice.

1. The telescope's lens has a small smear on it, but I can wipe it off with one of these microfiber towels.
2. The class's trip to the planetarium includes Mr. Hahn's lecture, two experiments, and lunch.
3. The comets' tails are made of dust and gases.
4. Jupiter's largest moons are Io, Europa, Ganymede, and Callisto.
5. Venus, the second planet from the sun, was named for the ancient Romans' goddess of love and beauty.

One sentence above contains an appositive. Write the appositive on the line below.

____

Review

NAME ______________________

Review Chapter 1 Lessons 1–8

Review: Personal Pronouns, Intensive and Reflexive Pronouns, Indefinite Pronouns, Pronoun Shifts

Underline the word that best completes each sentence below.

1. Each of the chemicals (produce, produces) toxic gases.
2. The children amused (ourselves, themselves) in the backyard while (their, our) parents discussed the school's new policies.
3. Anyone who (is, are) interested in learning to write science fiction (are, is) welcome to join us.
4. Both the chickadees and the sparrows (has, have) visited the new feeder.
5. Jorge (himself, myself) has three paintings in the new exhibit at the Winthrop Gallery.
6. Several students on the tennis team (represent, represents) the school in the finals.
7. If we don't want to have to wait at the restaurant, (you, we) should call ahead.
8. I attempted to explain (itself, myself) to Mr. Weber, but apparently he was very upset.
9. Grandpa and (I, me) are planning to camp at three national parks this summer.
10. Although Rex and Ruby play together well, (they, them) do get a little wild sometimes.

Identify the underlined pronoun in each sentence as a subject pronoun (**SP**), object pronoun (**OP**), or possessive pronoun (**PP**).

1. ______ <u>Her</u> composition will be performed in front of an audience of more than 300.
2. ______ Destiny asked <u>them</u> to make a gluten-free batch of muffins.
3. ______ <u>We</u> watch the fireworks each year at Uncle Phillip's house.
4. ______ Peyton just put <u>something</u> in the shed.
5. ______ <u>Our</u> family reunion is scheduled to take place at Long Creek Park.
6. ______ Dad paid <u>us</u> to rake the yard and dispose of the leaves.
7. ______ <u>Someone</u> sent me flowers on my birthday!
8. ______ I'm hoping to earn some money by selling some of <u>my</u> old books online.

Review

NAME ______________________

Lesson 1.9 Action Verbs

Action verbs tell the action of the sentence. The action can be physical or mental.

Ryder and Myles *made* Stella a cheese sandwich for lunch. (physical action)
The squirrel *leaped* onto the fence. (physical action)

I *wish* you could come to dinner with us. (mental action)
Nico *wondered* where he had left his sweatshirt. (mental action)

Identify It

Circle the action verbs in the sentences below. Then, categorize them as either physical or mental actions, and write them under the appropriate headings.

1. J. K. Rowling wrote the wildly popular series of Harry Potter books.
2. In 2008, Hillary Rodham Clinton ran for the Democratic nomination for president.
3. Martin Luther King, Jr. believed in equality and justice for all Americans.
4. Zoey expects that her classmates will elect her class president next Tuesday.
5. Satellites move in orbits around planets.
6. The woodpecker pecked a hole in the old oak tree next to the garage.
7. Female athletes from Saudi Arabia competed in the Olympics for the first time in 2012.
8. Aaron noticed the battery light flashing on his camera.
9. Dr. Abdul remembered something unusual in Becca's test results.
10. William the Conqueror, a Frenchman, invaded England in 1066.
11. Jogging burns about eight calories per minute.
12. Diego recognizes more than 50 birdcalls.

Physical Actions	Mental Actions
______________________	______________________
______________________	______________________
______________________	______________________
______________________	______________________
______________________	______________________
______________________	
______________________	
______________________	
______________________	

Lesson 1.9 Action Verbs

Solve It

Make a list of the action verbs you find in the sentences below. Find each verb in the word search puzzle.

1. Jazmin grilled eggplant in a marinade of olive oil, garlic, and salt.
2. Anton forgot the loaf of crusty French bread.
3. Mr. Rinaldi baked a berry crumble with fresh blackberries, blueberries, and raspberries.
4. Linh dropped a cup full of sparkling cranberry juice.
5. Our sweet golden retriever, Harley, stole a hot dog off the picnic table!
6. Molly wanted blue cheese dressing on her salad.
7. I knew that the burgers were meatless.
8. Dylan ate a baked sweet potato with sour cream, green onions, and cheese.
9. Addison decided that Japanese wasabi is much too spicy for her.
10. A sparrow nibbled at the crumbs on the patio.

Action verbs: ______________________

____

____

____

____

____

____

____

f	k	o	e	n	z	k	n	e	w
f	o	r	g	o	t	h	a	q	m
m	r	j	r	a	u	e	v	s	k
i	l	r	i	w	c	w	a	d	b
y	n	b	l	b	e	a	t	e	u
s	t	o	l	e	d	n	j	c	d
z	q	t	e	j	v	t	t	i	e
y	f	d	d	e	c	e	x	d	k
d	r	o	p	p	e	d	s	e	a
d	e	l	b	b	i	n	g	d	b

Try It

Choose two words from each column in the lists you made on page 23, and write your own sentences.

1. ______________________
2. ______________________
3. ______________________
4. ______________________

NAME ____________________

Lesson 1.10 Subject-Verb Agreement

Subject-verb agreement means that the verb must agree in number with the subject of the sentence. If the subject is singular, use a singular verb. If the subject is plural, use a plural verb.

The girl *flips* the pages of the book. The girls *flip* the pages of the book.

When a sentence contains a compound subject connected by the word and, use a plural verb.

The truck **and** the bus *stop* at the railroad tracks.

When a sentence contains a compound subject connected by the words **or** or **nor**, use a verb that agrees with the subject that is closer to the verb.

Neither the teacher **nor** her students *saw* that movie.

Either the athletes **or** the coach *plans* the potluck.

If the subject and the verb are separated by a word or words, be sure that the verb still agrees with the subject.

The *scanner*, as well as the printer, *is* broken.

Identify It

In each item, underline the correct form of the verb in parentheses.

1. Jaya (is, are) very talented at identifying animal tracks.
2. She and her mom (goes, go) hiking in a nearby nature preserve at least once a week.
3. Deer (stop, stops) near the edge of the pond to sip the cool water.
4. Jaya quickly (identify, identifies) their tracks.
5. Neither Jaya nor Mrs. Sharma (know, knows) what kind of animal gnawed on the bark of a tree bedside the trail.
6. There is a shuffling sound in the bushes, and a chipmunk, in addition to several blue jays, (peeks, peek) out before scurrying away.
7. Beavers (has, have) constructed a dam of tightly stacked twigs and branches.
8. Possums and raccoons (leave, leaves) behind scat that allows Jaya and her mother to identify them.
9. The animal track guide (is, are) scuffed and worn from frequent use.
10. Either a coyote or some neighborhood dogs (have, has) passed this way.

NAME ______________________

Lesson 1.10 Subject-Verb Agreement

Complete It

Complete each sentence below with the correct form of the verb in parentheses.

1. Boston cream pie (to be) ______________ the official dessert of the state of Massachusetts.
2. Fort Knox, located in Kentucky, (hold) ______________ most of the gold that the U.S. federal government owns.
3. Both Maine and Massachusetts (claim) ______________ the chickadee as their state bird.
4. Neither New Mexico nor Arizona (have) ______________ any ocean coastline.
5. Alligators (live) ______________ in many bodies of water throughout the state of Florida, which is why they are Florida's state reptile.
6. The world's oldest living things, a stand of bristlecone pine trees, (make) ______________ their home in California.
7. America's longest Main Street (run) ______________ through Island Park, Idaho.
8. Four states, New Hampshire, New Jersey, New York, and New Mexico, (have) ______________ the word *new* in their names.
9. Either Hawaii or Vermont (to be) ______________ known as the healthiest state to live in.
10. Idaho (grow) ______________ more potatoes than any other state.

Try It

Write a paragraph about states you have visited or would like to visit. Circle each verb you use, and underline the subject it agrees with.

____

____

____

____

____

____

____

____

NAME ______________________________

Lesson 1.11 Helping and Linking Verbs

Helping verbs help to form the main verb in a sentence. They add additional detail to the verb, such as clarifying time or possibility. The primary helping verbs are forms of the verbs *be, have,* and *do*. They are the most common helping verbs.

I ***had*** *hoped* you would arrive before the show started.
The robins ***were*** *singing* this morning as Martin left for work.
Did you *remember* to turn off the lights?

Other helping verbs are *can, could, will, would, may, might, shall, should,* and *must.*

The painters ***can*** *spread* drop cloths over the furniture.
The crew ***might*** *cancel* the flight due to mechanical problems.

Linking verbs connect a subject to a noun or adjective. They do not express an action.

The most common linking verbs are forms of the verb *to be,* such as *is, are, was, were, been,* and *am.*

Nevaeh *is* the highest ranked student on the chess team.
Most turtles *are* shy and will quickly withdraw inside their shells.

Other common linking verbs relate to the five senses (*smell, look, taste, feel, sound*) or a state of being (*appear, seem, become, grow, remain*).

The rocks *feel* slimy when they are submerged in water.
The children *grew* restless waiting for the speaker to arrive.

Identify It

In each sentence below, circle the verb. On the line, write **LV** or **HV** to identify it as a linking verb or helping verb.

1. ______ The mysterious statues of Easter Island have fascinated scholars for almost 300 years.
2. ______ The giant statues lining the coasts seem like guardians protecting the island.
3. ______ Do you know what the local people call Easter Island?
4. ______ Rapa Nui is the island's name in the local language.
5. ______ At first, historians could only guess how these massive statues got there.
6. ______ Most scholars have concluded that the native people rolled the statues on logs.
7. ______ The statues weigh many tons, so how could the people stand them up?
8. ______ The answer might not surprise you.
9. ______ Ropes, levers, and ramps were used to hoist a statue into an upright position.
10. ______ Religion is the most likely reason the native people built the statues.

NAME ______________________

Lesson 1.11 Helping and Linking Verbs

Complete It

Add helping verbs and linking verbs to the following paragraph. There may be more than one possible option for each blank, but be sure the verb you choose makes sense in the sentence.

You ______________ know that the top of Mount Everest ______________ the highest place on Earth, but ______________ you know where the deepest place ______________? The Mariana Trench in the Pacific Ocean plunges more than 36,000 feet below the ocean's surface. The intense pressure that far underwater ______________ be deadly without the right equipment. If you ______________ to swim that deep, the weight of the water ______________ like dozens of semi trucks stacked on your body! But humans ______________ visited the bottom of the trench several times by traveling in specially made submarines. The first trip to the bottom ______________ in 1960. Since then, other people, and even robots, ______________ made the trip.

Believe it or not, but life ______________ exist that far below the surface. Most of the creatures ______________ single-celled organisms and bacteria. They ______________ to live mostly around hydrothermal vents. Some small crustaceans, snails, and bivalves ______________ survive there as well. The snails' shells ______________ softer than normal snail shells, because hard shells ______________ too difficult to grow where water pressure ______________ so intense.

Try It

What is a strange, or even impossible, place you would like to visit? Write a paragraph describing where it is and why you would like to go there. Use at least three linking verbs and three helping verbs in your paragraph. Underline the linking verbs and circle the helping verbs.

____

____

____

____

____

____

____

____

NAME ______________________________

Lesson 1.12 Verbs: Active and Passive Voice

When a sentence is written in the **active voice**, the subject performs the action of the verb.

Mr. Sanchez painted the house a bright shade of red.
The bus driver opened the door to allow passengers to exit.

When a sentence is written in the **passive voice**, the subject receives the action of the verb. A form of the helping verb *be* is used with the main verb, and a phrase beginning with *by* often follows the verb.

The house was painted a bright shade of red *by* Mr. Sanchez.
The door was opened by the bus driver to allow the passengers to exit.

In general, using the active voice creates stronger writing that is more interesting to read. The passive voice can be used when you want to emphasize the receiver of an action, or when you do not want to emphasize the performer of an action.

The door was opened by the bus driver. (She did not open a window.)
The house was painted a bright shade of red. (The color of the house is important, not who painted it.)

Identify It

On the line, write **A** or **P** to identify which sentences use the active voice and which use the passive voice.

1. ______ Before leaving home, Hector always brushes his hair and cleans his glasses.
2. ______ The nuthatches were being fed by a group of children.
3. ______ The electronic switch was flicked by Mr. Strothman, and the building crumbled to the ground.
4. ______ Mount Takawa shielded the desert from any storms approaching from the west.
5. ______ On the day of the flood, Kate was riding her horse, Petulia, near the creek.
6. ______ The Caribbean was the site of many pirate attacks during the early 1700s.
7. ______ Jupiter is the largest planet in the solar system.
8. ______ The rocket was launched by NASA in 1972.
9. ______ When she stepped in the fire ant nest, Niki's foot was bitten multiple times by the swarming insects.
10. ______ Lucas was talking by the water fountain when the bell rang.
11. ______ An American flag was draped across the windows on the top floor of the building.
12. ______ Three jellyfish were accidentally caught by the ship's net.

NAME ______________________

Lesson 1.12 Verbs: Active and Passive Voice

Rewrite It

The sentences below have been written using the passive voice. Rewrite each sentence using the active voice.

1. Every Saturday, the front yard is mowed by my brother Charley.

   ____

2. The comet is accompanied by a long tail of dust and gas.

   ____

3. The phone was finally answered by Ms. Hosaka, the school librarian.

   ____

4. The nation of Japan is called *Nippon* by the Japanese people.

   ____

5. An increase in the desert's size was caused by the overgrazing of cattle.

   ____

6. A tiny robot was inserted into the patient's bloodstream by Dr. Lang.

   ____

7. In Greek mythology, the Gorgon Medusa's head was cut off by Perseus.

   ____

8. The statistics in the safety report were compiled by the staff at the Department of Transportation.

   ____

9. Solar panels were installed on the roof by a group of local electricians.

   ____

10. The company my dad works for was founded in 1968 by Mayor Reynolds.

    ____

Try It

Write two sentences using the active voice and two sentences using the passive voice.

1. active voice: ______________________

   ____

2. active voice: ______________________

   ____

3. passive voice: ______________________

   ____

4. passive voice ______________________

   ____

NAME ______________________

Lesson 1.13 Verb Moods: Indicative, Imperative, and Subjunctive

Most sentences contain verbs in the **indicative mood**. Verbs in the indicative mood state or ask about facts or opinions.

Where is the hospital?
Tomas will leave for the airport at four o'clock.

Verbs in the **imperative mood** make commands or requests. The subject is implied as *you*.

Slice those carrots, please.
Watch out for that squirrel!

Verbs in the **subjunctive mood** describe things that are hypothetical, or not true. They also express wishes or indirect requests. The word *If* often appears in subjunctive sentences.

If the furnace **were** to stop working, I would know who to call.
Tawnia wishes she **were** better at tennis.
I insisted that my brother **shut** the door.

In the subjunctive mood, the verb *be* is usually in past tense, and singular present verbs usually drop the final *–s* or *–es.*

Identify It

On the line, write **IN**, **IM**, or **S** to identify which sentences use the indicative, the imperative, or the subjunctive mood.

1. ______ If I were you, I would not buy those shoes.
2. ______ Please head out onto the field and form two teams.
3. ______ The light bulbs cost more at the grocery store than they do here.
4. ______ When will Uncle Tashi be arriving from Tel Aviv?
5. ______ I wish the beach was a shorter drive away than three hours.
6. ______ Ms. Stacy recommends that each girl practice for at least two hours per week.
7. ______ Before writing the invitations, purchase some nice stationery.
8. ______ New Zealand lies to the southeast of Australia.
9. ______ If you were to rewrite this section, your report would be ready to hand in.
10. ______ Click this link to unsubscribe from the newsletter.
11. ______ The council's requirement is that each speaker arrive 15 minutes early.
12. ______ On Earth, water exists naturally as a solid, liquid, and gas.

NAME ______________________

Lesson 1.13 Verb Moods: Indicative, Imperative, and Subjunctive

Try It

Write a sentence for each purpose described below. Use the verb mood indicated in parentheses.

1. Tell your friend to help you finish a school project. (imperative)

   ____

2. Warn your brother about what could happen if he forgets to tie his shoelaces. (subjunctive)

   ____

3. Share one fact you know about trees. (indicative)

   ____

4. Describe an activity you wish you were doing today. (subjunctive)

   ____

5. Tell where you would like to live someday. (indicative)

   ____

6. Warn someone about a dangerous situation. (imperative)

   ____

7. Ask a question about the Grand Canyon. (indicative)

   ____

8. Request a second helping of vegetables. (imperative)

   ____

9. Describe a request you made for an aunt to do something. (subjunctive)

   I requested that my aunt ______________________

10. Describe your favorite sport or other activity. (indicative)

    ____

11. Describe what would happen if two feet of snow were to fall tonight. (subjunctive)

    ____

12. Encourage your teammates to play well. (imperative)

    ____

13. Share one thing that you think is essential for creating a good atmosphere for studying. (subjunctive)

    It is essential that a student ______________________

14. Share one fact you know about American history. (indicative)

    ____

15. Request that an object be handed to you. (imperative)

    ____

Lesson 1.14 Gerunds, Participles, and Infinitives

Gerunds, participles, and **infinitives** are other kinds of verbs. These verbs take the role of another part of speech in some circumstances.

A **gerund** is when a verb is used as a noun. A verb can take the form of the noun when the ending *-ing* is added.

Jumping on the trampoline is Eddie's favorite afternoon activity.
(The subject *jumping* is a noun in the sentence.)

A **participle** is when a verb is used as an adjective. A verb can take the form of an adjective when the endings *-ing* or *-ed* are added.

Carrie extended a *trembling* hand to her grandmother.
(*trembling* modifies *hand*)
The *injured* raccoon limped slowly into the woods.
(*injured* modifies *raccoon*)

An **infinitive** is when a verb is used as a noun, adjective, or adverb. A verb can take the form of a noun, adjective, or adverb when preceded by the word *to.*

To *travel* abroad is something that everyone should have the chance to do.
(The verb to *travel* acts as the subject, or noun, of the sentence.)
Josiah has a book report to *finish* by tomorrow.
(The verb to *finish* acts as an adjective modifying *book report.*)
On Thursday, the inspector arrived to *check* the leaks.
(The verb to *check* acts as an adverb modifying *arrived.*)

Complete It

Rewrite each of the verbs in parentheses as a gerund to complete the sentence.

1. ______________ more than one language is a skill that an increasing number of Americans have. (to speak)
2. ______________ a second language at an early age is an excellent idea. (to learn)
3. Although it is never too late to learn another language, ______________ bilingual when you are young is much easier than waiting until adulthood. (to become)
4. It is also true that ______________ a foreign language helps you understand other cultures. (to understand)
5. ______________ in America, you are less likely to speak a foreign language than in many other places in the world. (to live)
6. ______________ your family and friends with a few words in another language can be fun! (to surprise)

NAME ______________________________

Lesson 1.14 Gerunds, Participles, and Infinitives

Identify It

In the sentences below, underline the gerunds and circle the infinitives.

1. If you want to protect the planet, there are many things you can do.
2. Hanging clothes out to dry instead of using an electric dryer saves energy.
3. It's easy to save water by turning off the tap while you brush your teeth.
4. Reusing items for new purposes keeps them from ending up in the trash.
5. You can purchase a reusable water bottle, and then you won't need to wash as many glasses each day.
6. Cleaning with old t-shirts or rags saves money and paper towels.
7. If you'd like to reduce your energy bills, lower the thermostat two degrees in winter.
8. Forget about plastic bags! Buying reusable lunch bags saves money and reduces the amount of plastic in landfills.
9. Most people are already in the habit of recycling, but if you aren't, it's not too late to start!
10. Try to remember to turn off the lights when you leave a room.

Try It

Write a sentence for each of the participles in the box.

broken	laughing	painted	caring	bruised	winding

1. ______________________________
2. ______________________________
3. ______________________________
4. ______________________________
5. ______________________________
6. ______________________________

NAME ______________________

Lesson 1.15 Verb Tenses: Progressive

Progressive verb tenses describe ongoing, or continuing, actions.

A **present progressive** verb describes an action or condition that is ongoing in the present. A present progressive verb is made up of the present tense of the helping verb *be* and the present participle of the main verb.

Mr. Yokima *is planning* a surprise birthday party for his wife.
The tall pines trees behind our house *are swaying* in a strong breeze.

A **past progressive** verb describes an action or condition that was ongoing at some time in the past. A past progressive verb is made up of the past form of the helping verb *be* and the present participle of the main verb.

The jaguar *was stalking* a tapir through most of the night.
Soldiers *were trekking* across the hot sands of the desert.

Rewrite It

Rewrite each sentence using the progressive tense. If a sentence contains a past tense verb, replace the verb with a past progressive verb, and use a present progressive verb to replace present tense verbs.

1. The Mastersons sailed from Miami to Key West.

____

2. The library holds its annual book sale on the first Saturday in June.

____

3. General MacArthur wrote an autobiography before he died.

____

4. Louisa wears high heels to the dance.

____

5. The campfire burned brightly enough to be seen from several miles away.

____

6. The Cardinals won the Central Division championship game.

____

7. A giraffe eats leaves from the topmost branches of the tree.

____

8. India becomes the most populated nation on Earth.

____

NAME ______________________

Lesson 1.15 Verb Tenses: Progressive

Complete It

Complete each sentence with the progressive tense form of the verb in parentheses. Use the present progressive or the past progressive as indicated.

1. The sun ______________ over the far edge of the desert. (**rise**, present progressive)
2. Chef Charles ______________ each ingredient carefully. (**weigh**, past progressive)
3. The director ______________, but the actors apparently did not hear her. (**yell**, past progressive)
4. As the tide rolls out, the dock ______________ farther below the bank. (**sink**, present progressive)
5. The phone ______________, so would you please answer it? (**ring**, present progressive)
6. Ms. Patel ______________ the students about her trip to New York City. (**tell**, past progressive)
7. For his science fair project, Terrell ______________ a robot that can draw a picture. (**design**, present progressive)
8. Dinosaurs ______________ Earth for more than 160 million years. (**roam**, past progressive)
9. The old tire factory ______________ torn down today. (**be**, present progressive)
10. Bees ______________ around the entrance to their hive. (**swarm**, present progressive)
11. The jet engine's blades ______________ at almost full speed. (**rotate**, past progressive)
12. A few of the floats ______________ into position along the street, ready for the parade to officially begin. (**move**, past progressive)
13. My sister and I ______________ an old chair that we will use for the play. (**paint**, present progressive)
14. Chad ______________ his mom to tell him what his birthday present would be. (**beg**, past progressive)
15. After the match, the hockey team ______________ to a nearby pizza place to celebrate. (**go**, present progressive)

Try It

Write a sentence using each indicated verb form.

1. plural present progressive: ______________________________

____

2. singular past progressive: ______________________________

____

3. plural past progressive: ______________________________

____

4. singular present progressive: ______________________________

____

Lesson 1.16 Verb Tenses: Perfect

Verb tenses tell when in time something happened. The **present perfect** tense shows that something happened in the past, but the action may still be going on. The present perfect is formed with the present tense of the verb *have* (*have* or *has*) and a past participle.

The violinists *have taken* their seats in the orchestra pit.

The **past perfect** tense shows that an action was completed before another action in the past. It is formed with the verb *had* and a past participle.

Workers *had demolished* the cabin before sunrise.

The **future perfect** tense shows that an action will be completed before a before future time or a future action. It is formed with the words *will have* and a past participle.

I *will have taken* my final exam by this time next year.

Match It

Write the letter of the verb tense that each sentence uses.

1. a. present perfect tense b. past perfect tense c. future perfect tense

______ The team has broken an old league record each of the past two seasons.

______ By the end of the season, the team will have broken the old league record.

______ Before the season ended, the team had broken the old league record.

2. a. present perfect tense b. past perfect tense c. future perfect tense

______ Dr. Wabara had discovered two new viruses before he turned 25.

______ Dr. Wabara has discovered two new viruses by utilizing an electron microscope.

______ Dr. Wabara will have discovered more viruses before he retires.

3. a. present perfect tense b. past perfect tense c. future perfect tense

______ By next week, Jada will have played the piano for three years.

______ Before her first recital, Jada had played the piano only for her family.

______ During the last few months, Jada has played the piano every day.

4. a. present perfect tense b. past perfect tense c. future perfect tense

______ Despite a love for history, Tyler has never studied the Renaissance.

______ By graduation, Tyler will have never studied the Renaissance, because his history classes did not cover that time period.

______ Tyler had never studied the Renaissance until his first history class at college.

NAME ______________________

Lesson 1.16 Verb Tenses: Perfect

Rewrite It

Rewrite each sentence using the perfect tense indicated in parentheses. Change details as needed in order for the new sentence to make sense.

1. By next week, the caribou will have passed our town on their way north. (past perfect)

____

2. The delays during the last month have cost our company thousands of dollars. (future perfect)

____

3. Joshua will have completed 30 hours of community service by next Thursday. (present perfect)

____

4. By the time I got there, the chickens had eaten the entire bag of pellets. (future perfect)

____

5. By midnight, the band will have played for nearly three hours. (past perfect)

____

6. Mr. Moriarty had given us the perfect gift: a new set of cookbooks. (present perfect)

____

7. I have swum more miles than I could count since joining the gym. (past perfect)

____

8. The children had donated clothes to the shelter as part of their unit on volunteerism. (future perfect)

____

9. Once it arrives at the zoo, the hippopotamus will have traveled nearly 2,000 miles. (present perfect)

____

10. Levi has built a bicycle, skateboard, and scooter this year. (past perfect)

____

Try It

Write three sentences about some of your favorite school activities. Write one in the past perfect, one in the present perfect, and one in the future perfect.

____

____

____

____

NAME ______________________

Review Chapter 1 Lessons 9–16

Review: Action Verbs, Subject-Verb Agreement, Helping and Linking Verbs, Active and Passive Voice, Verb Moods: Indicative, Imperative, and Subjunctive

Read each sentence below. Then, fill in the blank with the type of verb indicated.

1. Drew Brees, quarterback for the New Orleans Saints, threw touchdown passes for 54 games in a row!
   action verb: ______________________
2. Quinn has watched *The X Factor* every week this season.
   helping verb: ______________________
3. The boys appeared nervous as they prepared to go onstage.
   linking verb: ______________________
4. Elizabeth wrote a series of alliterative poems.
   action verb: ______________________
5. Beatriz is expecting to make the basketball team this fall.
   helping verb: ______________________
6. Solar panels convert sunlight into electricity.
   action verb: ______________________
7. At the end of the Spanish-American War, Puerto Rico, Guam, and the Philippines became U.S. territories.
   linking verb: ______________________

For each sentence below, circle **A** or **P** to indicate whether the sentence uses the active or passive voice.

1. **A P** I quickly flipped the omelet.
2. **A P** The cattle were fed by Uncle Chris each evening at dusk.
3. **A P** The rain pounded fiercely against the roof.
4. **A P** Matt and Teddy hiked the Dragonfly Trail at Reedy Creek Park.
5. **A P** The mural was painted by the students in Mr. Albertson's art class.

On the line, write **IN**, **IM**, or **S** to identify which sentences use the indicative, the imperative, or the subjunctive mood.

1. ______ Jonas can help you with your Spanish homework.
2. ______ If you were to lose that ring, Grandma would be heartbroken.
3. ______ Play the last song on that CD again.
4. ______ What time does the baseball game start?
5. ______ Ask Ms. Schneider which worksheet to complete.

Complete each sentence below with the correct form of the verb in parentheses.

1. Onions ______________ a chemical that makes your eyes water. (contain)
2. Sugar ______________ faster in hot water than in cold water. (dissolve)
3. Both Austria and Switzerland ______________ Germany. (border)
4. Neither the goose nor the ducks ______________ the hawk approaching. (saw)

NAME ______________________

Review Chapter 1 Lessons 9–16

Review: Gerunds, Participles, Infinitives, Verb Tenses, Progressive and Perfect Tenses

Identify the underlined word(s) using the key in the box. Write your answer on the line.

a. gerund	**b.** participle	**c.** infinitive

1. ______ Joey's brother plans to enlist in the Navy after high school.
2. ______ Skiing is Hayden's favorite way to spend a winter afternoon.
3. ______ The exhausted mother finally got the baby to sleep.
4. ______ I can't believe that winning is so important to Claudia.
5. ______ The wind is going to knock the potted plants off the porch.
6. ______ The gleaming silverware shone in the drawer.

Review

Rewrite each sentence below in the tense indicated in parentheses.

1. (present progressive) The lamp illuminates the papers on the desk.

   ____

2. (past progressive) The librarian checks in the overdue books.

   ____

3. (past progressive) Thea attends a book group on the first Thursday of the month.

   ____

4. (present progressive) Abe picks fresh tomatoes from the vine.

   ____

Underline the perfect tense verb in each sentence. On the line, write whether the verb is past, present, or future perfect.

1. Sam has celebrated Hanukkah with his grandparents since he was a baby. ______
2. The university had expected larger donations this fall. ______
3. Anita has used a hearing aid for four years. ______
4. Mags will have led thousands of yoga classes by the time she retires. ______
5. It will have rained at least a dozen times before we get the roof fixed. ______
6. The dance troupe had performed at more than 80 venues last year. ______

NAME ______________________

Lesson 1.17 Adjectives and Predicate Adjectives

An **adjective** is a word that describes a noun or pronoun. It offers more information about the word it modifies. Adjectives often come before the noun or pronoun they describe. They answer the question *What kind? How many?* or *Which one?*

Tasha climbed into the *wooden* canoe and grabbed the *battered old* paddles.
Blake picked out *two* bunches of *fresh* carrots at the *downtown* market.

Proper adjectives are capitalized.

Alexander made roasted *Brussels* sprouts on *Sunday* night.
Priya has never attended an authentic *Indian* wedding before.

A **predicate adjective** follows a linking verb (a form of the verb *to be, smell, look, taste, feel, sound, appear, seem, become, grow,* or *remain*). A predicate adjective modifies the subject of the sentence.

The windows on the back of the shed appeared *broken.*

In this example, *broken* is a predicate adjective, following the linking verb *appeared.* It modifies *windows,* the subject of the sentence.

Identify It

In the sentences below, underline adjectives once and proper adjectives twice. Circle predicate adjectives.

1. Did you know that butterfly wings are covered with tiny overlapping scales?
2. The amazing monarch butterfly migrates a distance of more than 2,000 miles.
3. There are more than 28,000 species of butterflies in the world.
4. The moth's speckled wings blended into the bumpy bark of the American elm.
5. Samuel remained still, and dozens of colorful butterflies settled on his arms, shoulders, and head.
6. The tiny moth used its long proboscis to suck sweet nectar from a honeysuckle flower.
7. The butterfly's wings looked iridescent in the bright sunlight.
8. On Easter morning, the brand-new butterflies emerged from the papery cocoons at the botanical gardens.
9. When a chrysalis breaks open, the butterfly's wings are wet and crinkly.
10. Many rare butterflies are found in tropical rainforests.
11. Beautiful peacock butterflies have purple eyespots on their hind legs.
12. Butterflies need warm, sunny weather—otherwise, they cannot fly!
13. Are you going to the Butterfly Ball on Saturday night?
14. Queen Alexandra's Birdwing butterfly is the rarest and largest.

NAME ______________________

Lesson 1.17 Adjectives and Predicate Adjectives

Complete It

Complete each sentence below with an adjective of your choosing. The word in parentheses will tell you what type of adjective to use.

1. The ______________ goose landed easily on the ______________ water of the pond beside the meadow. (adjectives)
2. For the potluck next week, Ana will be bringing a ______________ dish. (proper adjective)
3. Although the oranges smelled ______________, they ended up being dry and flavorless. (predicate adjective)
4. The ambulance's ______________ siren cut through the ______________ night and awoke residents in many of the ______________ apartment buildings. (adjectives)
5. Paulomi's voice sounded ______________ as she shouted for help. (predicate adjective)
6. Although Shannon speaks several languages, she is still anxious about her ______________ test next week. (proper adjective)
7. The ______________ students lined up outside the cafeteria doors, laughing and jostling as they waited for the ______________ bell to sound. (adjectives)
8. Tyson is ______________ and ______________, but his mother feels sure he'll grow out it. (predicate adjective)
9. Cristina peered behind the ______________ boxes in the attic, finally finding the ______________, rusty birdcage she had been looking for. (adjectives)
10. Marcus's mother thinks that the loveliest place in the world is the ______________ countryside. (proper adjective)
11. Benji and Alfie hopped up into the open window and purred as the sun warmed their ______________ fur. (adjective)
12. Silas has swim lessons on ______________ afternoons. (proper adjective)

Try It

Imagine that you are spending the day at a butterfly exhibit at a nature center. Describe what you see in detail. Use adjectives and predicate adjectives in your description.

____

____

____

____

____

____

NAME ______________________

Lesson 1.18 Comparative and Superlative Adjectives

Comparative adjectives compare two nouns, and **superlative adjectives** compare three or more nouns.

calm, calmer, calmest — shy, shyer, shyest — polite, politer, politest

For adjectives that end in *y*, change *y* to *i* before adding the suffixes *-er* or *-est*.

healthy, healthier, healthiest — windy, windier, windiest

Comparing two nouns:

Coach Wachter is known for being *meaner* than Coach Pickens.
My new desk is much *sturdier* than the old one.

Comparing three or more nouns:

The *gentlest* llama is the one with the spotted coat.
Zora's birthday fell on the *sunniest* day this week.

Comparative and superlative adjectives can also be formed by adding the words *more* (comparative) and *most* (superlative) before the adjective. Use *more* and *most* with longer adjectives.

Uncle Dan is *more impulsive* about making decisions than Dad is.
The *most eccentric* family in our neighborhood lives in the old Randolph house at the end of the street.

Complete It
Complete the chart below with the correct forms of the adjectives.

Adjective	Comparative Adjective	Superlative Adjective
jealous	______	______
______	slimmer	______
______	______	quietest
dramatic	______	______
______	______	most agile
______	grumpier	______
cheerful	______	______
______	______	most elegant
dainty	______	______
______	more fearful	______

NAME ______________________

Lesson 1.18 Comparative and Superlative Adjectives

Proof It

Read each sentence below. If the correct form of the boldfaced word(s) is used, make a check mark on the line. If the incorrect form is used, write the correct form on the line.

1. ______________ You must use the **most precisest** measurements when you are constructing the fence.
2. ______________ There's no doubt that Maggy is **more outspoken** than Missy.
3. ______________ Jenna's suggestion for a fundraiser was **popularer** than Sam's.
4. ______________ That silver cleaner doesn't work very well, but the silver does look slightly **more shiny** now.
5. ______________ When Johan went snorkeling, he encountered one of the **most unusual** fish he had ever seen.
6. ______________ I think Willow Springs is a **quainter** town than the town where we stayed last year.
7. ______________ Last weekend, Rilla and I watched the **most intensest** movie I'd ever seen.
8. ______________ The ingredients in Grandma's recipe are **unusualer** than in the recipe Mom uses.
9. ______________ Dr. Santiago was the **most brilliant** professor I had in my four years at the university.
10. ______________ I think you've given me the **wisest** advice I could have hoped for.
11. ______________ Hasaan's response was **more enthusiastic** than his brother's.
12. ______________ Ms. Matsuda is the **resourcefulest** Girl Scout leader we've ever had.

Try It

Write a sentence following the instruction for each item below.

1. Use the comparative of *curious*. ______________________________

   ____
2. Use the superlative of *fluffy*. ______________________________

   ____
3. Use the comparative of *wise*. ______________________________

   ____
4. Use the superlative of *suspicious*. ______________________________

   ____
5. Use the comparative of *artistic*. ______________________________

   ____
6. Use the superlative of *gloomy*. ______________________________

   ____

NAME ______________________

Lesson 1.19 Adverbs and Intensifiers

Adverbs modify, or describe, verbs. An adverb tells *how, when,* or *where* an action occurs.

Malia waited *patiently.* (tells *how* Malia waited)
My brother was sent to the principal's office *yesterday.* (tells *when* he was sent)
Kirby hid *behind* the sycamore tree. (tells *where* Kirby hid)

Adverbs can also modify adjectives or other adverbs.

The gas tank was *completely* empty. (*completely* modifies the adjective *empty*)
Earthquakes in the South are *quite* rare. (*quite* modifies the adverb *rare*)

Many, but not all, adverbs are formed by adding *-ly* to adjectives.

Intensifiers are adverbs that add emphasis or intensity to adjectives or other adverbs. The following are common intensifiers.

absolutely	just	quite	so	such
almost	nearly	rather	particularly	too
extremely	practically	really	somewhat	very

Mr. Singh travels for work *quite* often.
Felicia felt *extremely* impatient as she waited for the train to pass.

Complete It

Add an intensifier from the box above to each sentence below. Circle the word it modifies.

1. Mr. Crawley was ______________ embarrassed by the incident at work yesterday.
2. The actors were ______________ talented, and the sets were exquisite.
3. The door was ______________ open, and I was worried that the cats had escaped.
4. Carmen was ______________ asleep by the time her parents returned from the game.
5. It's not a ______________ funny movie, but I found myself laughing at the strangest parts.
6. Dr. Yusef was ______________ worried when he received the results of his wife's biopsy.
7. I found the documentary about sea turtles to be ______________ captivating.
8. Although Kiko's shoes were ______________ new, they were already scuffed and dirty.
9. The children were ______________ bored by the speech, but they were not permitted to leave.
10. The whole situation was just ______________ strange to explain.

NAME ______________________

Lesson 1.19 Adverbs and Intensifiers

Identify It

Circle the adverb in each sentence below. Make an arrow from the adverb to the word it modifies.

1. The biologist bitterly explained how deforestation was affecting the lives of rainforest animals.
2. Oscar smiled awkwardly at Amelia, ducked his head bashfully, and asked her to dance.
3. Although Noah was dressed quite suitably for the occasion, he wore bright green high-top sneakers.
4. "It's just that, well . . . I'm really sorry," replied Scott haltingly.
5. I pedaled vigorously, sure that I could make it to the summit of the trail.
6. Inez was highly recommended for the position by her friend and mentor, Dr. Bradley.
7. Soon, Caitlyn will be a teenager.
8. The sky was particularly lovely when the storm ended and the sun began to set.
9. Grandma smoothly blended the ingredients and carefully poured them into the dish.
10. Abby graciously accepted the award.
11. Daisy barked at strangers quite often, but she was exceptionally affectionate with her family.
12. Raylon stared intently at the television screen, waiting anxiously for news of the survivors.

Try It

Write four sentences using adverbs from the box. Underline each intensifier you use.

once	immediately	absolutely	yesterday
loosely	quite	skillfully	temporarily
extremely often	almost	surprisingly	early
nearly	furiously	rather	soon

1. ______________________________
____
2. ______________________________
____
3. ______________________________
____
4. ______________________________
____

NAME ____________________

Lesson 1.20 Comparative and Superlative Adverbs

Like comparative adjectives, **comparative adverbs** compare two actions.

Aaron answered his mother *more cheerfully* than his brother.
Dad rises *earlier* in the summer than he does during the rest of the year.

Superlative adverbs compare three or more actions.

Alison behaved *most cautiously* of any of the gymnasts.

Short adverbs are formed using *-er* for comparatives and *-est* for superlatives. Long adverbs use the words *more* or *most*, or for negative comparisons, use *less* or *least*.

The moon shone *more brightly* tonight than earlier this week.
Karl answered the question *less truthfully* than his brother.

Some comparative and superlative adverbs do not follow these patterns. The following are examples of irregular comparative and superlative adverbs.

well better best badly worse worst

Complete It

For each sentence below, write the correct comparative or superlative form of the adverb in parentheses.

1. Although the boys usually fight on road trips, the trip to Florida went ______________ than Mrs. Nesbit had expected. (smoothly)
2. Valentina arrived at school ______________ than her classmates. (early)
3. When the tornado warning sounded, my family reacted ______________ of anyone on our street. (quickly)
4. Bandit and Roxy clean their food bowls ________________ than the other dogs we foster. (thoroughly)
5. When Maggy's party was canceled because of the rain, she behaved ________________ than her parents had expected. (graciously)
6. The restaurant near the dock prepares fish sandwiches ______________ of all. (well)
7. Of all our cousins, I think Erik was ______________ happy to see us. (genuinely)
8. Uncle Gabe is ________________ knowledgeable of any of my relatives. (medically)
9. Joseph helped with the farm chores ______________ than his three sisters did. (eagerly)
10. I really didn't expect this year's birthday cake to turn out ______________ than last year's! (badly)

NAME ______________________________

Lesson 1.20 Comparative and Superlative Adverbs

Complete It

Complete the chart below with the correct forms of the adverbs.

Adverb	Comparative Adverb	Superlative Adverb
politely	____________	____________
well	____________	____________
____________	more persuasively	____________
____________	faster	____________
____________	more sincerely	____________
____________	____________	most intelligently
naturally	____________	____________
____________	____________	most brightly
exceedingly	____________	____________
____________	more childishly	____________
____________	____________	most hungrily
carelessly	____________	____________
____________	____________	most often

Try It

Write a sentence following the instruction for each item below.

1. Use the comparative of *well.* ______________________________
____
2. Use the superlative of *intently*. ______________________________
____
3. Use the comparative of *honestly*. ______________________________
____
4. Use the superlative of *badly*. ______________________________
____

Lesson 1.21 Adjectives and Adverbs

Some adjectives and adverbs are easy to confuse with one another. Use a predicate adjective after a linking verb (forms of the verb *to be* and verbs like *seem, taste, grow,* and *become*) to describe the subject. Use an adverb to describe an action verb.

The police dog seemed *proud* to be standing next to Officer Shari.
The police dog stood *proudly* next to Officer Shari.

In the first example, the adjective *proud* follows the linking verb *seemed* and modifies the subject *police dog*. In the second example, the adverb *proudly* modifies the action verb *stood*.

The words *good, well, bad,* and *badly* are often used incorrectly. *Good* and *bad* are adjectives, and *well* and *badly* are adverbs.

The hot bath felt *good* after such a long hike.
These eggs smell *bad*, so don't eat them.

The Rockets played *badly* last night and lost the game.
Cara performed *well* at the audition and earned a role in the play.

Identify It

Read each item below. On the line, write **Adj.** or **Adv.** to identify each **boldface** word as an adjective or adverb. If the word is an adjective, underline the noun it modifies. If the word is an adverb, underline the action verb it modifies.

1. ________ Music blared **loudly** from a pair of speakers placed in the window.
2. ________ As we were about to leave, my brother suddenly appeared **queasy**, so we stayed home.
3. ________ The coconut smoothie tasted so **good**, we ordered a second one.
4. ________ Rosa's room is **always** a bit cooler than the rest of the apartment.
5. ________ Mr. Swift felt **bad** about breaking his promise to the students.
6. ________ Paxton tried **hard** not to laugh when the gum got stuck in his friend's hair.
7. ________ The lamp shines so **brightly**, we use it only when we have to.
8. ________ The mosquitoes down by the lake are particularly **bad** this year.
9. ________ A few pebbles tumbled **quietly** down the slope and into the ravine.
10. ________ The children grew **quiet** as their mother entered the room.

NAME ______________________

Lesson 1.21 Adjectives and Adverbs

Proof It

Some of the sentences below contain errors in adjective and adverb usage. Use proofreading marks to make corrections. If the sentence is correct, place a checkmark on the line.

1. ______ Aunt Mae smiled proud as she presented the elaborate gingerbread house.
2. ______ During their trip to Myrtle Beach, the Connors ate well every day.
3. ______ A thresher moved slow through the fields like a dinosaur roaming the plains.
4. ______ When a toddler smells badly, it usually means it's time for a diaper change.
5. ______ Emperor penguins look majestically as they stand tall on the Antarctic ice.
6. ______ The scientists' prediction about where the module would land appeared to be successfully.
7. ______ The plumage of some parrots is beautifully to behold.
8. ______ The fresh coffee brewing in the café smelled good.
9. ______ The gentle movement of the curtains great amused a kitten.
10. ______ A dilapidated shack lay abandonedly and forgotten deep within the woods.
11. ______ Wallace stored his files safe by uploading them to the cloud.
12. ______ After reaching a height of nearly 400 feet, the roller coaster track plunges steep back to ground level.
13. ______ Lance's femur was broken so bad, the pieces had to be bolted back together.
14. ______ Coal burning power plants provide electricity more reliable than wind turbines.
15. ______ Historically, theatrical performances as we know them date back to the Ancient Greeks.
16. ______ A squirrel ran quick along the top of the fence, trying desperately to outrun the neighbor's dog.
17. ______ The manatee seems contently to float around and munch sea grass all day.
18. ______ The massive ship looks deceptively small when seen from a great distance.

Try It

Write two sentences containing adverbs and two containing predicate adjectives. Circle the adverbs in your sentences and underline the adjectives.

____

____

____

____

NAME ___________________________

Lesson 1.22 Prepositions and Prepositional Phrases

Prepositions are words that show the relationship between a noun or pronoun and another word in the sentence.

A fence ran *alongside* the creek.
Please memorize the poems *in* this book.

Some common prepositions are *above, across, after, along, around, at, away, because, before, behind, below, beneath, beside, between, by, down, during, except, for, from, in, into, near, of, off, on, outside, over, to, toward, under, until, up, with, within,* and *without.*

Compound prepositions consist of more than one word. Some common compound prepositions are *about, according to, aside from, across from, along with, because of, far from, in front of, in place of, instead of, on account of,* and *on top of.*

Prepositional phrases include the prepositions and the objects (nouns or pronouns) that follow the prepositions. A prepositional phrase includes the preposition and the object of the preposition, as well as any modifiers of the object.

Three dogs ran *through an empty field.* (The preposition is *through*; the object of the preposition is *field*; the words *an empty* modify the object *field.*)

A sentence may contain more than one prepositional phrase.

The teacup *inside the cupboard* sat *on top of a saucer.*

A prepositional phrase followed by a comma can start a sentence.

Because of the rain, we stayed indoors and played chess.

Identify It

Underline each prepositional phrase in the sentences below. Circle each preposition or compound preposition. Some sentences contain more than one prepositional phrase.

1. Along with good nutrition, exercise keeps your body in top shape.
2. Stretching before you exercise will help loosen the muscles throughout your body.
3. During times of bad weather, you might use a stationary bike at a gym instead of riding a real bike along a trail or around the block.
4. Something as simple as running up and down the stairs can be a great activity for a workout.

Lesson 1.22 Prepositions and Prepositional Phrases

Rewrite It

Rewrite each simple sentence below so that it contains one or more prepositions. The number of prepositions you need to include is shown in parentheses. The first sentence has been completed as an example.

1. The crew was nervous. (2)

   Example: The crew *of the fishing boat* was nervous *about an approaching storm.*

2. The clouds darkened. (1)

   ____

3. Wind blew. (3)

   ____

4. The captain yelled. (2)

   ____

5. The crew lowered the sails. (2)

   ____

6. The captain and crew sought shelter. (2)

   ____

7. The storm raged. (2)

   ____

8. The seas calmed. (1)

   ____

9. The crew emerged. (3)

   ____

10. The crew cheered. (2)

   ____

Try It

Write a sentence with a prepositional phrase that includes a preposition, its object, and at least one modifier of the object. Identify each part of the prepositional phrase.

____

____

preposition: __________ object of the preposition: __________ modifier(s): __________

NAME ______________________

Lesson 1.23 Conjunctions and Interjections

Conjunctions connect individual words or groups of words in sentences.

Coordinate conjunctions connect words, phrases, or independent clauses that are equal or of the same type. Coordinate conjunctions are *and, but, or, nor, for,* and *yet.*

Ask Russell *or* Jake to watch the baby this afternoon.

Correlative conjunctions come in pairs and are used together. *Both/and, either/or,* and *neither/nor* are examples of correlative conjunctions.

Both the pencils *and* pens are kept in the top drawer of the desk.

Subordinate conjunctions connect dependent clauses to independent clauses in order to complete the meaning. *After, although, as long as, because, since, unless, whether,* and *while* are examples of subordinate conjunctions.

As long as Ms. Burles says it is okay, our class can leave early today.

An **interjection** is a word or phrase used to express surprise or strong emotion. Common interjections include:

ah	alas	aw	awesome	eeek	hey	hi	hurray
oh	oh, no	oops	ouch	phew	wow		

An exclamation mark or a comma is used after an interjection to separate it from the rest of the sentence.

Ouch! I stubbed my toe! *Phew,* that's a huge relief!

Identify It

Circle the conjunction in each sentence. On the line, write **coordinate, correlative**, or **subordinate** to identify the type of conjunction used in the sentence.

1. ______________ Rudy will care for our rabbit, Hudson, while we are gone next week.
2. ______________ Mr. Isaacs plans to build a gazebo, but he won't be able to do it until next year.
3. ______________ The bus leaves at six o'clock sharp, unless it has some kind of mechanical problem.
4. ______________ Neither my mother nor my father likes driving long distances.
5. ______________ The car was parked in the garage, yet it still got wet somehow.
6. ______________ While you are at the library, please check to see if I have any books on hold.
7. ______________ Coach Randolph reviewed his notes about the game after all the players had left.
8. ______________ William can help me clean the birdhouse, or he can fill the feeder with birdseed.

NAME ______________________

Lesson 1.23 Conjunctions and Interjections

Complete It

Conjunctions have been removed from the following passage. Choose conjunctions from the box to complete the passage. The number in parentheses tells how many times that conjunction should appear in the passage.

and (3)	so (1)	while (1)
either (1)/or (1)	whether (1)	although (1)
after (1)	but (3)	since (1)

New Orleans, Louisiana, is considered the birthplace of jazz, ______________ it's also the birthplace of jazz great Louis Armstrong. ______________ countless musicians have made their mark in jazz since his time, many still consider Armstrong to be the greatest musician of all time.

Armstrong was born in 1901. His family was quite poor, ______________ Armstrong left school by 5th grade in order to help support them. He sold newspapers, delivered coal, ______________ even sang on the street to earn money.

On the last day of 1912, Armstrong made a mistake that got him into big trouble, ______________ it also set a positive course for the rest of his life. ______________ he was celebrating New Years Eve, Armstrong fired a gun into the air. He was quickly arrested ______________ sent to a home for troubled youths. ______________ the punishment was fair might be debatable, ______________ during the 18 months Armstrong spent in the home, he learned how to play the bugle. ______________ he was allowed to leave, Armstrong knew exactly where his life was headed: a career as a musician.

For the next two decades, Armstrong established his name as a top trumpet player ______________ bandleader in the popular new musical genre of jazz. He spent most of his time playing in ______________ Chicago ______________ New York, but he also traveled to California a few times.

______________ Armstrong died in 1971, his reputation has continued to grow. Today, he is universally recognized as a towering figure in jazz history.

Try It

Review the list of interjections on page 53. Choose three interjections and use each in a sentence.

1. ____

2. ____

3. ____

NAME ______________________________

Review Chapter 1 Lessons 17–23

Review: Adjectives and Predicate Adjectives, Comparative and Superlative Adjectives, Adverbs and Intensifiers, Comparative and Superlative Adverbs

Identify the adjective in each sentence. If it is a predicate adjective, underline it. Circle other adjectives. On the line, write **C** if the adjective is comparative, write **S** if the adjective is superlative, and leave the line blank if the adjective is neither comparative nor superlative.

1. ______ The most beautiful greenhouse I ever visited was in Athens, Greece.
2. ______ The orchids in particular looked spectacular.
3. ______ Purple flowers dangled delicately at the ends stems.
4. ______ Even the tiniest buds had a hint of color.
5. ______ Flowers bloomed brilliantly throughout the greenhouse's lush interior.
6. ______ The plants thrived and appeared healthier than plants grown in the wild.
7. ______ As I wandered the grounds outside the greenhouse, the sweetest scent filled the air.
8. ______ The plants displayed outside were larger than the ones grown inside the greenhouse.
9. ______ Olive trees marched in rows up a hillside in the distance.
10. ______ Unfortunately, the farther I looked across the sprawling city, the more clearly I saw the pollution.
11. ______ A haze obscured the most distant buildings and roads.
12. ______ Back inside the greenhouse, the view wasn't expansive.
13. ______ However, it was much cleaner.

As indicated, rewrite each sentence to change the adverb to a comparative or superlative adverb. If the original sentence contains an intensifier, circle the intensifier.

1. The locomotive chugged somewhat noisily along the railroad tracks.
Comparative: ______________________________
2. The Great Wall of China marches steadily through the hilly countryside.
Superlative: ______________________________
3. As dawn broke, General Macklin saw that the Fourth Regiment had fought successfully through the night.
Superlative: ______________________________
4. My new telescope can show the planets clearly when you adjust this knob.
Comparative: ______________________________
5. Last Saturday's potluck was planned well by Ms. Harrison's class.
Comparative: ______________________________
6. The shed was built sturdily to withstand strong winds coming over the mountain.
Comparative: ______________________________
7. I sleep very soundly when the room is pitch dark and a fan is running.
Superlative: ______________________________

Review

NAME ____________________

Review Chapter 1 Lessons 17–23

Review: Adjectives and Adverbs, Prepositions and Prepositional Phrases, Conjunctions and Interjections

Circle the correct adjective or adverb to complete each sentence.

1. The Pittsfield Pirates played (bad, badly) last night and lost the game.
2. "That burning bagel smells (awfully, awful)!" exclaimed Finn.
3. Allie danced (good, well) at ballet practice today.
4. We ate (quick, quickly) so we wouldn't be late getting to the bus.
5. Darrell grew (impatient, impatiently) as the time for his flight was changed yet again.

Identify the boldface word in each sentence. On the line, write **P** if it is a preposition, **C** if it is a conjunction, or **I** if it is an interjection. For sentences that contain a preposition, also underline the prepositional phrase.

1. ______ Mr. Inouye poured hot tea **into** his favorite mug.
2. ______ **Huh**, I didn't see that coming.
3. ______ Be sure to bring an umbrella, **for** you never know when it might rain.
4. ______ **Before** heading to practice, Hector always puts on his lucky shirt.
5. ______ The sunrise is still an hour away, **but** I can see a faint glow to the east.
6. ______ **While** you are in the kitchen, could you turn off the oven timer?
7. ______ **Oh, no!** The bell just rang!
8. ______ Millie cleaned the spot where she dropped a biscuit **onto** the floor.
9. ______ Don't sit in front of the window, **or** I won't be able to see.
10. ______ Thousands of bugs are swarming **under** the streetlamp's glow.

Write a sentence that contains a coordinate conjunction: ____________________

____

Write a sentence that contains a correlative conjunction: ____________________

____

Write a sentence that contains a subordinate conjunction: ____________________

____

Write a sentence that contains two prepositional phrases: ____________________

____

NAME ______________________

Lesson 1.24 Sentence Types

A **declarative sentence** makes a statement about a place, person, thing, or idea, and it ends with a period.

In 1983, Sally Ride became the first American woman to go into space.

An **interrogative sentence** asks a question and ends with a question mark.

Did you know that approximately half of our trash ends up in landfills?

An **exclamatory sentence** shows urgency, strong surprise, or emotion, and it ends with an exclamation mark.

They'll announce the winner in five minutes!

An **imperative sentence** demands that an action be performed. The subject of an imperative sentence is usually not expressed, but is understood as *you*. Imperative sentences can be punctuated with a period or an exclamation mark.

Place your drawings on Ms. Hadley's desk.
Look out for the rocks!

Complete It

Complete each sentence below by circling the appropriate end mark.

1. Did you know that it's not possible to tickle yourself . ? !
2. Venus is the Roman goddess of love and beauty . ? !
3. The longest word in the English language has 45 letters . ? !
4. Take the subway to the 11th Street stop . ? !
5. What is the most exotic food you've ever sampled . ? !
6. Watch out for the deer . ? !
7. In summer, the surface temperature of the Kalahari Desert is literally hot enough to fry an egg . ? !
8. Where is Mt. Rushmore located . ? !
9. Emperor penguins are the largest species of penguin . ? !
10. Beta carotene, which is found in carrots, may protect eyesight . ? !

NAME ______________________________

Lesson 1.24 Sentence Types

Identify It

Read the passage below. Use the line following each sentence to identify the sentence type. Write **D** for declarative, **IN** for interrogative, **E** for exclamatory, and **IM** for imperative.

Picture a modern day elephant with smaller ears and 3-foot-long fur. ______ This is what the ancient woolly mammoths looked like. ______ Their long, shaggy fur kept them warm in icy, frigid temperatures. ______ Their four-inch layer of solid fat helped, too! ______ One of the reasons that today's elephants have such long, floppy ears is that they help to keep the giant beasts cool in tropical places. ______ The smaller ear size of woolly mammoths actually helped them conserve heat. ______

Another difference between elephants and mammoths is tusk size. ______ The largest elephant tusks measure about 10 feet in length. ______ The largest mammoth tusks were about 15 feet long! ______ What was the purpose of such enormous tusks? ______ They were most likely used for protection and as a characteristic that attracted females. ______

Do you know what caused these giants to die out 4,000 years ago? ______ Think of how strong they were and how well-suited for surviving freezing weather. ______ Unfortunately, there was not enough food for the mammoths to survive the Ice Age. ______ In addition, they were hunted by early humans for their meat and their fur. ______ Humans were an even bigger threat than saber toothed cats! ______

It's fortunate that mammoths lived in such icy places. ______ Scientists have learned so much from their well-preserved remains. ______ In fact, they may be able to use the DNA they've found to clone a woolly mammoth some day! ______

Try It

Write one sentence of each type.

1. Declarative: ______________________________
____
2. Interrogative: ______________________________
____
3. Exclamatory: ______________________________
____
4. Imperative: ______________________________
____

NAME ______________________________

Lesson 1.25 Simple and Compound Sentences

An **independent clause** presents a complete thought and can stand alone as a sentence.

Simple sentences are sentences with one independent clause. Simple sentences can have one or more subjects and one or more predicates.

The roosters crowed in unison as the sky lightened. (one subject, one predicate)
Socrates and Plato are important Greek philosophers. (two subjects, one predicate)
Marcel and Naomi *set the table* and *served dinner to their parents*. (two subjects, two predicates)

Compound sentences are sentences with two or more simple sentences, or independent clauses. A compound sentence can be two sentences joined with a comma and a coordinate conjunction. The most common coordinating conjunctions are *and, but, or, yet,* and *so. For* and *nor* can also act as coordinating conjunctions.

The marching band needs to raise money, so band members will sell raffle tickets.

A compound sentence can also be two simple sentences joined by a semicolon.

The marching band needs to raise money; band members will sell raffle tickets.

Identify It

Read each sentence and determine whether it is a simple or compound sentence. On the line at the beginning of the sentence, write **S** for simple or **C** for compound. On the two lines following the sentence, identify the total number of subjects and predicates in each sentence.

______ 1. Our three dogs and four cats love hanging out together on the couch. **S:** ______ **P:** ______

______ 2. When you sleep, your heart rate, breathing, and brain activity all slow down. **S:** ______ **P:** ______

______ 3. The *Wizard of Oz* was released in 1930; it became one of the most popular films of all time. **S:** ______ **P:** ______

______ 4. A lioness and her cubs watched a herd of gazelles and several ostriches moving across the savannah. **S:** ______ **P:** ______

______ 5. The Kremlin and the Hermitage Museum are famous Russian landmarks, so they are often crowded with tourists. **S:** ______ **P:** ______

______ 6. Neptune and Uranus are gas giants and orbit farthest from the sun compared to the other planets. **S:** ______ **P:** ______

NAME ____________________

Lesson 1.25 Simple and Compound Sentences

Rewrite It

Combine each set of simple sentences into a single compound sentence using the conjunction and/or punctuation shown in parentheses.

1. NASA planned to launch the probe last Friday. Due to bad weather, it still hasn't left Earth. (, but)

2. Music is an important part of African culture. Dance is an important part of African culture. Lagos, Nigeria, will be the site of a major international performing arts center. (, so)

3. More than a million types of insects have been discovered. About a third of them are species of beetles. (;)

4. Elizabeth might want to become a vet. Elizabeth might want to become a professional dancer. Elizabeth has not made up her mind yet. (;)

5. The Eiffel Tower was built as part of the 1889 World's Fair in Paris, France. For nearly 40 years, it was the tallest structure on Earth. (, and)

6. Sound waves travel through air at about 1,000 feet per second. Sound waves travel four times faster than that through water. (, but)

Try It

Write a few sentences about a recent outing. It could be a trip to the grocery store or a trip to a foreign country. Include a variety of simple and compound sentences in your description.

NAME ___________________________

Lesson 1.26 Complex Sentences

A **dependent clause** does not present a complete thought and cannot stand alone as a sentence.

Complex sentences have one independent clause and one or more dependent clauses. The independent and dependent clauses are connected with a subordinate conjunction or a relative pronoun. The dependent clause can be anywhere in the sentence.

Complex sentence (connected with subordinate conjunction):

> You can sense sound *because* your inner ear contains an eardrum and tiny bones.

Complex sentence (connected with a relative pronoun):

> The Sydney Opera House, *which* was designed by architect Jorn Utzon, is a famous Australian landmark.

The dependent clause can either be the first or second part of the sentence.

> *After* you finish cleaning the fish tank, please put it back in the cupboard.
> Please put the fish tank back in the cupboard *after* you finish cleaning it.

Identify It

For each sentence, circle the subordinate conjunction or relative pronoun, and underline the dependent clause.

1. Uncle Ramos spent an hour sifting through the soil because we needed worms for fishing.
2. Until she turns thirteen, Monique must ride in the backseat of the car.
3. The suspension bridge sways a little bit whenever a strong breeze blows across it.
4. Even though Dr. Neils is an accomplished chess player, he still loves playing checkers with his niece.
5. Michael Jordan, who is well known as one the greatest basketball players of all time, also played professional baseball.
6. Before Randall leaves the house each morning, he makes sure the lights are off.
7. The French flag, which has three stripes, was designed in the late 1700s.
8. Unless you are a feline expert, you might not recognize *ragdoll, Abyssinian,* and *Cornish rex* as popular cat breed names.

NAME ______________________

Lesson 1.26 Complex Sentences

Complete It

For each unfinished complex sentence, choose a subordinate conjunction from the list and use it to write the missing dependent clause. Do not use the same conjunction more than once.

after	if	unless	where
although	once	until	wherever
because	since	when	whether
before	though	whenever	while

1. ____,
   the deer seek shelter under the thick brush in the ravine.
2. Captain Spinks was steering the yacht toward a small lagoon
   ____.
3. We plan to drive north to the Arizona Nevada border
   ____.
4. ____,
   Jamal rebooted his laptop and crossed his fingers.
5. The polished metal sculptures in the park shine
   ____.
6. ____,
   we learned that the Mongol Empire spread across most of Asia.
7. ____,
   Han might see Johnny Depp or another famous movie star.
8. The Museum of Fine Arts has been located on Elm Street
   ____.
9. In 2012, Park Geunhye became the first woman president of South Korea
   ____.
10. ____,
    the femur, or thigh bone, is the largest bone in the human body.

Try It

Write three of your own complex sentences: one that starts with a dependent clause first, one that ends with a dependent clause, and one that contains a relative pronoun.

1. ____
   ____
2. ____
   ____
3. ____
   ____

NAME ___________________

Lesson 1.27 Adjective, Adverb, and Noun Clauses

An **adjective clause** is a dependent clause that modifies a noun or pronoun. An adjective clause usually follows the word it modifies. The clause begins with a relative pronoun, such as *that, which, who, whom, whose,* or *whoever.*

Grandma Mia, *who lives in Arizona,* will visit us next week.
Comets have tails *that consist of dust and gas.*

An **adverb clause** is a dependent clause that modifies a verb, an adjective, or an adverb. An adverb clause answers the question *How? When? Where? Why?* or *Under what condition?* The first word of an adverb clause is a subordinate conjunction, such as *although, until, once, however, unless, if,* or *while.*

If the space shuttle is going overhead, we can see it with a pair of binoculars.
Most students should do fine on the test *unless they choose not to study.*

A **noun clause** is a dependent clause that acts like a noun.

How you behave at school can affect your grades. (subject)
An abstract painting can be *whatever you want it to be.* (predicate noun)
Maisie will decide *where we go to dinner tonight.* (direct object)
The lead role will be given to *whichever student earns it.* (object of the preposition *to*)

Identify It

Underline the dependent clause in each sentence. On the line, identify the type of clause by writing **Adj** for adjective, **Adv** for adverb, or **N** for noun.

1. _________ Although Venus is the planet closest to Earth, it is very different from Earth.
2. _________ Dinosaurs, which ruled Earth for millions of years, exist today only as fossils.
3. _________ Whatever you leave in the basket will be donated to the animal shelter.
4. _________ The community garden was planted in that empty lot located on First Avenue.
5. _________ The monkey that stole Monica's bracelet climbed to the top of the visitors center.
6. _________ If you drive from Halifax to Vancouver, you will be in the car for more than a week.
7. _________ Phinn tried to describe to his sister what a cello sounds like.

NAME ______________________

Lesson 1.27 Adjective, Adverb, and Noun Clauses

Try It

Write a sentence that fits each description.

1. a sentence containing an adjective clause with the relative pronoun *that*

   ____

   ____

2. a sentence containing an adverb clause with the subordinate conjunction *once*

   ____

   ____

3. a sentence containing a noun clause with the subordinate conjunction *wherever*

   ____

   ____

4. a sentence beginning with an adverb clause with the subordinate conjunction *as long as*

   ____

   ____

5. a sentence containing a noun clause subject with the subordinate conjunction *where*

   ____

   ____

6. a sentence containing an adjective clause with the relative pronoun *who*

   ____

   ____

7. a sentence containing an adverb clause with the subordinate conjunction *after*

   ____

   ____

NAME ______________________________

Review Chapter 1 Lessons 24–27

Review: Sentence Types, Simple and Compound Sentences

Read the sentences below. Use the line following each sentence to identify the sentence type. Write **D** for declarative, **IN** for interrogative, **E** for exclamatory, and **IM** for imperative.

1. Bears are not the only mammals that hibernate. ______
2. Can you name any other animals that hibernate? ______
3. Chipmunks dig tunnels and crawl underground to spend the coldest parts of winter hibernating. ______
4. Snakes, frogs, butterflies, and even a few types of birds hibernate. ______
5. What happens when an animal is hibernating? ______
6. Hibernation is a kind of deep sleep; the animal's body temperature drops and its breathing and heart rate slow down greatly. ______
7. Some animals hibernate for months! ______
8. Search the library or online for more information about hibernation. ______

Identify each sentence below as simple (**S**) or compound (**C**).

1. ______ A bird might try to grab a lizard by the tail, but a lizard can break off its tail and escape.
2. ______ Students and teachers interact regularly during classroom time.
3. ______ An insulator prevents or hinders an electrical current; a conductor enables the current to flow.
4. ______ The two tallest buildings in the world are the Burj Khalifa and the Petronas Towers.
5. ______ A forklift carried the pallet of boxes to the back of the truck and raised the load, and then two men emptied the pallet.
6. ______ The Sydney Opera House was designed to look like ships sailing into the harbor.
7. ______ Tsetse flies carry a disease called *sleeping sickness,* and they pass along the disease through their bites.
8. ______ Stars are classified by their temperature and size.

NAME ______________________

Review Chapter 1 Lessons 24–27

Review: Complex Sentences; Adjective, Adverb, and Noun Clauses

Underline the dependent clause in each complex sentence below.

1. After losing its arm to an octopus, the starfish grew a new one.
2. Dr. Weinstein studies pediatric journals because she needs to keep her medical knowledge up to date.
3. Once the helicopter lifts off, the pilot will contact the observation tower.
4. Please take a photo before the rainbow disappears.
5. Although Evelyn Glennie is deaf, she is one of the best drummers in the world.
6. My dad can give us a lift to swim practice, unless you'd rather walk.
7. While Nelson examines the damage, have your father call the insurance company.
8. When everybody gets here, Mr. Langley will begin his lecture.
9. We haven't been able to get across town in less than half an hour since the city closed Harris Boulevard.

Review

Read the sentences below. Circle the adjective clauses, underline the adverb clauses, and underline the noun clauses twice. Some sentences may have more than one clause.

1. What I meant to tell her was that we would be bringing my sister, too.
2. Most residents of the Philippines, who are called *Filipinos*, live in the capital of Manila.
3. During the symphony's finale, Patrice got to play a timpani, which is also known as a kettledrum.
4. Between 1861 and 1865, the North and South fought one another in the American Civil War.
5. When you get up, please hand that pitcher of lemonade to Uncle Victor.
6. Although both amphibians and reptiles are cold-blooded animals, what differentiates amphibians in part is that they start life breathing through gills.
7. As light passes through a prism, it becomes separated into different wavelengths.
8. Centipedes, which have poisonous claws around their heads, feed on other insects.

Follow the directions for each item.

1. Write a complex sentence. ______________________________

   ____
2. Write a sentence with an adjective clause. ______________________________

   ____
3. Write a compound sentence. ______________________________

   ____

Chapter 2 Mechanics

NAME ______________________

Lesson 2.1 Capitalization: Sentences, Quotations, Letter Parts

Capitalize the first word of **every sentence**.

Crater Lake, located in southwestern Oregon, is the deepest lake in the U.S.

Capitalize the first word in **direct quotations**.

"Only one more week until I get my braces off!" exclaimed Sariya.

Do not capitalize indirect quotations.

Harriet said that the chess club will be holding a yard sale next weekend.

If a continuous sentence in a direct quotation is split and the second half is not a new sentence, do not capitalize it.

"You're going to need a root canal," said Dr. Wan, "*as* well as two fillings."

If a new sentence begins after the split, then capitalize it as you would any sentence.

"You will have 25 minutes to complete the essay," said Ms. Cruz. "*You* may begin writing whenever you're ready."

In a **letter**, capitalize the name of the street, the city, the state, and the month in the heading.

528 *W*est *M*onroe *R*oad
*T*raverse *C*ity, *M*ichigan 49684
*S*eptember 24, 2014

Capitalize the salutation, or greeting, as well as the name of the person who is receiving the letter. Capitalize the first word of the closing.

*D*ear *M*rs. *G*robin, *T*o whom it may concern: *Y*our friend,

Rewrite It

Rewrite each sentence below using correct capitalization.

1. "have you bought any new music lately?" Asked Jackson.

____

2. "i want to see my brother's band play on Tuesday night," said Maura, "But I have a test Wednesday morning."

____

____

3. Bashir said His dad likes to listen to vinyl records on an old turntable.

____

4. "david, are my CDs in the car?" Asked Mom. "if they are in the car, they might melt."

____

____

NAME ______________________

Lesson 2.1 Capitalization: Sentences, Quotations, Letter Parts

Proof It

Proofread the following letter for mistakes in capitalization. Underline a lowercase letter three times to make it a capital. m

longview farm
518 bluebell lane
lovettsville, virginia 20180

april 13, 2014

dear ms. weineke,

my name is Meera Danwell, and I believe you know my aunt, Jess Wendt. aunt jess knows how interested I am in farm life, and she suggested I contact you. i would love to have the opportunity to volunteer at Longview Farm this summer. although animals are my main interest, I'd also be happy to help out in the garden, in the house, and with the bees. i don't have any experience specifically with farm animals, but I've always helped to care for my family's two Labrador retrievers and our rabbit. in addition, I volunteer at Purrfect Pets Cat Shelter twice a month. my teachers say that I'm a hard worker and a fast learner. i'm looking forward to learning about farm life firsthand.

thank you for your time. i look forward to hearing from you.

sincerely,
Meera Danwell

Try It

On the lines below, write a short dialogue between two friends discussing summer vacation. Be sure to use capital letters where necessary.

____

____

____

____

____

____

____

____

NAME ______________________

Lesson 2.2 Capitalization: Names, Titles, and Places

Proper nouns are specific people, places, and things. Proper nouns are capitalized.

I think that *Ana* is planning to get a haircut after school. (specific person)
The largest city in *Wisconsin* is *Milwaukee*. (specific place)
Mom always buys *Soft Touch* fabric softener. (specific thing)

The titles of books, poems, songs, movies, plays, newspapers, and magazines are proper nouns and are capitalized. In a title, capitalize the first and last words, and capitalize all other words except *a, an,* and *the*. Do not capitalize short prepositions, such as *of, to, in, on,* and so on. Most titles are also underlined or set in italic font in text. Song titles, essays, poems, and other shorter works are placed in quotes.

Nina needs to return *The Skin I'm In* to the library by Friday.
Halle and Ira sang along to the Beatles' "Yellow Submarine."

Titles associated with names are also capitalized, but do not capitalize these titles if they are not directly used with the name.

Before *Dr.* Ames became a *doctor,* he taught biology at the university.

Proof It

Correct the mistakes in capitalization using proofreading marks. Underline a lowercase letter three times to make it a capital. m≡

1. My cousin, manny, grew up just a couple of blocks from lake erie.
2. I hope you bought creamy naturals peanut butter—it's the only kind my brother will eat.
3. The poem "afternoon on a hill" by edna st. vincent millay is one of my favorites; I memorized it last year.
4. While she was babysitting, Keiko put the twins to sleep by humming "you are my sunshine."
5. kat and todd love to go skiing in breckenridge, colorado.
6. Do you know if mayor peabody will be attending the ribbon-cutting ceremony?
7. Dylan is using *the war to end all wars: world war I* as the main source for his history report.
8. The first book that maggie's book club plans to read is *to kill a mockingbird.*
9. Last week, selma wrote a letter to the editor of the *los angeles times.*
10. arnold schwarzenegger spent two terms in office as the governor of california.

NAME ______________________

Lesson 2.2 Capitalization: Names, Titles, and Places

Rewrite It

Rewrite each name or title below using correct capitalization.

1. "stopping by woods on a snowy evening" ______________________
2. nelson mandela ______________________
3. the blue ridge mountains ______________________
4. hamburg, germany ______________________
5. the president of centerville middle school's 8th grade class ______________________
6. the eiffel tower ______________________
7. *the firefly letters: a suffragette's journey to cuba* ______________________
8. dr. alysha johnson ______________________
9. the great salt lake ______________________
10. *national geographic* ______________________
11. president kennedy ______________________
12. *a wrinkle in time* ______________________
13. cuyahoga county ______________________
14. "a dream deferred" by langston hughes ______________________

Try It

Answer each of the questions below in a complete sentence. Remember to use correct capitalization.

1. What is the best book you've read in the last year?

   ____

2. If you could only listen to one album for the next month, what would it be?

   ____

3. You just won a free subscription to any magazine or newspaper. Which one would you choose?

   ____

4. What is the name of your city's or town's mayor?

   ____

5. If you could travel anywhere, where would you choose to go?

   ____

6. What figure from history do you most admire?

   ____

NAME ______________________________

Lesson 2.3 Capitalization: Other Proper Nouns

Organizations, departments of government, and sections of the country are all **proper nouns** and all important words are capitalized.

The names of organizations, associations, and businesses are capitalized.

Habitat for Humanity
The Greater Cleveland Arts Council
General Mills, Inc.

Capitalize the names of departments of government.

Bureau of Engraving and Printing
House of Representatives

Directional words that point out particular sections of the country are capitalized. However, words that give directions are not capitalized.

A hurricane affected most of the *Eastern* Seaboard.
The geese flew *south* for the winter.

Historical events and documents, historical time periods, nationalities, languages, and team names are all **proper nouns** as well.

The *Declaration of Independence* marked the beginning of the *Revolutionary War.*
The *Iron Age* lasted from approximately 1000 BC to 400 AD.
Laurie served *French* toast to her friends at camp.
The *Columbus Crew* will play a total of 17 away games this season.

Rewrite It

On the lines, rewrite the proper nouns in boldface so they are capitalized correctly.

1. The **gulf of tonkin resolution** led to an increase of American involvement in the **vietnam war**. ______________________________
2. The **san diego chargers** play in the **american football conference**. ______________________________
3. The **rotary club of charlotte** meets each Wednesday in the **south end** neighborhood. ______________________________
4. Lin is studying the history of the **supreme court**. ______________________________
5. Uncle Vince joined the **marine corps** and is stationed on the **east coast**. ______________________________
6. The **magna carta** was issued during the **middle ages**. ______________________________

NAME ______________________________

Lesson 2.3 Capitalization: Other Proper Nouns

Proof It

Correct the mistakes in capitalization using proofreading marks. Underline a lowercase letter three times to make it a capital. m Lowercase a letter by making a slash through it. M

Philadelphia, Pennsylvania, is the second largest city on the east coast of the United States. Its name comes from the greek language and means "city of brotherly love." Philadelphia played an important role during the time of Early American History. The Founding Fathers met in Philadelphia to sign the declaration of independence, and the city served as a temporary capital for the United States during the revolutionary war. The continental congresses met in Philadelphia as well to eventually complete and sign the United States constitution.

Philadelphia also has a significant Historical role for african Americans specifically. Even during the time of Slavery, Philadelphia was home to a large free Black community. The african methodist episcopal church was founded in the city by free blacks in the late 1700s. In the 1900s, Philadelphia became a Major Destination during the great migration, in which millions of african Americans left the American south to move north.

Try It

Write one example for each category listed below. Be sure to capitalize each proper noun correctly.

Name of a government department or organization: ______________________________

Name of a local business: ______________________________

Name of a charity organization: ______________________________

Name of a U.S. region: ______________________________

Name of a historical event: ______________________________

Name of a historical time period: ______________________________

Name of a historical document: ______________________________

Name of a sports team: ______________________________

NAME ______________________

Lesson 2.4 End Marks

Periods are used at the end of declarative sentences and some imperative sentences.

Mount Fuji emerges ghostlike through the morning fog.
Please wash the teacup by hand.

Question marks are used at the end of interrogative sentences.

Can astronauts send e-mails from space?
How many drops of water are in a milliliter?

Exclamation points are used at the end of exclamatory sentences. They are also used at the end of imperative sentences or interjections that show urgency, strong surprise, or emotion.

The Phillies won the World Series!
Wow! Look at the color of that sunrise!

Identify It
Circle the end mark that correctly completes each sentence.

1. What is the scientific name for an elephant (. ? !)
2. There's a gorilla loose in the zoo (. ? !)
3. How many stars would you rate that movie (. ? !)
4. Originally, all of Earth's land was connected as a supercontinent called Pangaea (. ? !)
5. I am conducting a poll to find out which brand of tissue is most popular (. ? !)
6. Please stop writing when you hear the bell (. ? !)
7. What I want to know is why all the paintbrushes are still dirty (. ? !)
8. Tell me what you thought about Lois Lowry's new novel (. ? !)
9. Watch out for that bike (. ? !)
10. Continue along this path until you reach the big oak tree (. ? !)
11. Who owns most of the world's gold (. ? !)
12. Which is the tallest species of palm tree (. ? !)
13. Stop bugging me (. ? !)

NAME ______________________________

Lesson 2.4 End Marks

Complete It

Add end marks to the sentences in the passage.

Let's go to the movies___ First we buy our tickets, then we grab a treat from the concession stand, and finally we find the perfect seat inside the theater___ The lights dim, and the show begins___ But did you ever wonder how the images onscreen appear to move___ It's an illusion___ They don't really move at all___ What you see as movement on the screen is really a succession of still images___ If you slowed the film down, you would see each photograph or drawing appear for a moment before the next one appeared, looking just slightly different from the previous image___ When all the slightly different images are played back quickly enough, they create the illusion of smooth movement___

The key to this illusion is persistence of vision___ What is persistence of vision___ When the retina at the back of your eye perceives something, the image lingers for a brief fraction of a second, creating an afterimage___ When you watch a film, the still images are projected quickly enough that the afterimage of one photograph is still lingering on your retina as the next image is shown___ You do not perceive the gap between the two images___ Instead, the change from one image to the next appears fluid___ Presto___ You see what looks like movement on the screen rather than a slide show___ Pretty cool, isn't it___

Try It

Write a paragraph about your favorite film or TV show. Include at least one declarative sentence, one interrogative sentence, and one imperative sentence. Be sure to use appropriate end marks.

____

____

____

____

____

____

____

____

____

____

____

____

NAME ______________________________

Review Chapter 2 Lessons 1–4

Review: Capitalization of Sentences, Quotations, Names, Titles, Places, and Other Proper Nouns

Proofread each sentence below for capitalization. Lowercase a letter by making a slash through it M̸, and capitalize a letter by making three lines below it m.

1. The Walker fine art center is located at the corner of First avenue and Stone boulevard.
2. "The solar power plant will come online this saturday," Dr. Nichols explained, "So we need to contact general Rickert at the department of homeland security."
3. The Public School system we are familiar with today in the United States is only about 100 years old.
4. The words of many Western Languages use roots from latin or greek words.
5. The Spring issue of *Manhattan Medical journal* contains an article about working for the National Institutes Of Health.
6. The Moons of Jupiter vary greatly in size, although most are less than 10 Kilometers in diameter.
7. The Appalachian mountains are located in the east, while the Rocky mountains are in the west.
8. Situated on the 53rd floor of wilson oaks tower, the Doctors' offices have a spectacular view of Downtown Atlanta.
9. The assassination of an Archduke of the Hapsburg Empire is considered by most Historians as the event that began world war I.
10. "Which station is showing the Super Bowl this year?" Asked Roshelle. "is it fox or espn?"
11. Many castles were built throughout europe during the middle ages.
12. Jesse Owens's accomplishments at the 1936 summer olympics in berlin, germany, made him an International Celebrity.
13. The official Religion of Israel is judaism.
14. American Astronaut Buzz Aldrin was the second man to walk on the moon.
15. Max told his Friend Henry, "my grandfather was a Pilot for pan am world airways back in the Fifties."

NAME ______________________________

Review Chapter 2 Lessons 1–4

Review: Capitalization of Letter Parts, End Marks

Read each letter part below. If it is correct, make a check mark on the line. If it contains an error in capitalization, make an **X** on the line.

1. ______ Charlotte, NC 28270
2. ______ Sincerely,
3. ______ Dear Madam or Sir:
4. ______ june 12, 2015
5. ______ dear Mae,
6. ______ All the Best,
7. ______ august 14, 2014
8. ______ Yours truly,

Review

Add the appropriate end mark to each sentence below.

1. Are you familiar with the Hindu myth of Garuda___
2. Ms. Seely speaks 13 languages___
3. Tell me what you think of the museum's new Holocaust exhibit___
4. I wonder what the first cameras looked like___
5. Quick, shut that gate before the lamb gets out___
6. What I really want to know is the name of the first film that featured a robot___
7. Is water in the Dead Sea saltier than ocean water___
8. The native peoples of a place are called *aboriginals*___
9. If you were in the orchestra, which instrument would you play___
10. Judge Robinson will preside over the court this morning___
11. Petrochemicals are substances created from petroleum, or crude oil___
12. Can you believe how quickly this last month went by___
13. Name three devices invented by Thomas Edison___
14. Earth's tectonic plates float atop a layer of molten rock, or magma___

NAME ______________________

Lesson 2.5 Commas: Series, Direct Address, Multiple Adjectives

Series commas are used with three or more items listed in a sentence. The items can be words or phrases and are separated by commas.

Salamanders, newts, and frogs are amphibians.
At the Ohio State Fair, we rode on a merry-go-round, a rollercoaster, and a Ferris wheel.

Commas are used to separate the name of a person spoken to from the rest of the sentence. This is called a **direct address**.

When should I make my next appointment, Dr. Reese?
Cesar, you will have the role of narrator in the play.

When **multiple adjectives** describe a noun, they are separated by commas if they are coordinate adjectives.

The dog's wet, matted fur was difficult to comb.
Asla is a vast, diverse continent.

Coordinate adjectives equally modify the noun. If they are coordinate adjectives, you can switch the order without changing the meaning.

The assistant's *agile, experienced* fingers typed about 100 words per minute. (coordinate adjectives because *agile, experienced fingers* and *experienced, agile fingers* both make sense)

Non-coordinate adjectives do not use commas.

Mae and her grandmother completed a *difficult jigsaw* puzzle. (non-coordinate adjectives because *jigsaw difficult puzzle* does not make sense)

Match It

Read the sentences below. Decide what kind of comma, if any, is needed in each sentence. Write the letter of your answer on the line.

a. series comma b. direct address comma
c. multiple adjectives comma d. no comma needed

1. ______ Mr. Larson could you please set this microscope on the top shelf?
2. ______ Breyton helped remove the damaged wading pool.
3. ______ The museum displayed a rusty antique submarine.
4. ______ Plastic is used in making cars clothing and containers.

NAME ______________________

Lesson 2.5 Commas: Series, Direct Address, Multiple Adjectives

Proof It

Read the sentences below. Add commas where they are needed. If the sentence is correct as it is, make a check mark on the line.

1. ______ Lewis be sure to include a self-addressed stamped envelope.
2. ______ A platypus is an odd creature that has a beak like a duck a tail like a beaver and lays eggs like a reptile.
3. ______ Examples of nations in Europe include Liechtenstein Moldova and Albania.
4. ______ Jupiter's famous Great Red Spot is a giant storm that has lasted for hundreds of years.
5. ______ The website you had trouble viewing is available now Shawn.
6. ______ Octillion decillion and googol are the names of very large numbers.
7. ______ Fresh clean laundry billowed in a soft summer breeze.
8. ______ I left my new laptop computer in the third floor reading room.
9. ______ During the coldest winter days, you should wear that cozy striped sweater Manny.
10. ______ On your hike Raj you might walk through some sticky spider webs.
11. ______ The Koneyas will visit Los Angeles San Francisco Portland and Seattle.
12. ______ Chewy garlic-flavored pizza crust is the best, don't you agree Mom?
13. ______ Earth has four oceans: the Pacific the Atlantic the Indian and the Arctic.
14. ______ A glass of refreshingly cold ice water is the perfect thing on a dry hot day.
15. ______ Put that dirty measuring cup on the empty bottom shelf of the dishwasher.

Try It

For each number below, write a sentence that includes the items in parentheses.

1. (series commas) ______________________

____

2. (multiple adjectives) ______________________

____

3. (series commas and direct address) ______________________

____

4. (direct address) ______________________

____

5. (multiple adjectives and direct address) ______________________

____

NAME ______________________

Lesson 2.6 Commas: Combining Sentences, Setting Off Dialogue

Use a comma to **combine two independent clauses** with a coordinate conjunction.

Taylor and Imani held up a car wash sign, *and* Liza directed traffic.

In a complex sentence, **connect a dependent and an independent clause** with a comma and subordinate conjunction.

Although Stephen has a hard time sitting still, he loves to read.

Commas are used when **setting off dialogue** from the rest of the sentence.

"The finalists in the art competition will be announced at 2:00," said Ms. Weiss.
"I'd like the Greek pasta," replied Zachary, "with a side of asparagus."

Complete It

The sentences below are missing commas. Add commas where they are needed using proofreaders' marks ^.

1. George Washington had a lifetime of trouble with his teeth but he never wore wooden dentures as some myths report.
2. He began having decay and tooth loss in his twenties which caused him years of pain, embarrassment, and discomfort.
3. Although Washington tried a variety of cleaners, medications, and dentures nothing really solved his dental problems.
4. When Washington was inaugurated as president he had only one real tooth left!
5. Washington had several pairs of dentures but none were very comfortable.
6. Some of his false teeth were crafted of hippopotamus ivory whereas others were made from human teeth and carved elephant ivory.
7. Because the false teeth were difficult to wear while eating Washington's diet suffered.
8. For a presidential portrait Washington once put cotton balls in his mouth to support his lips!
9. Old fashioned dentures stained easily and they required quite a bit of cleaning.
10. Contemporary researchers performed laser scans of George's teeth and they found that the dentures were made of gold, lead, ivory, and human and animal teeth.
11. Throughout his life Washington was self conscious about smiling.
12. Modern dentures are much more comfortable but they were long after George Washington's time.

NAME ______________________________

Lesson 2.6 Commas: Combining Sentences, Setting Off Dialogue

Identify It

Read each sentence below. If the use of commas is correct, write **C** on the line. If it is incorrect, write **X** on the line and add commas where they are needed.

1. ______ "Dad," began Isaac, "I just finished doing a research report on Australia, and I'm practically an expert now."
2. ______ "You can ask me about it" continued Isaac "or I can just tell you some of the more interesting things I learned."
3. ______ "Well" said Mr. Jackson scratching his head "I know that Australia is both a country and a continent."
4. ______ "That's right!" said Isaac. "Australia covers more than three million square miles, but it's the smallest continent."
5. ______ He added "Australia's Great Barrier Reef is so massive, it can be seen from space."
6. ______ "I've heard that there are more sheep than people in Australia and New Zealand" said Mr. Jackson "but I don't know if that's true."
7. ______ "Yep," said Isaac, "that is true."
8. ______ "Some areas are pretty densely populated but much of Australia is desert" added Isaac.
9. ______ "If you had to pick the most fascinating thing you learned about Australia, what would it be?" asked Mr. Jackson.
10. ______ "That's easy," said Isaac. "Animals like the kangaroo, platypus, and koala are unique to Australia and they aren't found anywhere else in the world."

Try It

Write a short dialogue between two people, being sure to use commas correctly.

____

____

____

____

____

____

____

____

NAME ______________________

Lesson 2.7 Commas: In Letters and Introductory Phrases

Commas are used in both **personal** and **business letters**.

Personal Letters

Commas appear in four of the five parts of the personal letter.

Heading: 3698 Waltham Rd.
Bismarck, ND 58501
October 3, 2014
Salutation: Dear Crystal,
Body: comma usage in sentences
Closing: Yours truly,

Business Letters

Commas appear in four of the six parts of the business letter.

Heading: 566 Covewood Ct.
Baltimore, MD 21205
January 29, 2014
Inside Address: Ms. Julia Cohen
Redford Musical Conservatory
1311 W. Maple St.
Indianapolis, IN 46077
Body: comma usage in sentences
Closing: Sincerely,

Use a comma to indicate **a pause after an introductory word or phrase**.

No, I won't be able to attend the seminar on Tuesday.
Furthermore, the tombs of pharaohs were filled with treasures to accompany them to the afterlife.
Jumping over the creek, Yusef managed to keep his pants and boots dry.

Complete It

Complete each item below by adding commas where they are needed. If no changes are necessary, make a check mark on the line.

1. ______ First I'd like you to clean your paintbrushes.
2. ______ In the woods Kathleen carefully noted the first signs of spring.
3. ______ Without her mother's permission, Nola was not permitted to accompany her classmates to the amusement park.
4. ______ Nevertheless it was still important to inspire confidence in the company's investors.
5. ______ Beside the maple tree, clusters of lilies of the valley bloomed.
6. ______ Nearby an owl called and received an answer in the moonless night.

NAME ___________________________

Lesson 2.7 Commas: In Letters and Introductory Phrases

Rewrite It

Rewrite each item below, including commas where they are needed.

1. In spite of the rain we'll still be attending the rally.

   ____

2. Best wishes

   ____

3. In addition you'll need two cups of oats and half a cup of raisins.

   ____

4. Walking quickly George managed to catch up to the class.

   ____

5. May 5 2010

   ____

6. Next June Isla will be turning fourteen.

   ____

7. Once again Antonio has managed to impress us with his memory.

   ____

8. Dear Ms. Chun

   ____

9. If you are hoping to make the team you should start working out this summer.

   ____

10. Austin Texas

    ____

Try It

On the lines below, write a short letter to a friend or family member about something fun you've done recently. Remember to include commas in all the necessary places.

____

____

____

____

____

NAME ______________________

Lesson 2.8 Semicolons and Colons

Colons have several functions in a sentence.

Colons are used to introduce a series in a sentence. Colons are not needed when the series is preceded by a verb or preposition.

Use the following resources for your report: *books, magazines, or the Internet.*
At the zoo, we *saw a wolf, kangaroo, and three tiger kittens.* (no colon needed)

A colon is sometimes used instead of a comma to set off a clause or to set off a word or phrase for emphasis.

Mr. Hanson reminded the students: *"Do not leave your seats until the bell rings."*
As Darrell approached his front door, he couldn't believe what he saw: *a gift-wrapped box!*

A **semicolon** is a cross between a period and a comma.

Semicolons join two independent clauses when a coordinate conjunction is not used.

The tea was much too hot; I let it cool for a few minutes before taking a sip.

Semicolons are used to separate clauses when the main clause is long and already contains a comma.

When the deer heard us, they darted into the woods, ran just a few yards, and then stopped; but as hard as I looked, I could no longer see them.

Semicolons are used to separate clauses when they are joined by some conjunctive adverbs, such as *consequently, furthermore, however, moreover, nevertheless,* or *therefore.*

After Pilar pulled into the parking space, she realized she had forgotten her purse; consequently, she had to call her sister to ask for a favor.

Identify It
Identify whether a colon or semicolon is needed to correctly complete each sentence. Circle the correct punctuation.

1. (: ;) The following animals are often found in rain forests ___ toucans, leafcutter ants, and tree frogs.
2. (: ;) Although they were allies during World War II, the Soviet Union and the United States soon grew distrustful of each other ___ the result was a Cold War lasting for decades.
3. (: ;) Renewable resources used today include wind, solar, and water power ___ but most electricity is still created through nuclear power or by burning fossil fuels.
4. (: ;) Light travels amazingly fast ___ 299,792,458 meters per second!
5. (: ;) Andrew explained to his mother ___ "Even if I get there by nine, most of the seats will be taken."

NAME ______________________________

Lesson 2.8 Semicolons and Colons

Proof It

In the sentences below, colons and semicolons are missing or used incorrectly. Correct each sentence by adding, replacing, or deleting colons and semicolons as needed.

> **= deletes punctuation**
> **= inserts punctuation**

1. Electrical generators contain the following parts, a coil of wire, magnets, and carbon brushes.
2. If you see a white cloud billowing from the top of a nuclear power plant, it is not smoke: it is steam.
3. Batteries produce DC, or direct current, electricity: whereas the electricity you get from a plug is AC, or alternate current, electricity.
4. Both nuclear power plants and coal-burning power plants produce electricity by heating water to create steam that turns a generator, however, each produces a different kind of pollution.
5. The electrical power grid consists of electrical energy produced by: nuclear power, fossil fuels, wind turbines, and hydroelectric dams.
6. The chain reactions inside a nuclear reactor release a huge amount of heat, therefore, the reactor is housed inside a thick, concrete container.
7. For centuries, wind power has been used to move boats, to grind corn, or to pump water: but its use for generating electricity is much more recent.
8. Fossil fuels, nuclear energy, wind, water, and sunlight can all be used to create electricity, however, fossil fuels and nuclear energy are nonrenewable resources.
9. Although sunlight is a renewable resource, solar panels utilize a nonrenewable resource; silicon.
10. Wind farms need to be located in windy places, such as mountaintops, coastlines, or treeless plains, but dozens, or even hundreds, of wind turbines in these places might create a kind of visual pollution.

Try It

On the lines below, write your own sentences containing colons or semicolons. Write two sentences that use a colon and two sentences that use one or more semicolons.

1. ______________________________
____
2. ______________________________
____
3. ______________________________
____
4. ______________________________
____

NAME ____________________

Lesson 2.9 Quotation Marks

Quotation marks are used to show the exact words of a speaker. The quotation marks are placed before and after the exact words.

> *"Let's look for a game to play,"* said Cho. *"I think this rain is going to last all afternoon."*

Quotation marks are also used when a direct quotation contains another direct quotation.

> "Mom said, *'Ask Branson to help you pick up the yard,'"* Jaden told his brother.

Note that single quotation marks are used to set off the inside quotation. Single quotes express what Mom said. Double quotes express what Jaden said.

Quotation marks are used with some titles. Quotation marks are used with the titles of short stories, poems, songs, and articles in magazines and newspapers.

> Emily's favorite song on Kelly Clarkson's album *Stronger* is *"Mr. Know It All."*

If a title is quoted within a direct quotation, then single quotation marks are used.

> "Please read *'The Lottery'* over the weekend so we can discuss it in class on Monday," said Ms. Shin.

Complete It

Add double or single quotation marks where they are needed in each sentence.

1. Have you ever read the poem Jabberwocky by Lewis Carroll? asked Aiden.
2. Ms. Yates explained to the class, I was told by Principal Lincoln, Your students will receive the credit they deserve.
3. Noah's essay was titled Harris Jr. High: Clean and Green.
4. When we were at breakfast, said Rae, my brother said his favorite Edgar Allan Poe story is The Pit and the Pendulum.
5. It's break time! yelled the foreman. And remember what Mr. Powers said: Everyone must be back to work by 12:30.
6. O. Henry's The Gift of the Magi is one of the most famous short stories of all time.
7. After Ms. Hanna recited A Narrow Fellow in the Grass, she said, That poem was written by Emily Dickinson.
8. In his list of sources, Liam included A New Bike for a New Millennium, an article he found in the June 2000 issue of *Outdoor Magazine.*
9. In celebration of Arbor Day, Emma announced, I will be reading the poem Trees.
10. Aunt Victoria said, Please bring a side dish or a dessert, Louis reminded his mother.

NAME ______________________________

Lesson 2.9 Quotation Marks

Try It

Two classmates (you choose their names) are discussing a reading assignment. Their teacher (you choose his or her name) has told them to choose one of these poems, read it, and write a report: "On This Wondrous Sea" by Emily Dickinson, "A Noiseless, Patient Spider" by Walt Whitman, or "Eldorado" by Edgar Allan Poe. Use the lines below to write a short dialogue between the classmates as they discuss which poem each will choose. Include at least one quotation within a quotation in your dialogue, and be sure to punctuate the dialogue correctly.

NAME ______________________

Lesson 2.10 Using Italics and Underlining

When you are working on a computer, use **italics** for the titles of books, plays, movies, television series, magazines, and newspapers. If you are writing by hand, **underline** these titles.

Last Saturday, my friends and I watched *Ferris Bueller's Day Off*. (movie)
The Washington Post carried an ad for the senator's reelection. (newspaper)
The Atlanta Community Theater is presenting *Death of a Salesman*. (play)

Identify It

Underline the title or titles in each sentence that should be italicized.

1. Director Steven Spielberg attended the premiere of Jurassic Park.
2. Kayla enjoyed reading the novel Holes more than seeing the film they made of it.
3. Several nights a week, Vince and his family watch reruns of the TV show Home Improvement.
4. Although The Lion, the Witch, and the Wardrobe was the first book C. S. Lewis wrote in the Narnia series, the events in The Magician's Nephew take place at an earlier time.
5. We canceled our subscription to Time Magazine because most of the same articles are available online.
6. Winston Churchill earned the Nobel Prize in Literature for his nonfiction book The Second World War.
7. "The Beach Boys' best album is Pet Sounds," Chris insisted.
8. Cameron's stomach felt queasy with nerves as he waited to audition for the lead role in Bye Bye Birdie.
9. The season premiere of The Voice airs next Thursday at 8 PM.
10. I found a copy of The World Almanac for Kids 2014 at the library.
11. Joseph Campbell's classic book The Hero with a Thousand Faces was assigned as part of our unit on mythology.
12. The San Francisco Chronicle published an essay written by our history teacher, Mr. Sampson.
13. The latest episode of Glee featured music by the Beatles.
14. I used an article about polar bears from the June 2012 issue of National Geographic as a source for my report.

NAME ______________________

Lesson 2.10 Using Italics and Underlining

Try It

Write a few sentences answering each set of questions. Be sure to use complete sentences.

1. What is the most popular book among your friends or classmates? Have you read the book? If not, do you plan to?

___

___

___

2. What is the last movie you saw? Write a sentence comparing it to another movie you liked better.

___

___

___

3. What books, magazines, or newspapers have you used as resources for school projects or reports? Include a brief description of the report or project.

___

___

___

___

4. What TV show have others encouraged you to watch? What TV shows have you recommended to others?

___

___

___

5. Who is your favorite author? Which of his or her books have you read? Which book did you like most? Which did you like least?

___

___

___

___

___

NAME ____________________

Lesson 2.11 Apostrophes

Apostrophes are used in contractions to form possessives.

Apostrophes take the place of the omitted letters in contractions.

have not = haven't   she will = she'll

Possessives show possession, or ownership. To form the possessive of a singular noun, add an apostrophe and an *s*. This rule applies even if the noun already ends in *s*.

The flower**'s** petals were pale yellow.   I borrowed Ross**'s** CD.

To form the possessive of plural nouns ending in *s*, add an apostrophe. If the plural noun does not end in *s*, add both the apostrophe and an *s*.

The naturalists**'** tour of the new nature center was very informative.

The men**'s** glee club will be performing on Saturday night.

Match It

Read each sentence below. From the box, choose the type of apostrophe that is used and write the letter of your choice on the line.

a. contraction	**b.** singular possessive
c. plural possessive ending in *s*	**d.** plural possessive not ending in *s*

1. ______ Carlita's new journal
2. ______ the people's reaction
3. ______ the professor's last class
4. ______ the Boy Scouts' campout
5. ______ you're
6. ______ the coaches' meeting
7. ______ Darius's math homework
8. ______ couldn't
9. ______ the chickadees' nest
10. ______ the tree trunk's bark
11. ______ the geese's feathers
12. ______ the children's umbrellas

NAME ______________________

Lesson 2.11 Apostrophes

Proof It

In the sentences below, add the apostrophes where they are needed using this proofreading mark ∨̓ . Delete unnecessary apostrophes ⸿ .

1. The archeologists expedition was led by Professor Abdul Naasir.
2. King Tut's tomb was found in Egypts' Valley of the Kings.
3. An archaeologist named Howard Carter found a step under some workmens' huts.
4. Pharaohs' tombs were often a place for thieves to find amazing riches.
5. Tutankhamun's tomb held over 5,000 objects because it had remained undisturbed by robbers.
6. The kings canopic chest held his organs.
7. The mummy's coffin was made of solid gold.
8. It is'nt easy to imagine how the massive pyramids could've been built without the use of modern-day machinery.
9. Newspapers' reports that there was a curse on the tomb of Tutankhamun were purely rumor.
10. The Nile Rivers location in northeast Africa contributed to the development of the Ancient Egyptians advanced civilization.
11. Its estimated that the Pyramid of Khufu is constructed of blocks weighing almost six million tons!
12. The British Museums' website on Ancient Egypt is filled with interesting facts and isn't difficult to navigate.

Try It

Write a sentence for each of the various types of apostrophes.

1. contraction ______________________________
2. singular possessive ______________________________
3. plural possessive ending in *s* ______________________________
4. plural possessive not ending in *s* ______________________________

NAME ______________________

Lesson 2.12 Hyphens, Dashes, Parentheses, and Ellipses

Hyphens are used in compound modifiers only when the modifier precedes the word it modifies. Hyphens are not used for compound modifiers with adverbs ending in *-ly*.

Jiang's *well-written* paper received an A. I knew it would be *well written.*
The *gently snoring* child rolled over in her sleep.

Use hyphens in some compound nouns. You will need to check a dictionary to be sure which compound nouns need hyphens.

Mom has a very close relationship with her *mother-in-law,* my grandmother.

Hyphens are used between compound numbers from twenty-one through ninety-nine.

Julian needs to read another *forty-two* entries in the short fiction contest.

Dashes indicate a sudden break or a change in thought.

Aunt Jeanine—*she's a doctor*—will be visiting next month.

Parentheses show supplementary, or additional, material or set off phrases in a stronger way than commas.

We plan to go to the barbecue *(hosted by the Boy Scouts)* next weekend.

Ellipses can be used to indicate an omission, or words that have been left out.

The hearing will be at noon . . . at the courthouse downtown.

An ellipsis can also be used to indicate a pause in a sentence.

"I'm not really sure what to say . . . but I am sorry."

Complete It

Add hyphens where they are needed in the phrases below. If no hyphens are needed, make a check mark on the line.

1. ______ a close up photograph
2. ______ twenty four chapters
3. ______ a brightly lit room
4. ______ the last get together
5. ______ a life size statue
6. ______ sixty five students
7. ______ a teacher who is well known
8. ______ a patiently waiting dog
9. ______ a long distance race
10. ______ the worn out jeans

NAME ______________________

Lesson 2.12 Hyphens, Dashes, Parentheses, and Ellipses

Rewrite It

Each sentence below is missing hyphens, dashes, parentheses, or ellipses. Rewrite each sentence using the appropriate punctuation. There may be more than one correct answer for some items.

1. My neighbor he lives in the blue house has six cats.

   ____

2. Simone is participating in the spelling bee this weekend and she plans to win.

   ____

3. Audrey downloaded her photos she just got a digital camera and started to edit them.

   ____

4. Mr. Toshi just turned forty four.

   ____

5. Ian thought and thought he thought some more but couldn't think of an excuse.

   ____

6. Daniel babysits for a set of well behaved twins.

   ____

7. Traveling to Rochester to see Grandma even though it's a long trip is always the best part of summer.

   ____

   ____

8. After you've mixed the batter make sure the oven is preheated you can fill up the muffin cups.

   ____

   ____

9. The high today should be between seventy five and seventy eight degrees.

   ____

10. We should go now unless you'd like me to pick you up later.

    ____

NAME ______________________

Review Chapter 2 Lessons 5–12

Review: Commas, Colons, and Semicolons

Add commas where they are needed in each item below.

1. We can make the muffins if you have ripe bananas buttermilk blueberries flour sugar and eggs.
2. "I woke up this morning to the sound of birds chirping" said Aunt Sadie "so I'm pretty sure that spring is on its way."
3. Your truly

   Becca Stanich
4. "Kyra if you want to make it to cheerleading practice on time" said Mrs. Bell "we need to get going in 15 minutes."
5. 1452 Maple Grove Ln.

   Tulsa OK 74102
6. Eating an apple each day can boost your immune system and it can also help prevent tooth decay.
7. Rohit have you taken the recycling out to the curb yet?
8. At first Dr. Ortiz wasn't certain how to interpret the results of the experiment.
9. The rusty ancient car has been parked in our neighbor's driveway for over a year.
10. Monika has packed T-shirts shorts sundresses and two pairs of shoes.
11. The sleek silky baby otter searched for its mother as the thick gray clouds gathered on the horizon.
12. Hillary Clinton was the First Lady during Bill Clinton's presidency but she is also a politician in her own right.
13. Despite the unexpected storm the plane was still scheduled to land on time.
14. Maurice's dad is returning from his deployment in Iraq tomorrow and the whole family will be there to welcome him home.

Each sentence below is missing a colon or a semicolon. Circle the missing punctuation mark in parentheses.

1. The following items are not allowed in the auditorium (; :) food, beverages, cell phones, and cameras.
2. There was a sign posted on the studio door (; :) it said that classes were canceled.
3. Katrina grew to dislike her own name (; :) it never failed to remind her of the hurricane.
4. The daily lunch special includes the following (; :) half a sandwich, a cup of soup, an apple, and a fountain drink.

Review

NAME ____________________

Review Chapter 2 Lessons 5–12

Review: Quotation Marks, Using Italics and Underlining, Apostrophes, Hyphens, Dashes, Parentheses, Ellipses

Rewrite each sentence below to add quotation marks or apostrophes where they are needed. Two sentences also contain words that need to be underlined when you rewrite the sentences.

1. In spite of last nights loss, said Coach Trammel, I have a good feeling about next weeks game.

   ____

   ____

2. I think that the movie Oz: The Great and Powerful is a prequel to Frank L. Baums novels about Oz, commented Eva.

   ____

   ____

3. Why arent you doing your presentation on the Salem witch trials? asked Nates sister.

   ____

4. If youll be going on the field trip to Gaston County History Museum on Friday, announced Ms. Mahmood, please bring your lunch with you.

   ____

   ____

5. On Saturday, Rubens cousin is going to a performance of the play The King and I.

   ____

Add hyphens where they are needed in each item below.

1. twenty four roses
2. a one way street
3. chocolate covered strawberries
4. a mid August birthday
5. the well loved professor
6. five year old sister

Add the missing dashes, parentheses, or ellipses to each sentence below. There may be more than one correct answer for some items.

1. Reed's brother ______ he goes to school in Vermont ______ is coming home for summer.
2. Tilly looked for hours and hours ______ she just didn't know what else to do.
3. The theme for Andrea's birthday party ______ she turns 13 on May 15th ______ is the Eighties.
4. The weeds are taking over the garden ______ but at least we're still getting a decent harvest.

Review

Chapter 3 Usage

NAME ____________________

Lesson 3.1 Word Roots

The **root** of a word is the main part of the word. It tells the main meaning, and other word parts add to the main meaning.

The root *spect* means "look" or "see."
The word *in<u>spect</u>* means "to look closely or carefully."
The word *<u>spect</u>acle* means "something interesting to look at."

If an unfamiliar word contains a familiar root, knowing the meaning of the root can give you a clue to the meaning of the unfamiliar word.

Most roots in the English language come from the Latin or Greek languages.

Latin Root Examples	**Greek Root Examples**
audi means "hear"	*bio* means "life"
dict means "say"	*chrono* means "time"
mis means "send"	*geo* means "earth"
port means "carry"	*graph* means "write"
sens and *sent* mean "feel"	*phon* means "sound"
vid or *vis* mean "see"	*photo* means "light"

Identify It

Review the examples above. Then, underline the roots where they are used in the words below. On the line, write an example of another word that contains the same root. Use a dictionary if you need help.

1. synchronize ____________________
2. invisible ____________________
3. respectful ____________________
4. photosynthesis ____________________
5. graphically ____________________
6. prediction ____________________
7. autobiography ____________________
8. geothermal ____________________
9. transmission ____________________
10. auditory ____________________
11. insensitive ____________________
12. telephone ____________________
13. deportation ____________________
14. resentful ____________________

NAME ____________________

Lesson 3.1 Word Roots

Complete It

Fill in the missing information in the table below. Use a dictionary if you need help.

Root	Meaning	Example
	"first"	primitive
spher		hemisphere
dia	"across"	
bene	"good"	
	"great"	magnify
levi		levity
	"heavy"	gravity
script	"write"	
pos	"put"	
retro		retrospect
rupt		disrupt
	"self"	automatic
ped		centipede
giga	"billion"	
	"to know"	recognize
astr	"star"	
	"empty"	evacuate
duc	"make"	

Try It

Choose four roots from the list above. Think of a word other than the one shown for each root and use it in a sentence. Write your sentences on the lines below.

1. **root:** __________ **sentence:** ____

____

2. **root:** __________ **sentence:** ____

____

3. **root:** __________ **sentence:** ____

____

4. **root:** __________ **sentence:** ____

____

NAME ____________________

Lesson 3.2 Prefixes and Suffixes

Prefixes and suffixes change the meanings of root and base words. A **prefix** is a word part added to the beginning of a root or base word. For example, the prefix *pre-* means "before," so *precut* means "cut **before**."

Some common prefixes and their meanings are listed below.

in-, im-, ir-, il- = "not'"	irregular, impolite, illiterate
re- = "again"	refreeze
dis- = "not, opposite of"	disconnect
non- = "not"	nonslip
over- = "too much"	overcook
mis- = "wrongly"	miscalculate
pre- = "before"	precut
inter- = "between, among"	intercoastal

Rewrite It

Add a prefix from the list above to each base word, and write the new word on the first line. If necessary, check in a dictionary to be sure the prefix and base word form an accepted English word. Then, use the new word in a sentence.

1. understand ____________________

____

2. state ____________________

____

3. order ____________________

____

4. organized ____________________

____

5. applied ____________________

____

6. perfect ____________________

____

7. issue ____________________

____

8. excited ____________________

____

NAME ___________________________

Lesson 3.2 Prefixes and Suffixes

A **suffix** is a word part added to the end of a root or base word. Sometimes, the spelling of the root or base word changes when a suffix is added. For example, the suffix *-ness* means "state or condition of." *Happiness* means "**the state or condition of** being happy." Note that the final *-y* in *happy* changes to *i* before adding the suffix.

Some common suffixes and their meanings are listed below.

-ful, -y = "characterized by or tending to"	playful, chilly
-ly = "characteristic of"	angrily
-er, -or, -ist = "one who" or "person connected with"	dreamer, cellist
-ion, -tion, -ation, -ition = "act or process"	animation
-ic = "having characteristics of"	allergic
-less = "without"	harmless
-en = "made of" or "to make"	brighten
-ment = "act or process"	fulfillment
-ness, -ity = "state or condition of"	stubbornness, infinity

Complete It

Complete each sentence below by adding one of the suffixes listed above to the root word in boldface. Then, underline the suffix. Use a dictionary if you need help.

1. A stove covered in **grime** is ________________.
2. If you make something **light**er you ________________ it.
3. An **athlete** can be described as someone who is ________________.
4. A gift that has **meaning** to you is ________________.
5. Someone who **climbs** is a ________________.
6. If you don't have a **penny**, you are ________________.
7. A doctor who studies **paleontology** is called a ________________.
8. ________________ is the process of putting something in a specific **place**.
9. ________________ is the process of **graduat**ing from school.
10. Someone who works in **realty** is a ________________.
11. A **grumpy** person is in a state of ________________.
12. If you are very **thirsty** as you drink water, you drink it ________________.

NAME ____________________

Lesson 3.2 Prefixes and Suffixes

Adding a suffix to a base word, or changing an existing suffix, often changes the word's part of speech. For example, *generous* is an adjective. When the suffix *-ity* is added to *generous*, the word *generosity* is formed, which is a noun meaning "the state of being generous."

Identify It

On the first line, identify the part of speech of the word shown. Then, add the suffix and write the new word on the second line, followed by the part of speech of the new word. The first problem has been done as an example.

1. adjective happy + -ness = happiness noun
2. ____________ run + er = ____________ ____________
3. ____________ stress + ful = ____________ ____________
4. ____________ limit + less = ____________ ____________
5. ____________ animate + tion = ____________ ____________
6. ____________ purposeful + ly = ____________ ____________
7. ____________ squeak + y = ____________ ____________
8. ____________ violin + ist = ____________ ____________
9. ____________ moist + en = ____________ ____________
10. ____________ govern + ment = ____________ ____________

Try It

On each line below, write a sentence that includes a word with the prefix or suffix indicated.

1. the suffix *-ic* ____________________
2. the prefix *dis-* ____________________
3. the prefix *inter-* ____________________
4. the suffix *-y* ____________________
5. the prefix *in-* ____________________
6. the suffix *-ful* ____________________

Lesson 3.2 Prefixes and Suffixes

Solve It

Read each definition below. Fill in the correct space in the crossword puzzle with a word that begins with a prefix or ends in a suffix and matches the definition.

Across
2 not sane
4 state or condition of being sweet
6 one who directs
7 without hair
8 to calculate wrongly

Down
1 to wrongly file
3 the act or process of entertaining
4 to make straight

NAME ____________________

Lesson 3.3 Negatives and Double Negatives

Double negatives occur when two negative words are used in the same sentence. Negative words include *not, no, never, neither, nobody, nowhere, nothing, barely, hardly, scarcely,* and contractions containing the word *not.* Avoid using double negatives—they are grammatically incorrect.

Negative: Ava and Emma *couldn't* see any stars because of the clouds.
Double Negative: Ava and Emma *couldn't* see *no* stars because of the clouds.

To correct a double negative, you can delete one of the negative words or replace it with an affirmative, or positive, word. Affirmative words are the opposite of negative words. Examples include *some, somewhere, someone, anyone, any,* and *always.*

Double Negative: *No one* did *nothing* to fix the broken chair in the hall.
Possible correction: *No one* did *anything* to fix the broken chair in the hall.

Identify It

Underline the word or words in parentheses that best complete each sentence below.

1. The doors are still locked, so nobody (is, isn't) sitting in the waiting room yet.
2. The horses won't eat (no, any) feed until Mr. Yates fills the food trough.
3. I could barely hear (nothing, anything) because I was seated at the back of the auditorium.
4. Uncle Joshua (will, won't) never finish repairing your car at the rate he's going.
5. The turtle won't (ever, never) stick its head out of its shell if you're too loud.
6. Ms. Henks won't accept (no, any) papers that are turned in after Friday.
7. The bus is hardly (never, ever) late arriving to pick up students from school.
8. Justin couldn't remember (no one, anyone) ever cleaning out the bottom drawer of the desk.
9. Grandma's been sewing for two hours, but she still hasn't finished mending (none, any) of the socks.
10. Despite several announcements that taxes would be reduced, the governor (has, hasn't) still not followed through on his promise.
11. We scarcely (never, ever) visit this restaurant anymore.
12. Months after leaving the Dust Bowl of Oklahoma, the Judsons still hadn't found (no, any) suitable place to settle.
13. Please don't allow (anyone, no one) to enter the living room while I wrap presents.
14. Because of heavy snowfall, no trucks (could, couldn't) reach the delivery dock.

NAME ______________________

Lesson 3.3 Negatives and Double Negatives

Rewrite It

Each sentence below contains a double negative. Rewrite the sentences to eliminate the double negatives. There may be more than one correct answer for each item.

1. We couldn't get none of the sheep into the barn before the storm hit.

   ____

2. Carl seldom never plays chess, but when he does, he usually wins.

   ____

3. Marty wouldn't give nobody a turn riding his new skateboard.

   ____

4. Ms. Reynolds didn't want to hear nobody complaining about the due dates for our reports.

   ____

5. If it keeps raining like this, we will not be going nowhere this weekend.

   ____

6. Don't nobody come near this stove while it's hot.

   ____

7. Drew didn't find none of the books he needed at the library.

   ____

8. The Lewis twins can't hardly wait for the next *Star Wars* movie to be released.

   ____

Try It

Write three sentences using double negatives. Trade papers with a friend and correct each other's errors.

1. ____

   ____

2. ____

   ____

3. ____

   ____

NAME ______________________________

Lesson 3.4 Synonyms and Antonyms

Synonyms are words that have the same, or almost the same, meaning. Using synonyms can help you avoid repeating words and can make your writing more interesting. A thesaurus, either in book form or online, is good source for finding synonyms.

empty/vacant inspect/examine casual/informal
brief/concise

Antonyms are words that have opposite meanings. A thesaurus, either in book form or online, is a good source for finding antonyms.

blunt/sharp likely/unlikely bold/timid frequent/seldom

Match It

Read each set of words below. Circle the two words in each set that are synonyms.

1. renew reliable dependable unreliable
2. mock ridicule lodge comfort
3. faithful preserve loyal lonely
4. relative negotiate rejoice bargain
5. residence community singular dwelling
6. subject column topic explanation
7. assert divide nestle snuggle
8. putrid rotten fresh mysterious

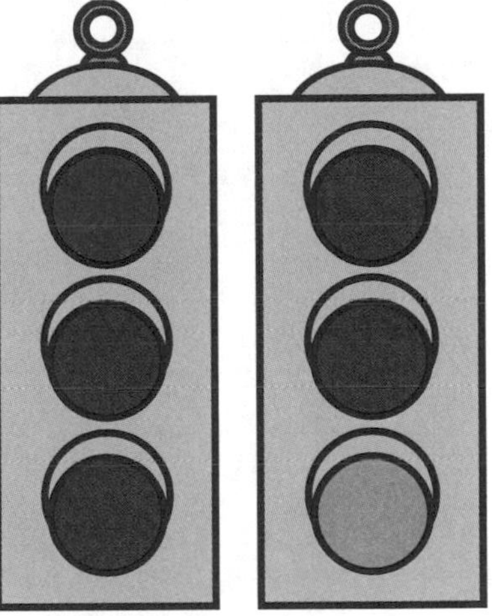

Now, circle the two words in each set that are antonyms.

9. patient advantage permanent disadvantage
10. optimist liquid depressed pessimist
11. temporary intelligence knowledge ignorance
12. attraction attract powerful repel
13. transparent horizontal voluntary vertical
14. demand qualified supply nonsense
15. feeble strong invisible plural
16. dishonest encourage discourage humble

NAME ______________________

Lesson 3.4 Synonyms and Antonyms

Identify It

Read each sentence below. The letter in parentheses will tell you whether to look in the box for a synonym or antonym for the boldface word. Write your answer on the line.

outstanding	**weaken**	**progress**	**observant**	**irregular**
reimbursed	**fertile**	**cheerful**	**unprofitable**	**attractive**

1. (S) ______________ The temperatures this month have been **erratic**, so we won't plant the seeds quite yet.
2. (A) ______________ The builder advised that we **fortify** the porch before we build the addition.
3. (S) ______________ Grandma says that the first time she saw my grandpa, she wondered, "Who on Earth is that **comely** boy?"
4. (A) ______________ The review said that the food at Tacos-to-Go is only **mediocre**.
5. (A) ______________ Fatima has come up with an idea for a summer job that we hope will be very **lucrative**.
6. (S) ______________ My dad will be **compensated** for the time he spends editing the proposal.
7. (A) ______________ I'm hoping that Jonathan doesn't **revert** to some of his old behaviors.
8. (A) ______________ The **barren** fields have not produced a harvest in years.
9. (S) ______________ Part of the reason Leah is such a good writer is that she is very **perceptive**.
10. (A) ______________ The **dour** expression on Viktor's face told me that he was in a difficult mood.

Find It

Use a dictionary, thesaurus, or online resource to find the following synonyms or antonyms. There may be more than one correct answer.

1. an antonym for *descend* ______________
2. a synonym for *animosity* ______________
3. a synonym for *rebuttal* ______________
4. an antonym for *vacant* ______________
5. an antonym for *expulsion* ______________
6. a synonym for *improbable* ______________
7. an antonym for *immense* ______________
8. a synonym for *illegible* ______________

NAME ____________________

Lesson 3.5 Analogies

An **analogy** is a comparison between two pairs of words. To complete an analogy, figure out how the pairs of words are related.

Attract is to *repel* as *conceal* is to *reveal.*
Attract is the opposite of *repel,* just as *conceal* is the opposite of *reveal.*

Pedal is to *bicycle* as *row* is to *canoe.*
You pedal a bicycle to move it, just as you row a canoe to move it.

Zipper is to *jacket* as *lead* is to *pencil.*
A zipper is part of a jacket, just as lead is part of a pencil.

Analogies are often presented without using the phrase *is to* and the word *as.* Instead, colons are used in place of *is to,* and two colons are used in place of *as* to separate the pairs being compared.

Horse is to *hoarse* as *road* is to *rode.*
horse : hoarse : : road : rode

Solve It

To solve each analogy below, unscramble the word in parentheses and write it on the line.

1. *Goose* is to ____________________ as *mouse* is to *mice.* (esege)
2. *Russia* is to ____________________ as *Paris* is to *city.* (rycntou)
3. *Five* is to *twenty-five* as ____________________ is to *one hundred forty-four.* (lvtewe)
4. *Satisfied* is to *unsatisfied* as ____________________ is to *rewrite.* (iewtr)
5. *Book* is to *read* as *ruler* is to ____________________. (eerasmu)
6. *Dance* is to *tango* as ____________________ is to *lullaby.* (gsno)
7. *Blender* is to ____________________ as *computer* is to *office.* (thckein)
8. *Pack* is to ____________________ as *school* is to *fish.* (sloevw)
9. ____________________ is to *letter* as *keyboard* is to *e-mail.* (npe)
10. *Doe* is to *deer* as ____________________ is to *pig.* (wso)
11. *Hola* is to *Spanish* as ____________________ is to *English.* (lhewlo)
12. *Inch* is to *yard* as ____________________ is to *meter.* (etceetimrn)

NAME ____________________

Lesson 3.5 Analogies

Complete It

Circle the letter of the word that best completes each analogy.

1. Skin : __________ : : crust : Earth.
   a. wheat b. apple c. nose d. moon
2. Bean : legume : : __________ : crustacean.
   a. chili b. shark c. peanut d. shrimp
3. Beef : cow : : __________ : pig.
   a. pork b. calf c. barnyard d. pen
4. __________ : yarn : : pulp : paper.
   a. knit b. draw c. wool d. cotton
5. Was : were : : __________ : dreamed.
   a. dream b. dreaming c. is d. am
6. Apple : McIntosh : : tree : __________.
   a. orange b. sycamore c. seed d. climb
7. Sandals : summer : : __________ : winter.
   a. flip-flops b. mittens c. sundress d. high heels
8. __________: amazing : : acknowledge : respond.
   a. expect b. unusual c. respectful d. extraordinary
9. Mad : __________ : : happy : overjoyed.
   a. furious b. exhausted c. confused d. suspect
10. Sixty-three : thirty-six : : __________ : eighty-two.
    a. twenty-six b. fifteen c. twenty-eight d. eighty-eight

Try It

Follow the directions to write your own analogies.

1. Write an analogy in which the words are homographs.

   ____

2. Write an analogy that shows a part-to-whole relationship.

   ____

3. Write an analogy that shows a numerical relationship.

   ____

4. Write an analogy that shows an object-use relationship.

   ____

5. Write an analogy in which the words are antonyms.

   ____

NAME ______________________________

Review Chapter 3 Lessons 1–5

Review: Word Roots, Prefixes and Suffixes, Negatives and Double Negatives

For each suffix or prefix, locate its meaning in the box. Write the meaning on the first line, and then write an example of a word that uses the prefix or suffix on the second line.

wrongly	**made of or to make**	**too much**	**state or condition of**
one who	**not or opposite of**	**without**	**having characteristics of**

1. *-or* ______________________ ______________________
2. *over-* ______________________ ______________________
3. *-en* ______________________ ______________________
4. *-ness* ______________________ ______________________
5. *mis-* ______________________ ______________________
6. *-less* ______________________ ______________________
7. *-ic* ______________________ ______________________
8. *non-* ______________________ ______________________

Each sentence below contains a root or base word with a familiar prefix or suffix. Underline the root or base word, and circle the familiar prefix or suffix. (Each root or base word, prefix, and suffix was used in a previous lesson.)

1. The gravity of the situation became clear as the judge entered the courtroom.
2. The crew anticipates that construction on the stadium will be completed next month.
3. In spite of the disruption the alarm caused, the students returned to the exam in just a few minutes.
4. Davis has inherited his mom's optimistic outlook on life.
5. We were horrified to find that the car was unrecognizable after the accident.
6. The weather station's prediction for Saturday was right on target.
7. Amina's love for photography began when she was still a teenager.
8. It is quite common for people to mispronounce my last name.

Underline the word or words in parentheses that best complete each sentence below.

1. Despite a lengthy e-mail correspondence last year, Brady hardly (never, ever) writes to his pen pal anymore.
2. The builder won't do (anything, nothing) until she's had a chance to speak with the architect.
3. Dante and Ava won't eat (none, any) of the foods at the potluck until they know what ingredients have been used.
4. Because the side streets had not been plowed yet, the buses couldn't go (nowhere, anywhere).

Review

NAME ______________________________

Review Chapter 3 Lessons 1–5

Review: Synonyms and Antonyms, Analogies

Read each word pair. Write **A** on the line if the words are antonyms, and write **S** on the line if the words are synonyms

1. ______ brief concise
2. ______ disgruntled pleased
3. ______ smug satisfied
4. ______ pertinent relevant
5. ______ approached departed
6. ______ necessary required
7. ______ captivity freedom
8. ______ endow grant
9. ______ majority minority
10. ______ positive negative
11. ______ previous former
12. ______ victory defeat
13. ______ plentiful scarce
14. ______ crooked askew
15. ______ artificial natural
16. ______ ominous sinister
17. ______ pollute contaminate
18. ______ qualified unqualified
19. ______ poverty wealth
20. ______ surly grumpy

Circle the word in parentheses that best completes each analogy.

1. *Reptile* is to *(vertebrate, snake)* as *mammal* is to *dolphin.*
2. *Clause* is to *claws* as *vain* is to *(vein, cat).*
3. *Past* is to *(present, memory)* as *peace* is to *war.*
4. *Pane* is to *window* as *(climb, rung)* is to *ladder.*
5. *(Artist, Mozart)* is to *compose* as *Monet* is to *paint.*
6. *Word* is to *dictionary* as *bristle* is to *(brush, page).*
7. *Happy* is to *happiness* as *(curious, sadness)* is to *curiosity.*
8. *(Classroom, Principal)* is to *school* as *surgeon* is to *hospital.*
9. *Hurricane* is to *ocean* as *tornado* is to *(cloud, land).*
10. *Potter* is to *clay* as *(sculpture, writer)* is to *words.*
11. *Dublin* is to *(Ireland, city)* as *Berlin* is to *Germany.*
12. *Leap* is to *bound* as *walk* is to *(stroll, swim).*

NAME ______________________

Lesson 3.6 Homophones

Homophones are words that sound the same but have different spellings and different meanings. There are hundreds of homophones in the English language.

pain - ache or soreness
pane - one section of glass in a window

gilt - covered in a thin layer of gold
guilt - remorse or regret

berries - small fruit
buries - places below ground

If you are unsure about which homophone to use, look up the meanings in a dictionary.

Complete It

Each sentence is followed by a pair of homophones in parentheses. Complete the sentence by choosing the correct homophone and writing it on the line.

1. During the avalanche, a ________________ rolled downhill and came to rest in the middle of the highway. (bolder, boulder)
2. Rapunzel tossed her long ________________ out the window when she heard the prince's call. (lox, locks)
3. According to geological time, we live in the Holocene ________________. (epoch, epic)
4. Aaron Burr and Alexander Hamilton fought a ________________ in 1804. (dual, duel)
5. Grandpa Taylor told me he was ________________ with guilt about forgetting my birthday. (wracked, racked)
6. Seventeen trapped ________________ were rescued yesterday in Australia. (minors, miners)
7. Chef Alexis ________________ the pizza dough for nearly ten minutes before rolling it out. (kneaded, needed)
8. Pa attached a harness to the ________________ encircling the oxen's necks. (yoke, yolk)
9. ________________ is generally considered the time period between puberty and adulthood. (Adolescents, Adolescence)
10. ________________ gym clothes were left in the locker overnight. (They're, Their)
11. After school today, ________________ going to pick up your father and head to the dentist. (were, we're)
12. Underneath the bark, the rotten wood was ________________ with beetles and other insects. (teeming, teaming)
13. On January 12, President Romero will step down and ________________ power to her successor. (seed, cede)
14. After hiking in his new boots, Andrew's right ________________ ached from a blister. (heal, heel)
15. The ________________ of King Louis XVI ended with the French Revolution. (rein, reign)

NAME ____________________

Lesson 3.6 Homophones

Proof It

Each sentence below contains at least one error in homophone usage, and some sentences contain two errors. Use proofreading marks to correct the mistakes.

deletes letters, words, punctuation
^ – **inserts letters, words, punctuation**

1. Library patrons are not aloud to raze their voices, because the noise may disturb others.
2. Louisa rapped a gift in colorful paper and placed a big green bow on top.
3. Please ewes the backdoor win you deliver the refrigerator.
4. Marvin found himself counting down each our until he would have too take the stage for his recital.
5. As costs rise in the future due to inflation, the impact of the new tax will lesson.
6. We red in the newspaper that an anime festival would be coming to the city.
7. A not in the rope keeps it from slipping through the whole in the board.
8. We new earlier in the year that we wood be traveling to Minnesota.
9. The cent of fresh flowers drifted in through the open window.
10. Some old jars are left down in the seller, along with a pare of windows from the barn.
11. Officer Ruiz let his patrol car idol by the curb as he went inside to investigate.
12. The flowers have groan sew much taller since you added some fertilizer.

Try It

Write sentences for each pair of homophones. Be sure to use the correct meaning of the homophone in your sentence. Use a dictionary if you need help.

1. **dessert:** ____________________

   desert: ____________________
2. **taught:** ____________________

   taut: ____________________
3. **serial:** ____________________

   cereal: ____________________
4. **medal:** ____________________

   meddle: ____________________

NAME ______________________

Lesson 3.7 Multiple-Meaning Words

Multiple-meaning words, or **homographs**, are words that are spelled the same but have different meanings. They may also sometimes have different pronunciations.

The word *refuse* can mean "trash or garbage," or it can mean "deny or reject."

> The empty lot was littered with *refuse*, including broken bottles and an old mattress.
>
> I *refuse* to believe that you read all of *War* and *Peace* in a single night.

Solve It

Read each pair of definitions below. Think of the multiple-meaning word that fits both definitions and write it on the lines. Then, take the first letters of the words and place them, in order, onto the lines at the end to answer the question.

1. a legal agreement; to become shorter

   ___ ___ ___ ___ ___ ___ ___ ___

2. part of a minute; after first

   ___ ___ ___ ___ ___ ___

3. a soft metal; have others following you

   ___ ___ ___ ___

4. a place to come in; fill with delight or wonder

   ___ ___ ___ ___ ___ ___ ___ ___

5. turned; an cut or other injury

   ___ ___ ___ ___ ___

6. make angry; a substance burned to create a pleasant odor

   ___ ___ ___ ___ ___ ___ ___

7. topic or course of study; a person who lives under the rule of a king

   ___ ___ ___ ___ ___ ___ ___

What famous author wrote: "Humility is not thinking less of yourself, it's thinking of yourself less."

___. ___. ___ ___ ___ ___ ___

NAME ____________________

Lesson 3.7 Multiple-Meaning Words

Rewrite It

Read each sentence below. Then, write a new sentence using a different meaning for the underlined word. Use a dictionary if you need help.

1. My grandmother has dozens of old *Reader's Digest* magazines stored in a closet.

   ____

2. The recipe called for half a teaspoon of almond extract to be added last.

   ____

3. "The kids at school were upset to learn that the arts program would lose funding," said Jamal.

   ____

4. When teenagers rebel, it's often to show their independence.

   ____

5. After evening the boards, Sandy glued them together.

   ____

6. The detective took the suspect into custody and prepared to question him.

   ____

7. "That pink is too strong for this room," said Ms. Ling. "Let's try a softer shade."

   ____

8. Bella lit a match and touched the flame to the wads of paper underneath the twigs.

   ____

9. With his baton held high, Maestro Kubelik prepared to conduct the orchestra.

   ____

10. First the waiters will clear the tables, and then they will serve dessert.

    ____

Try It

Choose your own multiple-meaning word and use each of its meanings in a different sentence.

Multiple-meaning word: ____________________

Meaning #1: ____________________

____

Meaning #2: ____________________

____

NAME ______________________

Lesson 3.8 Connotations and Denotations

A word's **denotation** is its actual, literal meaning. It is the meaning you would find if you looked the word up in a dictionary.

A word's **connotation** is the meaning associated with the word. The connotation may be more emotional, or tied to an idea or feeling about the word. Connotations can be positive, negative, or neutral.

For example, the words *aroma, smell,* and *stink* are all synonyms with approximately the same denotation, or actual, meaning: "odor." The connotation of these words, however, is different. *Aroma* has a positive connotation—it brings to mind the odor of baking bread or other good foods cooking. *Smell* is neutral because it can have a positive or negative connotation depending on how it is used. *Stink* has a negative connotation because it is almost always used to describe things that smell bad.

Complete It

Each row in the table lists three words with similar denotations but different connotations. The first row is completed as an example. Complete the other rows with appropriate words. Use a thesaurus or dictionary if you need help.

Positive	Neutral	Negative
prudence		paranoia
laid-back	relaxed	
home	house	
amusing		ridiculous
	interested	nosy
rustic		dilapidated
ornate	elaborate	
	less expensive	cheap

NAME ______________________________

Lesson 3.8 Connotations and Denotations

Rewrite It

Rewrite each sentence below, replacing the underlined word with a word that has a similar denotation but different connotation. Use a thesaurus or dictionary if you need help. Then, identify the connotation of the new word by writing **P** for positive or **N** for negative on the short line. Leave the line blank if the connotation is neutral.

1. Rudy collects old newspapers and stores them in his attic.

   ______________________________ ______

2. Energetic children raced around the rec center, chasing each other and making a lot of noise.

   ______________________________ ______

3. My sister has a unique way of riding her bike.

   ______________________________ ______

4. Lucas's flimsy model ship barely made it to school in one piece.

   ______________________________ ______

5. A youthful group of teens laughed and whispered throughout the performance.

   ______________________________ ______

6. Shawn's reckless behavior during the game resulted in a penalty.

   ______________________________ ______

7. The miserly owner seldom ever gave his employees bonuses or raises.

   ______________________________ ______

8. Ms. Sanchez was surprised at seeing Lauren in such a casual outfit.

   ______________________________ ______

Try It

Write a sentence for each word below. The words in each pair have similar denotations but different connotations.

1. fussy ______________________________

   detailed ______________________________

2. stare ______________________________

   glower ______________________________

3. calculated ______________________________

   thoughtful ______________________________

NAME ______________________

Lesson 3.9 Figures of Speech: Similes, Metaphors, and Personification

A **simile** is a figure of speech that compares two things using the words *like* or *as.*

The skin on my great-grandad's hands was like *the rough bark of an ancient tree.*
The fireflies in the jar were as bright as *tiny fallen stars.*

A **metaphor** is a figure of speech that compares two unlike things that are similar in some way.

The sound of the whirring fan was *a lullaby that quickly put me to sleep.*
The cheery yellow daffodils were *a sign announcing "Spring is here!"*

Personification is a figure of speech that gives human characteristics to something that is not human.

The blank computer screen *stared reproachfully* at Luke, *wondering* when he would begin his paper.

Identify It

Read each sentence below. Circle a boldface letter to indicate whether the sentence contains a metaphor, simile, or personification.

1. **S M P** When Paco lit the fire, the flames quickly and greedily ate the dry leaves.
2. **S M P** Tears ran down Grace's face, leaving shiny tracks like snails on the move.
3. **S M P** Dread was a mountain that loomed over Tanya.
4. **S M P** The baby's hair was as soft as a dandelion puff.
5. **S M P** Murphy's heart hung like a heavy steel weight in his chest.
6. **S M P** After the ice storm, the trees glittered with thousands of crystal ornaments.
7. **S M P** Fat snowflakes drifted to the ground like small parachutes.
8. **S M P** The balloon drifted higher and higher, teasing the boy who jumped for its string.
9. **S M P** The icy wind cut through the layers Esther wore like a freshly sharpened knife.
10. **S M P** The hurtful words Dominic had spoken were a wall between his mother and him.
11. **S M P** The stitches on Mark's leg were tiny railroad tracks leading to his ankle.
12. **S M P** The clock ticked impatiently, urging Toshi to hurry up.

NAME ______________________

Lesson 3.9 Figures of Speech: Similes, Metaphors, and Personification

Rewrite It

Rewrite each sentence below using a simile, metaphor, or personification to make the writing more descriptive or interesting to read. Make sure to use each type of figure of speech at least once.

1. Brandon worried about his upcoming math test.

____

____

2. The mug shattered on the floor.

____

____

3. A flock of starlings flew into the maple tree.

____

____

4. Myla's dog scurried under the couch when she heard the thunder.

____

____

5. The plane left a white trail behind it in the sky.

____

____

6. The giraffe nibbled at the leaves of the tree.

____

____

7. The morning glory vine twined around the mailbox post.

____

____

8. Connor flipped on the stereo and covered his ears as music blasted from the speakers.

____

____

9. Through the open window, I could hear the waves washing up on the beach.

____

____

10. Peter and Phong jumped as high as they could on the trampoline.

____

____

NAME ______________________

Lesson 3.10 Figures of Speech: Verbal Irony, Puns, and Hyperbole

Verbal irony is when a statement's literal meaning is different from, or even opposite of, its intended meaning.

When Beth saw her favorite teapot lying in pieces on the floor, she said, "Oh, great. I was hoping that would happen." (Beth is saying the opposite of what she means.)

A **pun** is a humorous play on words. Puns are often based on similar-sounding words or multiple-meaning words.

Vladimir Putin never slows down; he's always *Russian*. (*Russian* is used instead of *rushing*.)

"Where does a spy go at bedtime?" Rani asked. "Undercover!"(*Undercover* refers to both "in disguise" and "under the covers in bed.")

Hyperbole is exaggerating for effect. The exaggeration is extreme and obvious, so it is not meant to be taken seriously.

By the time we got to the theater, the ticket line was a hundred miles long, so we decided to leave.

Identify It

Identify each example below with **I** for irony, **P** for pun, or **H** for hyperbole.

1. ______ My brother left the door wide open when he came home, so I told him, "Thanks for airing out the front hall. Mom will really appreciate it."
2. ______ This song is so hard. It'll be years before I learn all the notes!
3. ______ I've been to the dentist plenty of times; I know the drill.
4. ______ Look at that sandwich. There must be a million ants crawling on it.
5. ______ The ringing bell tolled us it was time to leave.
6. ______ As Louis looked out at the pouring rain, he said, "It's just a lovely day, isn't it?"
7. ______ It was foggy this morning, but I woke up late and mist it.
8. ______ Today was so cold, I saw a penguin wearing a parka.
9. ______ Matthew handed the comic back to his younger brother and said, "Nothing makes me feel as grown-up as reading books with pictures."
10. ______ We must have walked a thousand miles to get to this side of the airport!

NAME ____________________

Lesson 3.10 Figures of Speech: Verbal Irony, Puns, and Hyperbole

Try It

Use the descriptions below to write your own examples of hyperbole and verbal irony.

1. A classmate disturbs you while you are studying. What do you say to him or her?

   verbal irony: ____________________

2. You visit the observation deck on the top floor of the tallest skyscraper in the city. What do you say as you look out the windows?

   hyperbole: ____________________

3. You visit the grocery store on the night before Thanksgiving. It is as crowded as you've ever seen it. What do you say?

   hyperbole: ____________________

4. You see a bicyclist weaving dangerously through the cars in a traffic jam. What do you say about it?

   verbal irony: ____________________

5. You arrive to class several minutes late. What do you say to the teacher if you're trying to be funny?

   verbal irony: ____________________

6. You've just completed a very difficult exam. How do you describe it?

   hyperbole: ____________________

Write the word that completes each pun.

1. Turtles talk on ____________ phones.
2. Fish are smart because they live in ____________ .
3. Wolves like cards because they come in ____________ .
4. Don't try to use that broken pencil; it's____________ .
5. You can't ____________ a hard-boiled egg for breakfast.
6. A golfer wore two pairs of pants to the course just in case he got a ____________ in one.

NAME ____________________

Review Chapter 3 Lessons 6–10

Review: Homophones, Multiple-Meaning Words

Read each definition. Choose the correct homophone from the box, and write it on the line beside the definition.

lightning	they're	mustered	mustard	fourth
ceiling	forth	sealing	their	lightening

1. ____________ the top of an enclosed room
2. ____________ making something less dark
3. ____________ onward or outward from a place or time
4. ____________ assembled or gathered
5. ____________ spicy yellow or brown sauce
6. ____________ a plural possessive pronoun
7. ____________ bright electrical discharge, usually from a cloud
8. ____________ after third
9. ____________ closing tightly
10. ____________ contraction formed from *they* and *are*

Read each sentence below. Then, write a new sentence using a different meaning for the underlined word. Use a dictionary if you need help.

1. Hank's library card was invalid because it had expired over the summer.
____
2. I'm avoiding Rachel today, because I refuse to subject myself to her rudeness.
____
3. Judge Unger ruled that a 5-year sentence would be excessive for minor vandalism.
____
4. Please conduct yourself with grace and humility when you meet the Queen.
____
5. Mr. Jenkins showed us several slides from his vacation to Europe during the 1970s.
____
6. Hydrogen is listed first on the periodic table of elements.
____
7. "I'll be with you in a minute, Mr. Fields," said Daisy.
____
8. Dr. Munson placed a cold compress on Eliza's bruised ankle.
____

NAME ______________________

Review Chapter 3 Lessons 6–10

Review: Connotations and Denotations, Figures of Speech

Write a sentence using each boldface word below. Follow the sentence by adding whether the word, as you used it, has a positive, neutral, or negative connotation.

1. **odd** ____
____
2. **pride** ____
____
3. **wild** ____
____
4. **immature** ____
____

Each sentence below contains a simile, a metaphor, or personification. Underline each figure of speech, and write **S**, **M**, or **P** on the line to tell what type of figure of speech it is.

1. The flag on top of the fort waved invitingly, announcing a warm, sheltered place for us to spend the evening. ______
2. The old photo album was a time machine carrying us back to more youthful days. ______
3. As the wrecking ball drew back for a final swing, the last wall of the abandoned factory bravely awaited its fate. ______
4. Like metal balls bouncing around inside a pinball machine, the squirrels chased each other in zigzag patterns across the lawn. ______
5. The red sun sank in the west, a ship carrying the final moments of the day out of sight beyond the horizon. ______
6. The field of wildflowers stretched before us like an ocean of green littered with confetti. ______

Identify each example below with **I** for irony, **P** for pun, or **H** for hyperbole.

1. After working all afternoon in the scorching heat, Matthew exclaimed, "I'm so hot, you could fry an egg on my head!" ______
2. When Emma's little sister asked her to tell the story of *Goldilocks and the Three Bears*, Emma replied, "I bear-ly remember how it goes!" ______
3. Paul noticed there were two dozen pies on the dessert table at the potluck, so he remarked, "Gee, do you think we have enough pie?" ______
4. At the little kids' tea party, Louisa pointed to her teddy bear and said, "He doesn't want any food. He's stuffed." ______

NAME ______________________

Chapter 4

Lesson 4.1 Writer's Guide: Prewriting

The five steps of the writing process are **prewriting**, **drafting**, **revising**, **proofreading**, and **publishing**.

Prewriting, the first stage of the writing process, involves planning and organizing. This is the stage where you get the ideas for your paper and start plotting it out.

When you prewrite, you:

- Think of ideas for your topic that are not too narrow or too broad. Write down your chosen ideas.
- Select your favorite topic, the one you think you can write about the best.
- Write down anything that comes to your mind about your chosen topic. Don't worry about grammar and spelling at this stage. This is called *freewriting*.
- Organize your information the way you might organize it in your paper. Use a graphic organizer. Graphic organizers visually represent the layout and ideas for a written paper. Graphic organizers include spider maps, Venn diagrams, story boards, network trees, and outlines.
- Use your graphic organizer to find out what information you already know and what information you need to learn more about.

Prewriting Example

Assignment: biography of a hero

Topic ideas: Martin Luther King, Jr., Eleanor Roosevelt, Jesse Owens, Cleveland Amory, Lance Armstrong, Rachel Carson

Freewriting of selected topic: Cleveland Amory hero of animals. Author. Founder of the Fund for Animals. Wrote The Cat Who Came for Christmas Read Black Beauty as a child and wanted a ranch for rescued animals. Established Black Beauty Ranch for rescued animals.

Graphic organizer:

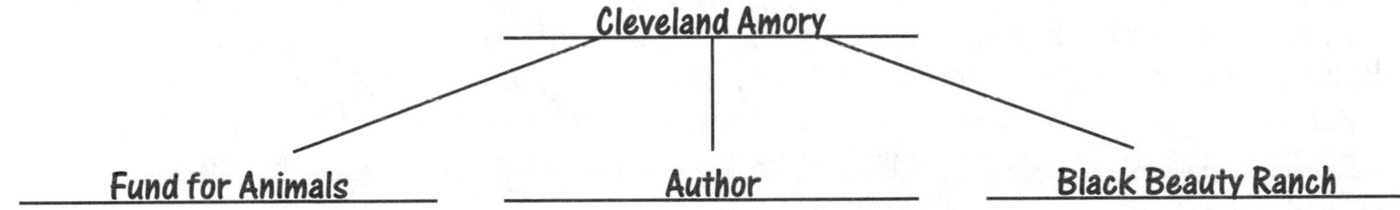

NAME ___________________________

Lesson 4.2 Writer's Guide: Drafting

Drafting involves writing your rough draft. Don't worry too much about grammar and spelling. Write down all of your thoughts about the subject, based on the structure of your graphic organizer.

When you draft, you:

- Write an **introduction** with a topic sentence. Get your readers' attention by stating a startling statistic or asking a question. Explain the purpose of your writing.
- Write the **body** of your paper. Use your graphic organizer to decide how many paragraphs will be included in your paper. Write one paragraph for each idea.
- Write your **conclusion**. Your conclusion will summarize your paper.

Drafting Example

My hero was a hero: a hero to animals. Cleveland Amory (1917-1998) was an author, an animal advocate, and an animal rescuer. Reading Black Beauty as a child inspired a dream for Amory. Cleveland Amory made his dream a reality.

Amory founded The Fund for Animals. The Fund for Animals is an animal advocacy group that campaigns for animal protection. Amory served as its president, without pay, until his death in 1998. Cleveland Amory was an editor. He was an editor for The Saturday Evening Post. He served in World War II. After world war II, he wrote history books that studied society. He was a commentator on The Today Show, a critic for TV guide, a columnist for Saturday Review. Amory especially loved his own cat, Polar Bear, who inspired him to write three instant best-selling books: The Cat Who Came for Christmas, The Cat and the Curmudgeon, and The Best Cat Ever.

When Amory read Black Beauty as a child. When he read Black Beauty, he dreamed of place where animals could roam free and live in caring conditions. The dream is real at Black Beauty Ranch, a sanctuary for abused and abandoned animals The ranch's 1,620 acres serve as home for hundreds of animals, including elephants, horses, burros, ostriches, chimpanzees, and many more. Black Beauty Ranch takes in unwanted, abused, neglected, abandoned, and rescued domestic and exotic animals.

Cleveland Amory is my hero because he is a hero. He worked to make his dreams realities. His best-selling books, the founding of The Fund for Animals, and the opening of Black Beauty Ranch are the legacy of his dreams. Words from Anna Sewell's Black Beauty, the words that inspired Cleveland Amory, are engraved at the entrance to Black Beauty Ranch: "I have nothing to fear; and here my story ends. My troubles are all over, and I am at home." Cleveland Amory died on October 15, 1998. He is buried at Black Beauty Ranch, next to his beloved cat, Polar Bear.

NAME ____________________

Lesson 4.3 Writer's Guide: Revising

Revising is the time to stop and think about what you have already written. It is time to rewrite.

When you revise, you:

- Add or change words.
- Delete unnecessary words or phrases.
- Move text around.
- Improve the overall flow of your paper.

Revising Example (body of paper)

Cleveland Amory did more than just write about the animals he loved.
in 1967 one of the world's most active
Amory founded The Fund for Animals.^ The Fund for Animals is^ ~~an~~ animal advocacy
rights and
group that campaigns for animal^ protection. Amory served as its president, without
Amory extended his devotion to animals with Black Beauty Ranch
started his writing career as
pay, until his death in 1998.^ Cleveland Amory^ ~~was~~ an editor. ~~He was an editor~~ for The
serving in
Saturday Evening Post. ~~He served in World War II~~. After^ world war II^ he wrote history
books that studied society. He was a commentator on The Today Show, a critic for
Amory's love of animals, as well as great affection for
TV guide, a columnist for Saturday Review.^ ~~Amory especially loved~~ his own cat, Polar
led
Bear, ~~who inspired~~^ him to ~~write~~ three instant best-selling books: The Cat Who Came for Christmas, The Cat and the Curmudgeon, and The Best Cat Ever.

Cleveland Amory made his childhood dream come true in 1979 when he
opened Black Beauty Ranch in Texas.
H
~~When Amory read Black Beauty^ as a child. When he read Black Beauty,~~ he
dreamed of place where animals could roam free and live in caring conditions. The
for hundreds of
dream is real^ at Black Beauty Ranch~~, a sanctuary for abused and abandoned animals~~
The ranch's 1,620 acres serve as home for ~~hundreds of animals, including~~ elephants,
animals
horses, burros, ostriches, chimpanzees, and many more.^ ~~Black Beauty Ranch takes in~~
unwanted, abused, neglected, abandoned, and rescued domestic and exotic animals.

NAME ______________________

Lesson 4.4 Writer's Guide: Proofreading

Proofreading is the time to look for more technical errors.

When you proofread, you:

- Check spelling.
- Check grammar.
- Check punctuation.

Proofreading Example (body of paper after revision)

Cleveland Amory started his writing career as an editor for The Saturday Evening Post. After serving in world war II, he wrote history books that studied society. He was a commentator on The Today Show, a critic for TV guide, a columnist for Saturday Review. Amory's love of animals, as well as great affection for his own cat, Polar Bear, led him to three instant best-selling books: The Cat Who Came for Christmas, The Cat and the Curmudgeon, and The Best Cat Ever.

Cleveland Amory did more than just write about the animals he loved. Amory founded The Fund for Animals in 1967. The Fund for Animals is one of the world's most active animal advocacy group that campaigns for animal rights and protection. Amory served as its president, without pay, until his death in 1998. Amory extended his devotion to animals with Black Beauty Ranch.

Cleveland Amory made his childhood dream come true in 1979 when he opened Black Beauty Ranch in Texas. He dreamed of place where animals could roam free and live in caring conditions. The dream is real for hundreds of unwanted, abused, neglected, abandoned, and rescued domestic and exotic animals at Black Beauty Ranch The ranch's 1,620 acres serve as home for elephants, horses, burros, ostriches, chimpanzees, and many more animals.

NAME ____________________

Lesson 4.5 Writer's Guide: Publishing

Publishing is the fifth and final stage of the writing process. Write your final copy and decide how you want to publish your work. Here is a list of some ideas:

- Read your paper to family and classmates.
- Illustrate and hang class papers in a "Hall of Fame" in your class or school.
- Publish your work in a school or community newspaper or magazine.

Publishing (compare to the other three versions to see how it has improved)

Biography of a Hero: Cleveland Amory

My hero was a hero: a hero to animals. Cleveland Amory (1917-1998) was an author, an animal advocate, and an animal rescuer. Reading Black Beauty as a child inspired a dream for Amory. Cleveland Amory made his dream a reality.

Cleveland Amory started his writing career as an editor for The Saturday Evening Post. After serving in World War II, Amory wrote history books that studied society. He was a commentator on The Today Show, a critic for TV Guide, and a columnist for Saturday Review. Amory's love of animals, as well as great affection for his own cat Polar Bear, led him to three instant best-selling books: The Cat Who Came for Christmas, The Cat and the Curmudgeon, and The Best Cat Ever.

Cleveland Amory did more than just write about the animals he loved. Amory founded The Fund for Animals in 1967. The Fund for Animals is one of the world's most active animal advocacy groups that campaigns for animal rights and protection. Amory served as its president, without pay, until his death in 1998. Amory extended his devotion to animals with Black Beauty Ranch.

Cleveland Amory made his childhood dream come true in 1979 when he opened Black Beauty Ranch in Texas. He dreamed of a place where animals could roam free and live in caring conditions. The dream is real for hundreds of unwanted, abused, neglected, abandoned, and rescued domestic and exotic animals at Black Beauty Ranch. The ranch's 1,620 acres serve as home for elephants, horses, burros, ostriches, chimpanzees, and many more animals.

Cleveland Amory is my hero because he is a hero. He worked to make his dreams realities. His best-selling books, the founding of The Fund for Animals, and the opening of Black Beauty Ranch are the legacy of his dreams. Words from Anna Sewell's Black Beauty, the words that inspired Cleveland Amory, are engraved at the entrance to Black Beauty Ranch: "I have nothing to fear; and here my story ends. My troubles are all over, and I am at home." Cleveland Amory died on October 15, 1998. He is buried at Black Beauty Ranch, next to his beloved cat, Polar Bear.

NAME ______________________

Lesson 4.6 Writer's Guide: Evaluating Writing

When you are evaluating your own writing and the writing of others, being a critic is a good thing.

You can learn a lot about how you write by reading and rereading papers you have written. As you continue to write, your techniques will improve. You can look at previous papers and evaluate them. How would you change them to improve them knowing what you know now?

You can also look at the writing of others: classmates, school reporters, newspaper and magazine writers, and authors. Evaluate their writing, too. You can learn about different styles from reading a variety of written works. Be critical with their writing. How would you improve it?

Take the points covered in the Writer's Guide and make a checklist. You can use this checklist to evaluate your writing and others' writing, too. Add other items to the checklist as you come across them or think of them.

Evaluation Checklist

- ❑ Write an introduction with a topic sentence that will get your readers' attention. Explain the purpose of your writing.
- ❑ Write the body with one paragraph for each idea.
- ❑ Write a conclusion that summarizes the paper, stating the main points.
- ❑ Add or change words.
- ❑ Delete unnecessary words or phrases.
- ❑ Move text around.
- ❑ Improve the overall flow of your paper.
- ❑ Check spelling.
- ❑ Check grammar.
- ❑ Check punctuation.
- ❑ ____
- ❑ ____
- ❑ ____

Lesson 4.7 Writer's Guide: Writing Process Practice

The following pages may be used to practice the writing process.

Prewriting

Assignment: ______________________

____

Topic ideas: ______________________

____

____

Freewriting of selected topic: ______________________

____

____

____

____

____

____

____

____

____

____

____

Graphic Organizer:

NAME ______________________________

Lesson 4.7 Writer's Guide: Writing Process Practice

Drafting

NAME ___

Lesson 4.7 Writer's Guide: Writing Process Practice

Revising

NAME ______________________

Lesson 4.7 Writer's Guide: Writing Process Practice

Proofreading

Lesson 4.7 Writer's Guide: Writing Process Practice

Publishing

Final Draft: Include illustrations, photographs, graphic aids, etc.

Answer Key

Common nouns name people, places, things, and ideas.

People: driver, musician, brother, pediatrician, firefighter
Places: tunnel, courthouse, zoo, backyard, desert, bedroom
Things: desk, helicopter, dictionary, microphone, pine tree
Ideas: nervousness, environmentalism, justice, religion

Proper nouns name specific people, places, and things. Proper nouns are capitalized. For proper nouns that consist of more than one word, capitalize the first letter of each important word.

People: Aunt Lucy, General Eisenhower, Juan, Ms. Braga
Places: New Mexico, People's Republic of China, Lake Michigan
Things: Eiffel Tower, Baja Bill's Burritos, Declaration of Independence
Ideas: Hinduism, Marxism

Rewrite It
Rewrite each sentence below. Replace the common nouns shown in boldface with proper nouns. **Answers will vary. Possible answers shown.**

1. I went to visit **my aunt** in **the city** last summer.
   I went to visit Aunt Carol in Chicago last summer.
2. On **a certain day of the week**, we took a taxi to **the museum**, where the works of **an artist** were being exhibited.
   On Monday, we took a taxi to the Chicago Center for Fine Arts, where the works of Picasso were being exhibited.
3. We stopped at **the street where the museum was located** and paid our fare.
   We stopped at Second Street and paid our fare.
4. As we exited the cab, I spotted **the tallest building in the city**.
   As we exited the cab, I spotted the Sears Tower.
5. Inside the museum, I realized I had left my **smart phone** in the taxi!
   Inside the museum, I realized I had left my iPhone in the taxi!
6. We spoke with **the security guard**, and he was kind enough to call **the cab company**.
   We spoke with Mr. Hinson, and he was kind enough to call Chicago Yellow Cab Company.
7. As we waited, I took a moment to admire a **specific religion's** tapestry.
   As we waited, I took a moment to admire an Islamic tapestry.
8. At last, we were told **the cab driver** had my phone, but he was now in **a suburb of the city**.
   At last, we were told Mr. Swann had my phone, but he was now in East Park.
9. We arranged to meet him at **a restaurant** later in the day, and I got my phone back.
   We arranged to meet him Luigi's Famous Italian later in the day, and I got my phone back.

5

Proof It
Correct the mistakes in the use of common and proper nouns using proofreading marks.

/ = lowercase letter
≡ = capitalize letter

1. The westide metropolitan library will host a Fundraising Event this Saturday.
2. The Major Religions of China are confucianism, taoism, and buddhism.
3. The Bill Of Rights are the first ten amendments of the United States constitution.
4. Elizabeth and her Cousin traveled to lake Ontario during june and july.
5. NASA Scientists are developing a robot that can explore mercury's surface.
6. Most of the arctic ocean is covered by Sea Ice during Winter.
7. Tony allen is a Nigerian Drummer who currently lives in Paris.
8. June 14 is national flag day.
9. Cane Toads in australia are an example of an Invasive Species.
10. On New Years eve each year, officer Markley visits his Nieces in New York city.
11. The Beauty Bouquet Flower Shop is at the Corner of Fourth street and Wilson boulevard.
12. The north sea is located between great Britain and the Nations of Scandinavia.
13. On fridays, my whole family gets together to play Cards and Board Games, like Monopoly and Scrabble.
14. Some of the Founding Fathers wrote about Freedom and the Pursuit of Happiness.
15. The statue of liberty and the Grand Canyon are well known United States Landmarks.

Try It
Write a paragraph about your favorite author or actor. Use at least six common and six proper nouns correctly.

Answers will vary.

6

Collective nouns are used to describe groups of specific animals, people, or things.

A group of birds is a *flock*.
A group of ships is a *fleet*.
A group of judges is a *panel*.

A collective noun refers to a single group, so it acts as a singular noun. When a collective noun is plural (refers to more than one group), it acts as a plural noun.

Incorrect: The *flock fly* south for the winter.
Correct: The *flock flies* south for the winter.
Correct: The *flocks fly* south for the winter.

Abstract nouns describe ideas rather than people, places, or things that can be perceived with the five senses.

pleasure grumpiness inability contentment

Complete It
Circle the verb in each sentence that correctly completes the sentence.

1. Next week, the committee (decide, decides) whether to approve the new bike lane.
2. A swarm of bees (chase, chases) a foolish young cub that wanted their honey.
3. Bunches of grapes (rot, rots) inside a misplaced crate.
4. This pair of shoes (hurts, hurt) my feet and (needs, need) to be returned to the store.
5. My staff (enjoys, enjoy) our weekly outings to a nearby restaurant for lunch.
6. The huge bouquets of daisies (fill, fills) the room with a bright, fresh scent.
7. A team of oxen (wait, waits) inside the barn, ready to be hitched to the wagon.
8. A pack of wolves (startle, startles) the sheep.
9. The panel of judges (award, awards) blue ribbons to the top performers.
10. Whenever the National Anthem begins, the audiences (stand, stands) at attention.
11. The fleet of ships (leave, leaves) at dawn.
12. Swarms of flies (cloud, clouds) the air above the pig sty.

7

Identify It
Circle the abstract nouns in the sentences below.

1. My uncle is convinced that the key to happiness is eating good food.
2. Louis plans to major in agriculture at the University of Minnesota.
3. Early childhood is often a time of freedom and exploration.
4. Your mathematical capabilities never cease to amaze me.
5. Can intelligence be measured accurately by testing?
6. Sometimes the truth is harder to believe than the reality.
7. The process of learning how to program a computer may be daunting.
8. What type of shoes do I need to buy for ballet class?
9. Mr. Thompson's greatest pleasure is spending the afternoon reading.
10. As the students continued to misbehave, Ms. Yang's patience was tested.
11. Imagine my delight when Grandpa Hennessy finally arrived from Ireland.
12. Never ignore the opportunity to help someone who is in trouble.
13. Hiro's dedication was recognized with an award given at the banquet.
14. My fear of snakes kept me from attending the most recent field trip.
15. Yoko demonstrated her maturity by being the first to apologize.

Try It
Collective nouns for specific animals are often unusual. Use a dictionary or the Internet to look up the collective noun for each type of animal and use it in a sentence.

1. crows: **murder**
2. baboons: **troop; congress**
3. vultures: **colony; committee; wake; venue; kettle**
4. stingrays: **fever**
5. raccoons: **nursery; gaze**
6. foxes: **leash**
7. emus: **mob**
8. eagles: **convocation; congress; aerie; brood**

Collective nouns are shown. Sentences will vary.

8

Answer Key

Although plural and possessive nouns often sound similar, they are spelled differently and have different meanings.

Plural noun: The *novelists* gathered in Chicago for a conference.
Singular possessive noun: The *novelist's* main character traveled to Chicago.
Plural possessive noun: The *novelists'* meeting was postponed until next month.

Proof It
Use proofreaders' marks to correct the mistakes in plural and possessive nouns in the sentences below.

1. Deserts cover about 20 percent of Earths surfaces.
2. Harsh conditions mean that deserts are home to animals with special adaptations.
3. Deserts inhabitant's include lizards, snakes, fennec foxes, and scorpions.
4. Our planets largest habitat is the marine biome.
5. Biomes relationships are vital to Earth's well-being.
6. Hippo's, rhino's, and lion's make their homes in grassland biomes.
7. The tundras extreme cold makes it a poor place for vegetation to flourish.
8. One reason that forest biomes are important to Earth is tree's ability to absorb carbon dioxide.
9. Hot, semiarid, coastal, and cold are the four types of desert's.
10. Mosquitoes ability to live in a tundra biome surprises many people.
11. Tropical forest's, such as rain forests, produce plants that are not found anywhere else in the world.
12. A coral reefs many structures provide homes to countless sea creature's.
13. The worlds youngest biome is the Arctic tundra.
14. An invasive animals behavior can eventually affect more than one biome.

9

Rewrite It
Rewrite each phrase below to make it a plural, a singular possessive, or a plural possessive.

1. the backpacks belonging to the girls **the girls' backpacks**
2. the tail of the raccoon **the raccoon's tail**
3. the experiment belonging to the scientists **the scientists' experiment**
4. the baseball glove of Roberto **Roberto's baseball glove**
5. more than one sweater **sweaters**
6. the cat belonging to the Browns **the Browns' cat**
7. the covers of the books **the books' covers**
8. the painting of Charles **Charles's painting**
9. more than one strawberry **strawberries**
10. the moon belonging to the planet **the planet's moon**
11. the leaves of the trees **the trees' leaves**
12. the buttons of the remote control **the remote control's buttons**

Try It
Write a sentence for each word in the box.

Answers will vary. Possible answers shown.

trains	train's	trains'	bird's

1. **Trains leave the stations all day long.**
2. **A railroad worker waved from a window in the train's caboose.**
3. **The trains' engines were stored in garages at the depot.**
4. **Birds perched along the roof's peak.**
5. **The bird's wing looked like it might be broken.**
6. **The birds' calls woke me up this morning.**

10

An **appositive** is a noun or phrase that renames another noun in a sentence. The appositive offers more information about the noun.

Lucille, my great aunt in Texas, owns a small art gallery.
The phrase *my great aunt in Texas* is an appositive that renames *Lucille*.

When the appositive is nonessential, or not necessary to the sentence, it should have a comma before and after it. In the example above, you can remove the appositive, and the sentence still makes sense.

When the appositive is essential to the meaning of the sentence, do not set it off with commas. In the following sentence, removing the appositive *Jane Austen* would make the sentence much less clear.

The author *Jane Austen* wrote six novels.

Identify It
In each sentence below, underline the appositive. On the line, write **E** if it is essential and **NE** if it is nonessential.

1. China, one of the world's most populated countries, is one of Earth's oldest civilizations. **NE**
2. Beijing, China's capital city, is also known as Peking. **NE**
3. Mount Everest, Earth's tallest mountain, lies on the border of China and neighboring Nepal. **NE**
4. The bicycle, China's main form of transportation, is a speedy and energy-efficient way to travel. **NE**
5. China is home to the giant panda, an animal that survives primarily on bamboo. **NE**
6. China's neighbor Mongolia shares the Gobi Desert with China. **E**
7. Students around the world are currently learning China's official language, Mandarin Chinese. **NE**
8. China, a country whose history is divided into dynasties, has a communist government today. **NE**
9. The Chinese, talented inventors, created things like paper, compasses, porcelain, and silk. **NE**
10. The Chinese leader Mao Tse-tung was instrumental in China's shift to a communist government. **E**

11

Complete It
There is an appositive in each sentence below. On the line, write **E** if it is essential and **NE** if it is nonessential, and add commas where necessary.

1. Ian my brother's best friend is moving to California in the fall. **NE**
2. Families from all over the county will be attending the summer's best entertainment the Highland County Fair. **NE**
3. Russian my mother's first language is difficult to learn because it uses a different alphabet. **NE**
4. Some athletes increase the amount of complex carbohydrates or starches they consume before an event. **NE**
5. An undersea earthquake can cause tsunamis or massive waves. **NE**
6. The artist Claude Monet was especially known for his paintings of water lilies. **E**
7. Alina whistled for Peter her new Jack Russell terrier and fed him his dinner. **NE**
8. Next weekend, we'll be going to my cousin Josh's bar mitzvah the Jewish ceremony in which a boy becomes a man. **NE**
9. The library does not have any available copies of Darren's favorite book, *Al Capone Does My Shirts*. **NE**
10. The dream that Quinn had since she was a little girl to meet tennis legend Venus Williams in person was finally coming true. **NE**
11. The British doctor Edward Jenner created the smallpox vaccine and saved many lives. **E**
12. Each Halloween Mia loves to read the chilling stories of horror writer Edgar Allan Poe. **NE**

Try It
Write four sentences that contain appositives. Write **E** or **NE** after each to tell whether you used an essential or nonessential appositive.

1. ______
2. ______
3. ______
4. ______

Answers will vary.

12

A **pronoun** is a word used in place of a noun. A **subject pronoun** can be used as the subject of a sentence. It can be singular (*I, you, he, she, it*) or plural (*we, you, they*).
They canceled the meeting because of bad weather.

An **object pronoun** is the object of a verb or a preposition. It can also be singular (*me, you, him, her, it*) or plural (*us, you, them*).
Please give *him* my thanks for the lovely bouquet.

A **possessive pronoun** shows possession. Singular possessive pronouns are *my, your, his, her*, and *its*, and plural possessive pronouns are *our, your*, and *their*.
Your teeth should be brushed at least twice a day.

Some singular and plural possessive pronouns can stand alone: *mine, yours, his, hers, its, ours, theirs*.
The pickup truck was *ours*. Wilma donated *hers* to the church bazaar.

Complete It
Circle the pronouns that correctly complete the sentences.

1. (Mine, (My)) friend Kyoko ordered butterfly eggs for ((our) ours) science experiment.
2. ((They) Theirs) soon arrived, safely shipped inside ((their) hers) sealed container.
3. ((We) Ours) opened ((it) hers) to find the eggs lying in rows on a leaf.
4. Kyoko lifted the leaf from (it, (its)) box and placed ((it) its) inside an aquarium.
5. The aquarium was (her, (hers)), so ((I) me) prepared the sugar water.
6. In just a couple of days, the caterpillars hatched and began wriggling (theirs, (their)) little bodies.
7. ((We) Our) fed (theirs, (them)) every day, and before long, (them, (they)) had grown much bigger.
8. Kyoko called ((me) mine) one day with exciting news: some of (they, (them)) had attached (theirs, (their)) bodies to twigs.
9. ((My) Mine) mother used ((her) hers) camera to record the process.
10. A caterpillar sheds ((its) their) striped skin and hardens to form a chrysalis.
11. ((You) Your) would be amazed by (them, (its)) beauty.
12. When ((it) its) finally splits open, a butterfly emerges and spreads (it, (its)) wings.

13

Rewrite It
The sentences below contain errors in pronoun usage. Rewrite each sentence to correct the errors.

1. Mine Aunt Helga was married last week to hers best friend.
   My Aunt Helga was married last week to her best friend.
2. Frogs enlarge them vocal sacs to make sounds that will attract a mate.
   Frogs enlarge their vocal sacs to make sounds that will attract a mate.
3. Them shipped theirs automobile overseas so its would be waiting for they in England.
   They shipped their automobile overseas so it would be waiting for them in England.
4. Henry painted yours portrait, framed it, and wrapped them as a gift.
   Henry painted your portrait, framed it, and wrapped it as a gift.
5. The St. Louis Cardinals played they last home game yesterday.
   The St. Louis Cardinals played their last home game yesterday.
6. Its is the largest hydroelectric dam anywhere near ours city.
   It is the largest hydroelectric dam anywhere near our city.
7. Theirs dog stands on it front paws and, to mine amazement, takes a few steps.
   Their dog stands on its front paws and, to my amazement, takes a few steps.
8. The library stores thems down in the basement, so us needs to find the stairs.
   The library stores theirs down in the basement, so we need to find the stairs.
9. I handed hims mine science textbook and told hims to open them to page 135.
   I handed him my science textbook and told him to open it to page 135.
10. Yours is on the top shelf, and mines is below it on the second shelf.
    Yours is on the top shelf, and mine is below it on the second shelf.

Try It
Write sentences containing each type of pronoun.

1. subject pronoun: ____________
2. object pronoun: ____________
3. possessive pronoun that comes before a noun: ____________
4. possessive pronoun that stands alone: ____________

Answers will vary.

14

Intensive and **reflexive pronouns** are pronouns that end in *-self* or *-selves*. The way the pronoun is used determines whether it is intensive or reflexive.

Intensive pronouns usually appear right after the subject of a sentence. They emphasize the subject.
You *yourself* will pull up the damaged sod and reseed the area.
Johan *himself* stacked the boxes and cleaned out the garage.

Reflexive pronouns appear elsewhere in the sentence and refer back to the subject.
I gave *myself* a pat on the back for completing the project.
The monkeys played among *themselves* while we watched.

Identify It
Identify whether the boldface word in each sentence is an intensive or reflexive pronoun. Write **I** on the line if it is intensive, and write **R** if it is reflexive. Then, underline the noun the pronoun refers to.

1. I Mr. Henkins explained that the garden **itself** would sit on a hill above the pond.
2. R After purchasing their tickets at the box office window, Madeline and Sonja bought **themselves** some popcorn and bottled water at the concession stand.
3. R For safety reasons, a roofer should always attach **himself** by rope to a well secured hook on the rooftop.
4. I The rocking chairs **themselves** will be hand delivered by my brother and uncle.
5. R The raccoon fed **itself** midstream while balanced on a rock.
6. R Before speaking with the principal, I reminded **myself** to take a deep breath and remain calm.
7. R My family and I treat **ourselves** to a pizza once in a while.
8. R With the day's last light illuminating its peak, the mountain presented **itself** as a lone beacon in the approaching dark.
9. I At tonight's meeting, Laurie **herself** will explain why the bill did not pass.
10. R Please allow **yourself** plenty of time to complete the project. You implied
11. I Sterling **himself** would have a hard time believing the mess we've made.
12. R The kittens saw **themselves** in the mirror and tried to play with their reflections.

15

Complete It
Complete each sentence below with a reflexive or an intensive pronoun.

1. Kyle and Luiz themselves worked all summer to build the two-story tree house.
2. Shawn scooped up a spoonful of jam and finished making himself a sandwich.
3. Please go downstairs and get the laundry yourself .
4. I myself plan to spend the morning sanding and staining this chair.
5. Moments before the first bell rings, the students at Lincoln Jr. High gather themselves at the front entrance.
6. The dishwasher itself will need to be installed by a plumber.
7. Deep inside the cave, a colony of bats can keep themselves well hidden throughout the day.
8. Grandma Tang herself collects snow globes and salt shakers.
9. Last winter, my brother and I built ourselves an igloo and camped in it overnight.
10. Coach Lewis told his players, "You yourselves must dig down deep to find the strength to win!"
11. Genes themselves are arranged on twisted strings of chemicals called DNA.
12. Hiroshi himself was born in Japan and raised as a Buddhist.
13. The MacGregor twins captured themselves on video rapping together.
14. A cat can give itself a bath with its tongue.
15. On Wednesdays I have band practice, but I also practice guitar by myself for an hour each day.

Try It
Write a short paragraph describing your proudest accomplishment, including what others thought of it. Use at least two reflexive pronouns and two intensive pronouns in your paragraph.

Answers will vary. Paragraphs should contain at least two reflexive pronouns and two intensive pronouns.

16

Answer Key

Indefinite pronouns are pronouns that do not refer to a specific noun.

another anybody anyone anything each everybody everyone everything nobody no one nothing one somebody someone

Does *anybody* know where the post office is?
No one chooses the green balloon.
Someone left a note on the front door.

Most indefinite pronouns are singular, but the following are plural:
both few many others several

Many of my friends are going to the play on Saturday.
Both landed at the airfield on the west side of town.

Some indefinite pronouns, such as *all, any, most, none,* and *some*, are either singular or plural, depending on their meaning in the sentence.

Any eligible child is encouraged to take part in the contest.
Any of these children are eligible to take part in the contest.

Proof It
Use proofreading marks to correct any errors in verb usage. If the sentence is correct, place a checkmark on the line.

ℯ = deletes a word or letter
^ = inserts a word or letter

1. _____ Both of the children reads for about an hour before bed each night. (s deleted)
2. _____ None of the classes is going to the planetarium this semester. (is → are)
3. ✓ Despite the rain, everybody stays in line, each person equally determined to get a ticket to the show.
4. _____ Few of the trees in the orchard is producing apples at this point in the season. (is → are)
5. ✓ If someone phones about the gift, please don't say anything to my mother.
6. _____ Each of the horses are provided with a separate stall inside the barn. (are → is)
7. _____ Most of the cupcakes is being saved for the party at school tomorrow. (is → are)
8. _____ Everyone heading out to pan for gold in the stream need to bring along spare clothes. (need → needs)
9. _____ I can hear thunder in the distance, so please be sure all the windows is shut. (is → are)
10. ✓ Several of Zander's teammates are heading into the locker room.

17

Complete It
Complete each sentence ... indefinite pronoun ... makes sense and agrees in number ...

Some answers may vary. Possible answers shown.

1. The game is rather simple, so **anyone** can explain the rules quickly to a new player.
2. The lights are off, and the driveway is empty, so most likely **no one** is home.
3. **Most** of the people in my yoga class have attended for several years.
4. **Any** soldier who leaves the base without permission is considered AWOL.
5. Brandon can't decide between two different brands of cell phone, because **either** provides an equal number of pros and cons.
6. At the top of the silo, **some** chickadees take turns perching at the highest point.
7. **Much** of the fence is rotted and falling apart, so **someone** will need to make repairs.
8. **Anyone** who knows how to restring a violin will be eligible for the position as music teacher's assistant.
9. **Some** child I don't know is waving to my little sister.
10. **Something** about the new art studio is making Maurice excited for the school year to start.
11. Hannah dropped the box of dishes, but miraculously **none** of the plates are broken.
12. Only a **few** of the sled dogs are going to be chosen to take part in the Iditarod.

Try It
Write a persuasive paragraph convincing others to try your favorite food. Include at least five indefinite pronouns in your paragraph.

Answers will vary.

18

A **pronoun shift** happens when a writer changes pronouns in the middle of a sentence or paragraph. This can confuse the reader.

In this example, the writer changes from *we* (first-person plural) to *you* (second-person singular):

Incorrect: If *we* want to learn to play hockey, *you* should sign up for the beginners' team at the rec center.

Correct: If *we* want to learn to play hockey, *we* should sign up for the beginners' team at the rec center.

In this example, there is no agreement between *weeds* (a plural noun) and *it* (third-person singular pronoun).

Incorrect: The *weeds* growing in the garden are a nuisance because *it* takes nutrients from the vegetable plants.

Correct: The *weeds* growing in the garden are a nuisance because *they* take nutrients from the vegetable plants.

Identify It
In the sentences below, underline each pronoun and the noun it refers to. If the sentence is correct, make a checkmark on the line. If a pronoun shift occurs, make an **X** on the line.

1. X Caroline doesn't want to try sushi, because you can get food poisoning from eating raw fish.
2. X If the students don't think the new policy is fair, he or she should tell the principal.
3. ✓ Layla's parents are expecting their new refrigerator to be delivered this afternoon.
4. X After we arrived at the theater, we realized that you should come at least half an hour early to find a decent parking space.
5. X The doctor gave the intern a short lecture on the kind of behavior they expected.
6. X An artist must always keep experimenting with new ideas and techniques in their artwork.
7. X Kris and Antonio wanted to skateboard at the park after finishing our dinner.
8. ✓ As long as you study, you should pass the exam with no problems.

19

Complete It
Circle the pronoun that correctly completes the sentence.

1. The grubs were destroying the garden, but Mom chose not to use pesticides to kill (it, **them**).
2. Maureen used fresh clams in the chowder because (its, **they**) have more flavor than canned ones.
3. Della's new assistant only began work a week ago, but (**she** you) is a quick learner.
4. If a child wants to ride the roller coaster, (they, **he or she**) must be 48 inches tall.
5. The rocking chair is missing paint from (**its** their) left armrest.
6. The photographer quickly kneeled as (you, **he**) attempted to capture an interesting view of the couple dancing.
7. The hospital board is meeting on Tuesday to approve (**its** your) new budget for the year.
8. Although the dancers had performed eight nights in a row, (she, **they**) were still filled with enthusiasm and energy.
9. Most people choose to visit the amusement park on weekends, so I guess (**they** we) don't mind crowds.
10. Roberto and Dani are planning to go to the van Gogh exhibit at the museum if (you, **they**) can still get tickets.
11. If a student is dissatisfied with a grade, (you, **he or she**) should talk to the teacher.
12. Dmitri's teammates cheered for him as (**he** they) rounded the bases.

Try It
On the lines below, write a short description of a time you were a member of a team. Circle each pronoun you use, and proofread your paragraph to be sure there are no pronoun shifts.

Answers will vary.
Pronouns in the paragraph should be circled.

20

Review: Common and Proper Nouns, Collective and Abstract Nouns, Plurals and Possessives, Appositives

Identify the underlined word using the key in the box. Write your answer on the line following each underlined word.

a. common noun **b.** proper noun **c.** collective noun **d.** abstract noun

1. It was hard to know how to handle my mother's sorrow d when Grandma Carol b passed away last February b .
2. Ella's visit to Latta Plantation b in North Carolina sparked some questions a about slavery d and the Civil War b .
3. A convoy c of army trucks passed us on the highway a , and I felt a sudden gratefulness d for the sacrifice d that American soldiers make.
4. Aziz stared in delight d at the flock c of seagulls and quickly snapped a series c of photographs a with his new camera.

In the sentences below, circle singular possessives, underline plurals, and underline plural possessives twice.

1. The (telescope's) lens has a small smear on it, but I can wipe it off with one of these microfiber towels.
2. The (class's) trip to the planetarium includes (Mr. Hahn's) lecture, two experiments, and lunch.
3. The comets' tails are made of dust and gases.
4. (Jupiter's) largest moons are Io, Europa, Ganymede, and Callisto.
5. Venus, the second planet from the sun, was named for the ancient Romans' goddess of love and beauty.

One sentence above contains an appositive. Write the appositive on the line below.

the second planet from the sun

21

Review: Personal Pronouns, Intensive and Reflexive Pronouns, Indefinite Pronouns, Pronoun Shifts

Underline the word that best completes each sentence below.

1. Each of the chemicals (produce, produces) toxic gases.
2. The children amused (ourselves, themselves) in the backyard while (their, our) parents discussed the school's new policies.
3. Anyone who (is, are) interested in learning to write science fiction (are, is) welcome to join us.
4. Both the chickadees and the sparrows (has, have) visited the new feeder.
5. Jorge (himself, myself) has three paintings in the new exhibit at the Winthrop Gallery.
6. Several students on the tennis team (represent, represents) the school in the finals.
7. If we don't want to have to wait at the restaurant, (you, we) should call ahead.
8. I attempted to explain (itself, myself) to Mr. Weber, but apparently he was very upset.
9. Grandpa and (I, me) are planning to camp at three national parks this summer.
10. Although Rex and Ruby play together well, (they, them) do get a little wild sometimes.

Identify the underlined pronoun in each sentence as a subject pronoun (**SP**), object pronoun (**OP**), or possessive pronoun (**PP**).

1. PP Her composition will be performed in front of an audience of more than 300.
2. OP Destiny asked them to make a gluten-free batch of muffins.
3. SP We watch the fireworks each year at Uncle Phillip's house.
4. OP Peyton just put something in the shed.
5. PP Our family reunion is scheduled to take place at Long Creek Park.
6. OP Dad paid us to rake the yard and dispose of the leaves.
7. SP Someone sent me flowers on my birthday!
8. PP I'm hoping to earn some money by selling some of my old books online.

22

Action verbs tell the action of the sentence. The action can be physical or mental.

Ryder and Myles *made* Stella a cheese sandwich for lunch. (physical action)
The squirrel *leaped* onto the fence. (physical action)

I *wish* you could come to dinner with us. (mental action)
Nico *wondered* where he had left his sweatshirt. (mental action)

Identify It

Circle the action verbs in the sentences below. Then, categorize them as either physical or mental actions, and write them under the appropriate headings.

1. J. K. Rowling (wrote) the wildly popular series of Harry Potter books.
2. In 2008, Hillary Rodham Clinton (ran) for the Democratic nomination for president.
3. Martin Luther King, Jr. (believed) in equality and justice for all Americans.
4. Zoey (expects) that her classmates will (elect) her class president next Tuesday.
5. Satellites (move) in orbits around planets.
6. The woodpecker (pecked) a hole in the old oak tree next to the garage.
7. Female athletes from Saudi Arabia (competed) in the Olympics for the first time in 2012.
8. Aaron (noticed) the battery light (flashing) on his camera.
9. Dr. Abdul (remembered) something unusual in Becca's test results.
10. William the Conqueror, a Frenchman, (invaded) England in 1066.
11. Jogging (burns) about eight calories per minute.
12. Diego (recognizes) more than 50 birdcalls.

Physical Actions	Mental Actions
wrote	believed
ran	expects
elect	noticed
move	remembered
pecked	recognizes
competed	
flashing	
invaded	
burns	

23

Solve It

Make a list of the action verbs you find in the sentences below. Find each verb in the word search puzzle.

1. Jazmin grilled eggplant in a marinade of olive oil, garlic, and salt.
2. Anton forgot the loaf of crusty French bread.
3. Mr. Rinaldi baked a berry crumble with fresh blackberries, blueberries, and raspberries.
4. Linh dropped a cup full of sparkling cranberry juice.
5. Our sweet golden retriever, Harley, stole a hot dog off the picnic table!
6. Molly wanted blue cheese dressing on her salad.
7. I knew that the burgers were meatless.
8. Dylan ate a baked sweet potato with sour cream, green onions, and cheese.
9. Addison decided that Japanese wasabi is much too spicy for her.
10. A sparrow nibbled at the crumbs on the patio.

Action verbs: grilled, forgot, baked, dropped, stole, wanted, knew, ate, decided, nibbled

f	k	o	e	n	z	k	n	e	w
f	o	r	g	o	t	h	a	q	m
m	r	j	r	a	u	e	v	s	k
i	l	r	i	w	c	w	a	d	b
y	n	b	l	b	e	a	t	e	u
s	t	o	l	e	d	n	j	c	d
z	q	t	e	j	v	t	t	i	e
y	f	d	d	e	c	e	x	d	k
d	r	o	p	p	e	d	s	e	a
d	e	l	b	b	i	n	g	d	b

Try It

Choose two words from each column in the lists you made on page 23, and write your own sentences.

1.
2. Answers will vary.
3.
4.

24

Answer Key

Subject-verb agreement means that the verb must agree in number with the subject of the sentence. If the subject is singular, use a singular verb. If the subject is plural, use a plural verb.

The girl *flips* the pages of the book. The girls *flip* the pages of the book.

When a sentence contains a compound subject connected by the word and, use a plural verb.

The truck **and** the bus *stop* at the railroad tracks.

When a sentence contains a compound subject connected by the words **or** or **nor**, use a verb that agrees with the subject that is closer to the verb.

Neither the teacher **nor** her students *saw* that movie.
Either the athletes **or** the coach *plans* the potluck.

If the subject and the verb are separated by a word or words, be sure that the verb still agrees with the subject.

The *scanner*, as well as the printer, *is* broken.

Identify It
In each item, underline the correct form of the verb in parentheses.

1. Jaya (is, are) very talented at identifying animal tracks.
2. She and her mom (goes, go) hiking in a nearby nature preserve at least once a week.
3. Deer (stop, stops) near the edge of the pond to sip the cool water.
4. Jaya quickly (identify, identifies) their tracks.
5. Neither Jaya nor Mrs. Sharma (know, knows) what kind of animal gnawed on the bark of a tree beside the trail.
6. There is a shuffling sound in the bushes, and a chipmunk, in addition to several blue jays, (peeks, peek) out before scurrying away.
7. Beavers (has, have) constructed a dam of tightly stacked twigs and branches.
8. Possums and raccoons (leave, leaves) behind scat that allows Jaya and her mother to identify them.
9. The animal track guide (is, are) scuffed and worn from frequent use.
10. Either a coyote or some neighborhood dogs (have, has) passed this way.

25

Complete It
Complete each sentence below with the correct form of the verb in parentheses.

1. Boston cream pie (to be) ___**is**___ the official dessert of the state of Massachusetts.
2. Fort Knox, located in Kentucky, (hold) ___**holds**___ most of the gold that the U.S. federal government owns.
3. Both Maine and Massachusetts (claim) ___**claim**___ the chickadee as their state bird.
4. Neither New Mexico nor Arizona (have) ___**has**___ any ocean coastline.
5. Alligators (live) ___**live**___ in many bodies of water throughout the state of Florida, which is why they are Florida's state reptile.
6. The world's oldest living things, a stand of bristlecone pine trees, (make) ___**make**___ their home in California.
7. America's longest Main Street (run) ___**runs**___ through Island Park, Idaho.
8. Four states, New Hampshire, New Jersey, New York, and New Mexico, (have) ___**have**___ the word *new* in their names.
9. Either Hawaii or Vermont (to be) ___**is**___ known as the healthiest state to live in.
10. Idaho (grow) ___**grows**___ more potatoes than any other state.

Try It
Write a paragraph about states you have visited or would like to visit. Circle each verb you use, and underline the subject it agrees with.

**Answers will vary.
Verbs should be circled, and subjects should be underlined.**

26

Helping verbs help to form the main verb in a sentence. They add additional detail to the verb, such as clarifying time or possibility. The primary helping verbs are forms of the verbs *be, have,* and *do.* They are the most common helping verbs.

I ***had** hoped* you would arrive before the show started.
The robins ***were** singing* this morning as Martin left for work.
Did you *remember* to turn off the lights?

Other helping verbs are *can, could, will, would, may, might, shall, should,* and *must.*

The painters ***can** spread* drop cloths over the furniture.
The crew ***might** cancel* the flight due to mechanical problems.

Linking verbs connect a subject to a noun or adjective. They do not express an action.

The most common linking verbs are forms of the verb *to be,* such as *is, are, was, were, been,* and *am.*

Nevaeh *is* the highest ranked student on the chess team.
Most turtles *are* shy and will quickly withdraw inside their shells.

Other common linking verbs relate to the five senses (*smell, look, taste, feel, sound*) or a state of being (*appear, seem, become, grow, remain*).

The rocks *feel* slimy when they are submerged in water.
The children *grew* restless waiting for the speaker to arrive.

Identify It
In each sentence below, circle the verb. On the line, write **LV** or **HV** to identify it as a linking verb or helping verb.

1. **HV** The mysterious statues of Easter Island (have fascinated) scholars for almost 300 years.
2. **LV** The giant statues lining the coasts (seem) like guardians protecting the island.
3. **HV** Do you (know) what the local people call Easter Island?
4. **HV** Rapa Nui (is) the island's name in the local language.
5. **HV** At first, historians (could) only (guess) how these massive statues got there.
6. **HV** Most scholars (have concluded) that the native people rolled the statues on logs.
7. **HV** The statues weigh many tons, so how (could) the people (stand) them up?
8. **HV** The answer (might not surprise) you.
9. **HV** Ropes, levers, and ramps (were used) to hoist a statue into an upright position.
10. **LV** Religion (is) the most likely reason the native people built the statues.

27

Complete It
Add helping verbs and linking ... be more than one ... the verb you choose makes sense in the sen...

Answers may vary. Possible answers shown.

You ___**might**___ know that the top of Mount Everest ___**is**___ the highest place on Earth, but ___**do**___ you know where the deepest place ___**is**___? The Mariana Trench in the Pacific Ocean plunges more than 36,000 feet below the ocean's surface. The intense pressure that far underwater ___**would**___ be deadly without the right equipment. If you ___**were**___ to swim that deep, the weight of the water ___**would be**___ like dozens of semi trucks stacked on your body! But humans ___**have**___ visited the bottom of the trench several times by traveling in specially made submarines. The first trip to the bottom ___**was**___ in 1960. Since then, other people, and even robots, ___**have**___ made the trip.

Believe it or not, but life ___**does**___ exist that far below the surface. Most of the creatures ___**are**___ single-celled organisms and bacteria. They ___**have**___ to live mostly around hydrothermal vents. Some small crustaceans, snails, and bivalves ___**can**___ survive there as well. The snails' shells ___**are**___ softer than normal snail shells, because hard shells ___**are**___ too difficult to grow where water pressure ___**is**___ so intense.

Try It
What is a strange, or even impossible, place you would like to visit? Write a paragraph describing where it is and why you would like to go there. Use at least three linking verbs and three helping verbs in your paragraph. Underline the linking verbs and circle the helping verbs.

Answers will vary. Paragraphs should contain at least three underlined linking verbs and three circled helping verbs

28

Answer Key

When a sentence is written in the **active voice**, the subject performs the action of the verb.
Mr. Sanchez painted the house a bright shade of red.
The bus driver opened the door to allow passengers to exit.

When a sentence is written in the **passive voice**, the subject receives the action of the verb. A form of the helping verb *be* is used with the main verb, and a phrase beginning with *by* often follows the verb.
The house was painted a bright shade of red *by* Mr. Sanchez.
The door was opened by the bus driver to allow the passengers to exit.

In general, using the active voice creates stronger writing that is more interesting to read. The passive voice can be used when you want to emphasize the receiver of an action, or when you do not want to emphasize the performer of an action.
The door was opened by the bus driver. (She did not open a window.)
The house was painted a bright shade of red. (The color of the house is important, not who painted it.)

Identify It
On the line, write **A** or **P** to identify which sentences use the active voice and which use the passive voice.

1. A Before leaving home, Hector always brushes his hair and cleans his glasses.
2. P The nuthatches were being fed by a group of children.
3. P The electronic switch was flicked by Mr. Strothman, and the building crumbled to the ground.
4. A Mount Takawa shielded the desert from any storms approaching from the west.
5. A On the day of the flood, Kate was riding her horse, Petulia, near the creek.
6. A The Caribbean was the site of many pirate attacks during the early 1700s.
7. A Jupiter is the largest planet in the solar system.
8. P The rocket was launched by NASA in 1972.
9. P When she stepped in the fire ant nest, Niki's foot was bitten multiple times by the swarming insects.
10. A Lucas was talking by the water fountain when the bell rang.
11. P An American flag was draped across the windows on the top floor of the building.
12. P Three jellyfish were accidentally caught by the ship's net.

29

Rewrite It
The sentences be[...] using the active v[...]nce

Answers may vary. Possible answers shown.

1. Every Saturday, the front yard is mowed by my brother Charley.
Every Saturday, my brother Charley mows the front yard.
2. The comet is accompanied by a long tail of dust and gas.
A long tail of dust and gas accompanies the comet.
3. The phone was finally answered by Ms. Hosaka, the school librarian.
Ms. Hosaka, the school librarian, finally answered the phone.
4. The nation of Japan is called *Nippon* by the Japanese people.
The Japanese people call the nation of Japan *Nippon*.
5. An increase in the desert's size was caused by the overgrazing of cattle.
The overgrazing of cattle caused an increase in the desert's size.
6. A tiny robot was inserted into the patient's bloodstream by Dr. Lang.
Dr. Lang inserted a tiny robot into the patient's bloodstream.
7. In Greek mythology, the Gorgon Medusa's head was cut off by Perseus.
In Greek mythology, Perseus cut off the Gorgon Medusa's head.
8. The statistics in the safety report were compiled by the staff at the Department of Transportation.
The staff at the Department of Transportation compiled the statistics in the safety report.
9. Solar panels were installed on the roof by a group of local electricians.
A group of local electricians installed solar panels on the roof.
10. The company my dad works for was founded in 1968 by Mayor Reynolds.
Mayor Reynolds founded the company my dad works for in 1968.

Try It
Write two sentences using the active voice and two sentences using the passive voice.

1. active voice:
2. active voice:
3. passive voice:
4. passive voice

Answers will vary.

30

Most sentences contain verbs in the **indicative mood**. Verbs in the indicative mood state or ask about facts or opinions.
Where is the hospital?
Tomas will leave for the airport at four o'clock.

Verbs in the **imperative mood** make commands or requests. The subject is implied as *you*.
Slice those carrots, please.
Watch out for that squirrel!

Verbs in the **subjunctive mood** describe things that are hypothetical, or not true. They also express wishes or indirect requests. The word *if* often appears in subjunctive sentences.
If the furnace **were** to stop working, I would know who to call.
Tawnia wishes she **were** better at tennis.
I insisted that my brother **shut** the door.

In the subjunctive mood, the verb *be* is usually in past tense, and singular present verbs usually drop the final *-s* or *-es*.

Identify It
On the line, write **IN**, **IM**, or **S** to identify which sentences use the indicative, the imperative, or the subjunctive mood.

1. S If I were you, I would not buy those shoes.
2. IM Please head out onto the field and form two teams.
3. IN The light bulbs cost more at the grocery store than they do here.
4. IN When will Uncle Tashi be arriving from Tel Aviv?
5. S I wish the beach was a shorter drive away than three hours.
6. S Ms. Stacy recommends that each girl practice for at least two hours per week.
7. IM Before writing the invitations, purchase some nice stationery.
8. IN New Zealand lies to the southeast of Australia.
9. S If you were to rewrite this section, your report would be ready to hand in.
10. IM Click this link to unsubscribe from the newsletter.
11. S The council's requirement is that each speaker arrive 15 minutes early.
12. IN On Earth, water exists naturally as a solid, liquid, and gas.

31

Try It
Write a senter[...]ed in parentheses.

Answers may vary. Possible answers shown.

1. Tell your friend to help you finish a school project. (imperative)
Help me finish creating this map of Africa.
2. Warn your brother about what could happen if he forgets to tie his shoelaces. (subjunctive) **If you were to leave those shoes untied, you would most likely trip on the laces.**
3. Share one fact you know about trees. (indicative)
Coniferous trees have needles and cones.
4. Describe an activity you wish you were doing today. (subjunctive)
I wish I were heading to the beach.
5. Tell where you would like to live someday. (indicative)
Someday, I will move to Los Angeles, California.
6. Warn someone about a dangerous situation. (imperative)
Look out for those bees!
7. Ask a question about the Grand Canyon. (indicative)
Is the Grand Canyon bigger than the Gobi Desert?
8. Request a second helping of vegetables. (imperative)
Please hand me that bowl of mashed potatoes.
9. Describe a request you made for an aunt to do something. (subjunctive)
I requested that my aunt **drive me to the mall.**
10. Describe your favorite sport or other activity. (indicative)
I love playing hockey.
11. Describe what would happen if two feet of snow were to fall tonight. (subjunctive)
If two feet of snow were to fall tonight, schools might be canceled.
12. Encourage your teammates to play well. (imperative)
Go team!
13. Share one thing that you think is essential for creating a good atmosphere for studying. (subjunctive)
It is essential that a student **play quiet music while studying.**
14. Share one fact you know about American history. (indicative)
Abraham Lincoln gave the Gettysburg Address.
15. Request that an object be handed to you. (imperative)
Give me that pencil, please.

32

Answer Key

Gerunds, participles, and **infinitives** are other kinds of verbs. These verbs take the role of another part of speech in some circumstances.

A **gerund** is when a verb is used as a noun. A verb can take the form of the noun when the ending *-ing* is added.
Jumping on the trampoline is Eddie's favorite afternoon activity.
(The subject *jumping* is a noun in the sentence.)

A **participle** is when a verb is used as an adjective. A verb can take the form of an adjective when the endings *-ing* or *-ed* are added.
Carrie extended a *trembling* hand to her grandmother.
(*trembling* modifies *hand*)
The *injured* raccoon limped slowly into the woods.
(*injured* modifies *raccoon*)

An **infinitive** is when a verb is used as a noun, adjective, or adverb. A verb can take the form of a noun, adjective, or adverb when preceded by the word *to*.
To *travel* abroad is something that everyone should have the chance to do.
(The verb to *travel* acts as the subject, or noun, of the sentence.)
Josiah has a book report to *finish* by tomorrow.
(The verb to *finish* acts as an adjective modifying *book report*.)
On Thursday, the inspector arrived to *check* the leaks.
(The verb to *check* acts as an adverb modifying *arrived*.)

Complete It
Rewrite each of the verbs in parentheses as a gerund to complete the sentence.

1. Speaking more than one language is a skill that an increasing number of Americans have. (to speak)
2. Learning a second language at an early age is an excellent idea. (to learn)
3. Although it is never too late to learn another language, becoming bilingual when you are young is much easier than waiting until adulthood. (to become)
4. It is also true that understanding a foreign language helps you understand other cultures. (to understand)
5. Living in America, you are less likely to speak a foreign language than in many other places in the world. (to live)
6. Surprising your family and friends with a few words in another language can be fun! (to surprise)

33

Identify It
In the sentences below, underline the gerunds and circle the infinitives.

1. If you want (to protect) the planet, there are many things you can do.
2. Hanging clothes out (to dry) instead of using an electric dryer saves energy.
3. It's easy (to save) water by turning off the tap while you brush your teeth.
4. Reusing items for new purposes keeps them from ending up in the trash.
5. You can purchase a reusable water bottle, and then you won't need (to wash) as many glasses each day.
6. Cleaning with old t-shirts or rags saves money and paper towels.
7. If you'd like (to reduce) your energy bills, lower the thermostat two degrees in winter.
8. Forget about plastic bags! Buying reusable lunch bags saves money and reduces the amount of plastic in landfills.
9. Most people are already in the habit of recycling, but if you aren't, it's not too late (to start)!
10. Try (to remember) (to turn) off the lights when you leave a room.

Try It
Write a sentence for each of the participles in the box.

Answers may vary. Possible answers shown.

1. We fixed a broken window in our clubhouse.
2. A laughing clown led the parade.
3. The painted horses on the carousel went round and round.
4. My grandmother is a very caring person.
5. I'll eat the bruised apple.
6. A winding staircase led up to the attic.

34

Progressive verb tenses describe ongoing, or continuing, actions.

A **present progressive** verb describes an action or condition that is ongoing in the present. A present progressive verb is made up of the present tense of the helping verb *be* and the present participle of the main verb.
Mr. Yokima *is planning* a surprise birthday party for his wife.
The tall pines trees behind our house *are swaying* in a strong breeze.

A **past progressive** verb describes an action or condition that was ongoing at some time in the past. A past progressive verb is made up of the past form of the helping verb *be* and the present participle of the main verb.
The jaguar *was stalking* a tapir through most of the night.
Soldiers *were trekking* across the hot sands of the desert.

Rewrite It
Rewrite each sentence using the progressive tense. If a sentence contains a past tense verb, replace the verb with a past progressive verb, and use a present progressive verb to replace present tense verbs.

1. The Mastersons sailed from Miami to Key West.
The Mastersons were sailing from Miami to Key West.
2. The library holds its annual book sale on the first Saturday in June.
The library is holding its annual book sale on the first Saturday in June.
3. General MacArthur wrote an autobiography before he died.
General MacArthur was writing an autobiography before he died.
4. Louisa wears high heels to the dance.
Louisa is wearing high heels to the dance.
5. The campfire burned brightly enough to be seen from several miles away.
The campfire was burning brightly enough to be seen from several miles away.
6. The Cardinals won the Central Division championship game.
The Cardinals were winning the Central Division championship game.
7. A giraffe eats leaves from the topmost branches of the tree.
A giraffe is eating leaves from the topmost branches of the tree.
8. India becomes the most populated nation on Earth.
India is becoming the most populated nation on Earth.

35

Complete It
Complete each sentence with the progressive tense form of the verb in parentheses. Use the present progressive or the past progressive as indicated.

1. The sun is rising over the far edge of the desert. (**rise**, present progressive)
2. Chef Charles was weighing each ingredient carefully. (**weigh**, past progressive)
3. The director was yelling, but the actors apparently did not hear her. (**yell**, past progressive)
4. As the tide rolls out, the dock is sinking farther below the bank. (**sink**, present progressive)
5. The phone is ringing, so would you please answer it? (**ring**, present progressive)
6. Ms. Patel was telling the students about her trip to New York City. (**tell**, past progressive)
7. For his science fair project, Terrell is designing a robot that can draw a picture. (**design**, present progressive)
8. Dinosaurs were roaming Earth for more than 160 million years. (**roam**, past progressive)
9. The old tire factory is being torn down today. (**be**, present progressive)
10. Bees are swarming around the entrance to their hive. (**swarm**, present progressive)
11. The jet engine's blades were rotating at almost full speed. (**rotate**, past progressive)
12. A few of the floats were moving into position along the street, ready for the parade to officially begin. (**move**, past progressive)
13. My sister and I are painting an old chair that we will use for the play. (**paint**, present progressive)
14. Chad was begging his mom to tell him what his birthday present would be. (**beg**, past progressive)
15. After the match, the hockey team is going to a nearby pizza place to celebrate. (**go**, present progressive)

Try It
Write a sentence using each indicated verb form.

1. plural present progressive:
2. singular past progressive:
3. plural past progressive:
4. singular present progressive:

Answers will vary.

36

Answer Key

Verb tenses tell when in time something happened. The **present perfect** tense shows that something happened in the past, but the action may still be going on. The present perfect is formed with the present tense of the verb *have* (*have* or *has*) and a past participle.

The violinists *have taken* their seats in the orchestra pit.

The **past perfect** tense shows that an action was completed before another action in the past. It is formed with the verb *had* and a past participle.

Workers *had demolished* the cabin before sunrise.

The **future perfect** tense shows that an action will be completed before a before future time or a future action. It is formed with the words *will have* and a past participle.

I *will have taken* my final exam by this time next year.

Match It

Write the letter of the verb tense that each sentence uses.

1. a. present perfect tense b. past perfect tense c. future perfect tense
   - a The team has broken an old league record each of the past two seasons.
   - c By the end of the season, the team will have broken the old league record.
   - b Before the season ended, the team had broken the old league record.
2. a. present perfect tense b. past perfect tense c. future perfect tense
   - b Dr. Wabara had discovered two new viruses before he turned 25.
   - a Dr. Wabara has discovered two new viruses by utilizing an electron microscope.
   - c Dr. Wabara will have discovered more viruses before he retires.
3. a. present perfect tense b. past perfect tense c. future perfect tense
   - c By next week, Jada will have played the piano for three years.
   - b Before her first recital, Jada had played the piano only for her family.
   - a During the last few months, Jada has played the piano every day.
4. a. present perfect tense b. past perfect tense c. future perfect tense
   - a Despite a love for history, Tyler has never studied the Renaissance.
   - c By graduation, Tyler will have never studied the Renaissance, because his history classes did not cover that time period.
   - b Tyler had never studied the Renaissance until his first history class at college.

37

Rewrite It

Rewrite each sentence using the perfect tense indicated in parentheses. Change details as needed in order for the new sentence to make sense.

1. By next week, the caribou will have passed our town on their way north. (past perfect)
   By last Saturday, the caribou had passed our town on their way north.
2. The delays during the last month have cost our company thousands of dollars. (future perfect) **By the end of the month, the delays will have cost our company thousands of dollars.**
3. Joshua will have completed 30 hours of community service by next Thursday. (present perfect)
   Joshua has completed 30 hours of community service this month.
4. By the time I got there, the chickens had eaten the entire bag of pellets. (future perfect) **By the time I get there, the chickens will have eaten the entire bag of pellets.**
5. By midnight, the band will have played for nearly three hours. (past perfect)
   By midnight, the band had played for nearly three hours.
6. Mr. Moriarty had given us the perfect gift: a new set of cookbooks. (present perfect)
   Mr. Moriarty has given us the perfect gift: a new set of cookbooks.
7. I have swum more miles than I could count since joining the gym. (past perfect)
   By the time I quit the gym, I had swum more miles than I could count.
8. The children had donated clothes to the shelter as part of their unit on volunteerism. (future perfect) **By the end of the semester, the children will have donated clothes to the shelter as part of their unit on volunteerism.**
9. Once it arrives at the zoo, the hippopotamus will have traveled nearly 2,000 miles. (present perfect)
   On its way to the zoo, the hippopotamus has traveled nearly 2,000 miles.
10. Levi has built a bicycle, skateboard, and scooter this year. (past perfect)
    Levi had built a bicycle, skateboard, and scooter while visiting his uncle.

Try It

Write three sentences about some of your favorite school activities. Write one in the past perfect, one in the present perfect, and one in the future perfect.

Answers will vary.

38

Review: Action Verbs, Subject-Verb Agreement, Helping and Linking Verbs, Active and Passive Voice, Verb Moods: Indicative, Imperative, and Subjunctive

Read each sentence below. Then, fill in the blank with the type of verb indicated.

1. Drew Brees, quarterback for the New Orleans Saints, threw touchdown passes for 54 games in a row!
   action verb: **threw**
2. Quinn has watched *The X Factor* every week this season.
   helping verb: **has**
3. The boys appeared nervous as they prepared to go onstage.
   linking verb: **appeared**
4. Elizabeth wrote a series of alliterative poems.
   action verb: **wrote**
5. Beatriz is expecting to make the basketball team this fall.
   helping verb: **is**
6. Solar panels convert sunlight into electricity.
   action verb: **convert**
7. At the end of the Spanish-American War, Puerto Rico, Guam, and the Philippines became U.S. territories.
   linking verb: **became**

For each sentence below, circle **A** or **P** to indicate whether the sentence uses the active or passive voice.

1. (A) P I quickly flipped the omelet.
2. A (P) The cattle were fed by Uncle Chris each evening at dusk.
3. (A) P The rain pounded fiercely against the roof.
4. (A) P Matt and Teddy hiked the Dragonfly Trail at Reedy Creek Park.
5. A (P) The mural was painted by the students in Mr. Albertson's art class.

On the line, write **IN**, **IM**, or **S** to identify which sentences use the indicative, the imperative, or the subjunctive mood.

1. IN Jonas can help you with your Spanish homework.
2. S If you were to lose that ring, Grandma would be heartbroken.
3. IM Play the last song on that CD again.
4. IN What time does the baseball game start?
5. IM Ask Ms. Schneider which worksheet to complete.

Complete each sentence below with the correct form of the verb in parentheses.

1. Onions **contain** a chemical that makes your eyes water. (contain)
2. Sugar **dissolves** faster in hot water than in cold water. (dissolve)
3. Both Austria and Switzerland **border** Germany. (border)
4. Neither the goose nor the ducks **saw** the hawk approaching. (saw)

39

Review: Gerunds, Participles, Infinitives, Verb Tenses, Progressive and Perfect Tenses

Identify the underlined word(s) using the key in the box. Write your answer on the line.

a. gerund	b. participle	c. infinitive

1. c Joey's brother plans to enlist in the Navy after high school.
2. a Skiing is Hayden's favorite way to spend a winter afternoon.
3. b The exhausted mother finally got the baby to sleep.
4. a I can't believe that winning is so important to Claudia.
5. c The wind is going to knock the potted plants off the porch.
6. b The gleaming silverware shone in the drawer.

Rewrite each sentence below in the tense indicated in parentheses.

1. (present progressive) The lamp illuminates the papers on the desk.
   The lamp is illuminating the papers on the desk.
2. (past progressive) The librarian checks in the overdue books.
   The librarian was checking in the overdue books.
3. (past progressive) Thea attends a book group on the first Thursday of the month.
   Thea was attending a book group on the first Thursday of the month.
4. (present progressive) Abe picks fresh tomatoes from the vine.
   Abe is picking fresh tomatoes from the vine.

Underline the perfect tense verb in each sentence. On the line, write whether the verb is past, present, or future perfect.

1. Sam has celebrated Hanukkah with his grandparents since he was a baby. **present**
2. The university had expected larger donations this fall. **past**
3. Anita has used a hearing aid for four years. **present**
4. Mags will have led thousands of yoga classes by the time she retires. **future**
5. It will have rained at least a dozen times before we get the roof fixed. **future**
6. The dance troupe had performed at more than 80 venues last year. **past**

40

Answer Key

An **adjective** is a word that describes a noun or pronoun. It offers more information about the word it modifies. Adjectives often come before the noun or pronoun they describe. They answer the question *What kind? How many?* or *Which one?*

Tasha climbed into the *wooden* canoe and grabbed the *battered old* paddles.
Blake picked out *two* bunches of *fresh* carrots at the *downtown* market.

Proper adjectives are capitalized.

Alexander made roasted *Brussels* sprouts on *Sunday* night.
Priya has never attended an authentic *Indian* wedding before.

A **predicate adjective** follows a linking verb (a form of the verb *to be, smell, look, taste, feel, sound, appear, seem, become, grow,* or *remain*). A predicate adjective modifies the subject of the sentence.

The windows on the back of the shed appeared *broken*.

In this example, *broken* is a predicate adjective, following the linking verb *appeared*. It modifies *windows*, the subject of the sentence.

Identify It
In the sentences below, underline adjectives once and proper adjectives twice. Circle predicate adjectives.

1. Did you know that butterfly wings are covered with tiny overlapping scales?
2. The amazing monarch butterfly migrates a distance of more than 2,000 miles.
3. There are more than 28,000 species of butterflies in the world.
4. The moth's speckled wings blended into the bumpy bark of the American elm.
5. Samuel remained (still) and dozens of colorful butterflies settled on his arms, shoulders, and head.
6. The tiny moth used its long proboscis to suck sweet nectar from a honeysuckle flower.
7. The butterfly's wings looked (iridescent) in the bright sunlight.
8. On Easter morning, the brand-new butterflies emerged from the papery cocoons at the botanical gardens.
9. When a chrysalis breaks open, the butterfly's wings are (wet) and (crinkly).
10. Many rare butterflies are found in tropical rainforests.
11. Beautiful peacock butterflies have purple eyespots on their hind legs.
12. Butterflies need warm, sunny weather—otherwise, they cannot fly!
13. Are you going to the Butterfly Ball on Saturday night?
14. Queen Alexandra's Birdwing butterfly is the (rarest) and (largest).

41

Complete It
Complete [...] parenthe[...] [...] type of adjective to use. [...] the word in

Answers may vary. Possible answers shown.

1. The **white** goose landed easily on the **smooth** water of the pond beside the meadow. (adjectives)
2. For the potluck next week, Ana will be bringing a **Spanish** dish. (proper adjective)
3. Although the oranges smelled **delicious**, they ended up being dry and flavorless. (predicate adjective)
4. The ambulance's **loud** siren cut through the **dark** night and awoke residents in many of the **tall** apartment buildings. (adjectives)
5. Paulomi's voice sounded **hoarse** as she shouted for help. (predicate adjective)
6. Although Shannon speaks several languages, she is still anxious about her **English** test next week. (proper adjective)
7. The **rambunctious** students lined up outside the cafeteria doors, laughing and jostling as they waited for the **lunch** bell to sound. (adjectives)
8. Tyson is **rude** and **immature**, but his mother feels sure he'll grow out it. (predicate adjective)
9. Cristina peered behind the **dusty** boxes in the attic, finally finding the **broken**, rusty birdcage she had been looking for. (adjectives)
10. Marcus's mother thinks that the loveliest place in the world is the **Irish** countryside. (proper adjective)
11. Benji and Alfie hopped up into the open window and purred as the sun warmed their **soft** fur. (adjective)
12. Silas has swim lessons on **Wednesday** afternoons. (proper adjective)

Try It
Imagine that you are spending the day at a butterfly exhibit at a nature center. Describe what you see in detail. Use adjectives and predicate adjectives in your description.

Answers will vary.

42

Comparative adjectives compare two nouns, and **superlative adjectives** compare three or more nouns.

calm, calmer, calmest — shy, shyer, shyest — polite, politer, politest

For adjectives that end in *y*, change *y* to *i* before adding the suffixes *-er* or *-est*.

healthy, healthier, healthiest — windy, windier, windiest

Comparing two nouns:

Coach Wachter is known for being *meaner* than Coach Pickens.
My new desk is much *sturdier* than the old one.

Comparing three or more nouns:

The *gentlest* llama is the one with the spotted coat.
Zora's birthday fell on the *sunniest* day this week.

Comparative and superlative adjectives can also be formed by adding the words *more* (comparative) and *most* (superlative) before the adjective. Use *more* and *most* with longer adjectives.

Uncle Dan is *more impulsive* about making decisions than Dad is.
The *most eccentric* family in our neighborhood lives in the old Randolph house at the end of the street.

Complete It
Complete the chart below with the correct forms of the adjectives.

Adjective	Comparative Adjective	Superlative Adjective
jealous	**more jealous**	**most jealous**
slim	slimmer	**slimmest**
quiet	**quieter**	quietest
dramatic	**more dramatic**	**most dramatic**
agile	**more agile**	most agile
grumpy	grumpier	**grumpiest**
cheerful	**more cheerful**	**most cheerful**
elegant	**more elegant**	most elegant
dainty	**daintier**	**daintiest**
fearful	more fearful	**most fearful**

43

Proof It
Read each sentence below. If the correct form of the boldfaced word(s) is used, make a check mark on the line. If the incorrect form is used, write the correct form on the line.

1. **most precise** You must use the **most precisest** measurements when you are constructing the fence.
2. ✓ There's no doubt that Maggy is **more outspoken** than Missy.
3. **more popular** Jenna's suggestion for a fundraiser was **populare**r than Sam's.
4. **shinier** That silver cleaner doesn't work very well, but the silver does look slightly **more shiny** now.
5. ✓ When Johan went snorkeling, he encountered one of the **most unusual** fish he had ever seen.
6. ✓ I think Willow Springs is a **quainter** town than the town where we stayed last year.
7. **most intense** Last weekend, Rilla and I watched the **most intensest** movie I'd ever seen.
8. **more unusual** The ingredients in Grandma's recipe are **unusualer** than in the recipe Mom uses.
9. ✓ Dr. Santiago was the **most brilliant** professor I had in my four years at the university.
10. ✓ I think you've given me the **wisest** advice I could have hoped for.
11. ✓ Hasaan's response was **more enthusiastic** than his brother's.
12. **most resourceful** Ms. Matsuda is the **resourcefulest** Girl Scout leader we've [...]ad.

Try It
Write a sentence f[...]

Answers will vary. Possible answers shown.

1. Use the comp[...] *curious*.
Our dog is more curious about than our cat.
2. Use the superlative of *fluffy*.
My aunt makes the fluffiest whipped cream I've ever had.
3. Use the comparative of *wise*.
I think your professor is wiser than mine.
4. Use the superlative of *suspicious*.
The man in the dark hat is the most suspicious of the people in the line up.
5. Use the comparative of *artistic*.
My sister is more artistic than I am.
6. Use the superlative of *gloomy*.
You have the gloomiest expression I've ever seen.

44

Adverbs modify, or describe, verbs. An adverb tells *how, when,* or *where* an action occurs.
Malia waited *patiently.* (tells *how* Malia waited)
My brother was sent to the principal's office *yesterday.* (tells *when* he was sent)
Kirby hid *behind* the sycamore tree. (tells *where* Kirby hid)

Adverbs can also modify adjectives or other adverbs.
The gas tank was *completely* empty. (*completely* modifies the adjective *empty*)
Earthquakes in the South are *quite* rare. (*quite* modifies the adverb *rare*)

Many, but not all, adverbs are formed by adding *-ly* to adjectives.

Intensifiers are adverbs that add emphasis or intensity to adjectives or other adverbs. The following are common intensifiers.

absolutely	just	quite	so	such
almost	nearly	rather	particularly	too
extremely	practically	really	somewhat	very

Mr. Singh travels for work *quite* often.
Felicia felt *extremely* impatient as she waited for the train to pass.

Complete It
Add an intensifier from the box above to each sentence below. Circle the word it modifies.

1. Mr. Crawley was **very** (embarrassed) by the incident at work yesterday.
2. The actors were **extremely** (talented) and the sets were exquisite.
3. The door was **almost** (open) and I was worried that the cats had escaped.
4. Carmen was **nearly** (asleep) by the time her parents returned from the game.
5. It's not a **particularly** (funny) movie, but I found myself laughing at the strangest parts.
6. Dr. Yusef was **quite** (worried) when he received the results of his wife's biopsy.
7. I found the documentary about sea turtles to be **absolutely** (captivating).
8. Although Kiko's shoes were **almost** (new) they were already scuffed and dirty.
9. The children were **somewhat** (bored) by the speech, but they were not permitted to leave.
10. The whole situation was just **too** (strange) to explain.

45

Identify It
Circle the adverb in each sentence below. Make an arrow from the adverb to the word it modifies.

1. The biologist (bitterly) explained how deforestation was affecting the lives of rainforest animals.
2. Oscar smiled (awkwardly) at Amelia, ducked his head (bashfully) and asked her to dance.
3. Although Noah was dressed quite (suitably) for the occasion, he wore bright green high-top sneakers.
4. "It's just that, well . . . I'm really sorry," replied Scott (haltingly).
5. I pedaled (vigorously) sure that I could make it to the summit of the trail.
6. Inez was (highly) recommended for the position by her friend and mentor, Dr. Bradley.
7. (Soon) Caitlyn will be a teenager.
8. The sky was (particularly) lovely when the storm ended and the sun began to set.
9. Grandma (smoothly) blended the ingredients and (carefully) poured them into the dish.
10. Abby (graciously) accepted the award.
11. Daisy barked at strangers quite (often) but she was (exceptionally) affectionate with her family.
12. Raylon stared (intently) at the television screen, waiting (anxiously) for news of the survivors.

Try It
Write four sentences using adverbs from the box. Underline each intensifier you use.

once	immediately	absolutely	yesterday
loosely	quite	skillfully	temporarily
extremely often	almost	surprisingly	early
nearly	furiously	rather	soon

1.
2.
3. **Answers will vary. Intensifiers should be underlined.**
4.

46

Like comparative adjectives, **comparative adverbs** compare two actions.
Aaron answered his mother *more cheerfully* than his brother.
Dad rises *earlier* in the summer than he does during the rest of the year.

Superlative adverbs compare three or more actions.
Alison behaved *most cautiously* of any of the gymnasts.

Short adverbs are formed using *-er* for comparatives and *-est* for superlatives. Long adverbs use the words *more* or *most,* or for negative comparisons, use *less* or *least.*
The moon shone *more brightly* tonight than earlier this week.
Karl answered the question *less truthfully* than his brother.

Some comparative and superlative adverbs do not follow these patterns. The following are examples of irregular comparative and superlative adverbs.
well better best badly worse worst

Complete It
For each sentence below, write the correct comparative or superlative form of the adverb in parentheses.

1. Although the boys usually fight on road trips, the trip to Florida went **more smoothly** than Mrs. Nesbit had expected. (smoothly)
2. Valentina arrived at school **earlier** than her classmates. (early)
3. When the tornado warning sounded, my family reacted **most quickly** of anyone on our street. (quickly)
4. Bandit and Roxy clean their food bowls **more thoroughly** than the other dogs we foster. (thoroughly)
5. When Maggy's party was canceled because of the rain, she behaved **more graciously** than her parents had expected. (graciously)
6. The restaurant near the dock prepares fish sandwiches **best** of all. (well)
7. Of all our cousins, I think Erik was **genuinely** happy to see us. (genuinely)
8. Uncle Gabe is **most medically** knowledgeable of any of his relatives. (medically)
9. Joseph helped with the farm chores **more eagerly** than his three sisters did. (eagerly)
10. I really didn't expect this year's birthday cake to turn out **worse** than last year's! (badly)

47

Complete It
Complete the chart below with the correct forms of the adverbs.

Adverb	Comparative Adverb	Superlative Adverb
politely	**more politely**	**most politely**
well	**better**	**best**
persuasively	more persuasively	**most persuasively**
fast	faster	**fastest**
sincerely	more sincerely	**most sincerely**
intelligently	**more intelligently**	most intelligently
naturally	**more naturally**	**most naturally**
brightly	**more brightly**	most brightly
exceedingly	**more exceedingly**	**most exceedingly**
childishly	more childishly	**most childishly**
hungrily	**more hungrily**	most hungrily
carelessly	**more carelessly**	**most carelessly**
often	**more**	most often

Try It
Write a sentence **Answers will vary. Possible answers shown.**

1. Use the comparative of *well.* **I play guitar better than my uncle does.**
2. Use the superlative of *intently.* **I looked most intently at the MP3 player, hoping I would get it for my birthday.**
3. Use the comparative of *honestly.* **I am able to speak more honestly with Ms. Rousseau than any other teacher.**
4. Use the superlative of *badly.* **Of all the children on the field trip, Matty and Brian behaved the worst.**

48

Some adjectives and adverbs are easy to confuse with one another. Use a predicate adjective after a linking verb (forms of the verb *to be* and verbs like *seem, taste, grow,* and *become*) to describe the subject. Use an adverb to describe an action verb.

The police dog seemed *proud* to be standing next to Officer Shari.
The police dog stood *proudly* next to Officer Shari.

In the first example, the adjective *proud* follows the linking verb *seemed* and modifies the subject *police dog*. In the second example, the adverb *proudly* modifies the action verb *stood*.

The words *good, well, bad,* and *badly* are often used incorrectly. *Good* and *bad* are adjectives, and *well* and *badly* are adverbs.

The hot bath felt *good* after such a long hike.
These eggs smell *bad*, so don't eat them.

The Rockets played *badly* last night and lost the game.
Cara performed *well* at the audition and earned a role in the play.

Identify It

Read each item below. On the line, write **Adj.** or **Adv.** to identify each **boldface** word as an adjective or adverb. If the word is an adjective, underline the noun it modifies. If the word is an adverb, underline the action verb it modifies.

1. Adv Music blared **loudly** from a pair of speakers placed in the window.
2. Adj As we were about to leave, my brother suddenly appeared **queasy**, so we stayed home.
3. Adj The coconut smoothie tasted so **good**, we ordered a second one.
4. Adv Rosa's room is **always** a bit cooler than the rest of the apartment.
5. Adj Mr. Swift felt **bad** about breaking his promise to the students.
6. Adv Paxton tried **hard** not to laugh when the gum got stuck in his friend's hair.
7. Adv The lamp shines so **brightly**, we use it only when we have to.
8. Adj The mosquitoes down by the lake are particularly **bad** this year.
9. Adv A few pebbles tumbled **quietly** down the slope and into the ravine.
10. Adj The children grew **quiet** as their mother entered the room.

49

Proof It

Some of the sentences below contain errors in adjective and adverb usage. Use proofreading marks to make corrections. If the sentence is correct, place a checkmark on the line.

1. ____ Aunt Mae smiled proud ^ly as she presented the elaborate gingerbread house.
2. ✓ During their trip to Myrtle Beach, the Connors ate well every day.
3. ____ A thresher moved slow ^ly through the fields like a dinosaur roaming the plains.
4. ____ When a toddler smells badly, it usually means it's time for a diaper change.
5. ____ Emperor penguins look majestically as they stand tall on the Antarctic ice.
6. ____ The scientists' prediction about where the module would land appeared to be successfully.
7. ____ The plumage of some parrots is beautifully to behold.
8. ✓ The fresh coffee brewing in the café smelled good.
9. ____ The gentle movement of the curtains great ^ly amused a kitten.
10. ____ A dilapidated shack lay abandonedly and forgotten deep within the woods.
11. ____ Wallace stored his files safe ^ly by uploading them to the cloud.
12. ____ After reaching a height of nearly 400 feet, the roller coaster track plunges steep ^ly back to ground level.
13. ____ Lance's femur was broken so bad ^ly the pieces had to be bolted back together.
14. ____ Coal burning power plants provide electricity more reliable ^ly than wind turbines.
15. ✓ Historically, theatrical performances as we know them date back to the Ancient Greeks.
16. ____ A squirrel ran quick ^ly along the top of the fence, trying desperately to outrun the neighbor's dog.
17. ____ The manatee seems contently to float around and munch sea grass all day.
18. ✓ The massive ship looks deceptively small when seen from a great distance.

Try It

Write two sentences containing adverbs and two containing predicate adjectives. Circle the adverbs in your sentences and underline the adjectives.

Answers will vary. Adverbs should be circled and adjectives should be underlined.

50

Prepositions are words that show the relationship between a noun or pronoun and another word in the sentence.

A fence ran *alongside* the creek.
Please memorize the poems *in* this book.

Some common prepositions are *above, across, after, along, around, at, away, because, before, behind, below, beneath, beside, between, by, down, during, except, for, from, in, into, near, of, off, on, outside, over, to, toward, under, until, up, with, within,* and *without*.

Compound prepositions consist of more than one word. Some common compound prepositions are *about, according to, aside from, across from, along with, because of, far from, in front of, in place of, instead of, on account of,* and *on top of*.

Prepositional phrases include the prepositions and the objects (nouns or pronouns) that follow the prepositions. A prepositional phrase includes the preposition and the object of the preposition, as well as any modifiers of the object.

Three dogs ran *through an empty field*. (The preposition is *through*; the object of the preposition is *field*; the words *an empty* modify the object *field*.)

A sentence may contain more than one prepositional phrase.

The teacup *inside the cupboard* sat *on top of a saucer*.

A prepositional phrase followed by a comma can start a sentence.

Because of the rain, we stayed indoors and played chess.

Identify It

Underline each prepositional phrase in the sentences below. Circle each preposition or compound preposition. Some sentences contain more than one prepositional phrase.

1. (Along with) good nutrition, exercise keeps your body (in) top shape.
2. Stretching (before) you exercise will help loosen the muscles (throughout) your body.
3. (During) times of bad weather, you might use a stationary bike (at) a gym (instead of) riding a real bike (along) a trail or (around) the block.
4. Something as simple as running (up) and (down) the stairs can be a great activity (for) a workout.

51

Rewrite It

Rewrite each simple sentence below so that it contains one or more prepositions. The number of pr[epositions] ... [se]ntence has been co[mpleted] ...

Answers will vary. Possible answers are shown.

1. The crew was nervous. (2)
   Example: The crew *of the fishing boat* was nervous *about an approaching storm*.
2. The clouds darkened. (1)
   The clouds above the ship darkened.
3. Wind blew. (3)
   Wind blew across the ship and into the faces of the crew.
4. The captain yelled. (2)
   The captain yelled at the crew to get below deck.
5. The crew lowered the sails. (2)
   Before heading below deck, the crew lowered the sails to protect the ship.
6. The captain and crew sought shelter. (2)
   Rain poured onto the ship, and the captain and crew sought shelter from the storm.
7. The storm raged. (2)
   Above the ship, the storm raged for several hours.
8. The seas calmed. (1)
   After several house, the seas calmed.
9. The crew emerged. (3)
   Because of the silence, the crew emerged from inside the ship and into the fresh air.
10. The crew cheered. (2)
    Beneath a clear sky, the crew cheered with relief.

Try It

Write a sentence with a prepositional phrase that includes a preposition, its object, and at least one modifier of the object. Identify each part of the prepositional phrase.

Answers will vary.

preposition: ________ object of the preposition: ________ modifier(s): ________

52

Conjunctions connect individual words or groups of words in sentences.

Coordinate conjunctions connect words, phrases, or independent clauses that are equal or of the same type. Coordinate conjunctions are *and, but, or, nor, for,* and *yet.*
Ask Russell *or* Jake to watch the baby this afternoon.

Correlative conjunctions come in pairs and are used together. *Both/and, either/or,* and *neither/nor* are examples of correlative conjunctions.
Both the pencils *and* pens are kept in the top drawer of the desk.

Subordinate conjunctions connect dependent clauses to independent clauses in order to complete the meaning. *After, although, as long as, because, since, unless, whether,* and *while* are examples of subordinate conjunctions.
As long as Ms. Burles says it is okay, our class can leave early today.

An **interjection** is a word or phrase used to express surprise or strong emotion. Common interjections include:
ah alas aw awesome eeek hey hi hurray
oh oh, no oops ouch phew wow

An exclamation mark or a comma is used after an interjection to separate it from the rest of the sentence.
Ouch! I stubbed my toe! *Phew,* that's a huge relief!

Identify It
Circle the conjunction in each sentence. On the line, write **coordinate**, **correlative**, or **subordinate** to identify the type of conjunction used in the sentence.

1. subordinate Rudy will care for our rabbit, Hudson, (while) we are gone next week.
2. coordinate Mr. Isaacs plans to build a gazebo, (but) he won't be able to do it until next year.
3. subordinate The bus leaves at six o'clock sharp, (unless) it has some kind of mechanical problem.
4. correlative (Neither) my mother (nor) my father likes driving long distances.
5. coordinate The car was parked in the garage, (yet) it still got wet somehow.
6. subordinate (While) you are at the library, please check to see if I have any books on hold.
7. subordinate Coach Randolph reviewed his notes about the game (after) all the players had left.
8. coordinate William can help me clean the birdhouse, (or) he can fill the feeder with birdseed.

53

Complete It
Conjunctions have been removed from the following passage. Choose conjunctions from the box to complete the passage. The number in parentheses tells how many times that conjunction should appear in the passage.

and (3)	so (1)	while (1)
either (1)/or (1)	whether (1)	although (1)
after (1)	but (3)	since (1)

New Orleans, Louisiana, is considered the birthplace of jazz, **but** it's also the birthplace of jazz great Louis Armstrong. **Although** countless musicians have made their mark in jazz since his time, many still consider Armstrong to be the greatest musician of all time.

Armstrong was born in 1901. His family was quite poor, **so** Armstrong left school by 5th grade in order to help support them. He sold newspapers, delivered coal, **and** even sang on the street to earn money.

On the last day of 1912, Armstrong made a mistake that got him into big trouble, **but** it also set a positive course for the rest of his life. **While** he was celebrating New Years Eve, Armstrong fired a gun into the air. He was quickly arrested **and** sent to a home for troubled youths. **Whether** the punishment was fair might be debatable, **but** during the 18 months Armstrong spent in the home, he learned how to play the bugle. **After** he was allowed to leave, Armstrong knew exactly where his life was headed: a career as a musician.

For the next two decades, Armstrong established his name as a top trumpet player **and** bandleader in the popular new musical genre of jazz. He spent most of his time playing in **either** Chicago **or** New York, but he also traveled to California a few times.

Since Armstrong died in 1971, his reputation has continued to grow. Today, he is universally recognized as a towering figure in jazz history.

Try It
Review the list of interjections on page 53. Choose three interjections and use each in a sentence.

1. _____
2. _____
3. _____

Answers will vary.

54

Review: Adjectives and Predicate Adjectives, Comparative and Superlative Adjectives, Adverbs and Intensifiers, Comparative and Superlative Adverbs

Identify the adjective in each sentence. If it is a predicate adjective, underline it. Circle other adjectives. On the line, write **C** if the adjective is comparative, write **S** if the adjective is superlative, and leave the line blank if the adjective is neither comparative nor superlative.

1. S The (most beautiful) greenhouse I ever visited was in Athens, Greece.
2. ___ The orchids in particular looked spectacular.
3. ___ (Purple) flowers dangled delicately at the ends stems.
4. S Even the (tiniest) buds had a hint of color.
5. ___ Flowers bloomed brilliantly throughout the greenhouse's (lush) interior.
6. C The plants thrived and appeared healthier than plants grown in the wild.
7. S As I wandered the grounds outside the greenhouse, the (sweetest) scent filled the air.
8. C The plants displayed outside were larger than the ones grown inside the greenhouse.
9. ___ (Olive) trees marched in rows up a hillside in the distance.
10. ___ Unfortunately, the farther I looked across the (sprawling) city, the more clearly I saw the pollution.
11. S A haze obscured the (most distant) buildings and roads.
12. ___ Back inside the greenhouse, the view wasn't expansive.
13. C However, it was much cleaner.

As indicated, rewrite each sentence to change the adverb to a comparative or superlative adverb. If the original sentence contains an intensifier, circle the intensifier.

1. The locomotive chugged (somewhat) noisily along the railroad tracks.
Comparative: **The locomotive chugged more noisily along the railroad tracks.**
2. The Great Wall of China marches steadily through the hilly countryside.
Superlative: **The Great Wall of China marches most steadily through the hilly countryside.**
3. As dawn broke, General Macklin saw that the Fourth Regiment had fought successfully through the night. **As dawn broke, General Macklin saw that the**
Superlative: **Fourth Regiment had fought most successfully through the night.**
4. My new telescope can show the planets clearly when you adjust this knob.
Comparative: **My new telescope can show the planets more clearly when you adjust this knob.**
5. Last Saturday's potluck was planned well by Ms. Harrison's class.
Comparative: **Last Saturday's potluck was planned better by Ms. Harrison's class.**
6. The shed was built sturdily to withstand strong winds coming over the mountain.
Comparative: **The shed was built more sturdily to withstand strong winds coming over the mountain.**
7. I sleep (very) soundly when the room is pitch dark and a fan is running.
Superlative: **I sleep most soundly when the room is pitch dark and a fan is running.**

55

Review: Adjectives and Adverbs, Prepositions and Prepositional Phrases, Conjunctions and Interjections

Circle the correct adjective or adverb to complete each sentence.

1. The Pittsfield Pirates played (bad, (badly)) last night and lost the game.
2. "That burning bagel smells (awfully, (awful))!" exclaimed Finn.
3. Allie danced (good, (well)) at ballet practice today.
4. We ate (quick, (quickly)) so we wouldn't be late getting to the bus.
5. Darrell grew ((impatient) impatiently) as the time for his flight was changed yet again.

Identify the boldface word in each sentence. On the line, write **P** if it is a preposition, **C** if it is a conjunction, or **I** if it is an interjection. For sentences that contain a preposition, also underline the prepositional phrase.

1. P Mr. Inouye poured hot tea **into** his favorite mug.
2. I **Huh**, I didn't see that coming.
3. C Be sure to bring an umbrella, **for** you never know when it might rain.
4. P **Before** heading to practice, Hector always puts on his lucky shirt.
5. C The sunrise is still an hour away, **but** I can see a faint glow to the east.
6. P **While** you are in the kitchen, could you turn off the oven timer?
7. I **Oh, no!** The bell just rang!
8. P Millie cleaned the spot where she dropped a biscuit **onto** the floor.
9. C Don't sit in front of the window, **or** I won't be able to see.
10. P Thousands of bugs are swarming **under** the streetlamp's glow.

Write a sentence that contains a coordinate conjunction: _____

Write a sentence that contains a correlative conjunction: _____

Write a sentence that contains a subordinate conjunction: _____

Write a sentence that contains two prepositional phrases: _____

Answers will vary.

56

A **declarative sentence** makes a statement about a place, person, thing, or idea, and it ends with a period.
In 1983, Sally Ride became the first American woman to go into space.

An **interrogative sentence** asks a question and ends with a question mark.
Did you know that approximately half of our trash ends up in landfills?

An **exclamatory sentence** shows urgency, strong surprise, or emotion, and it ends with an exclamation mark.
They'll announce the winner in five minutes!

An **imperative sentence** demands that an action be performed. The subject of an imperative sentence is usually not expressed, but is understood as *you.* Imperative sentences can be punctuated with a period or an exclamation mark.
Place your drawings on Ms. Hadley's desk.
Look out for the rocks!

Complete It **Answers 4 and 7 have two possible answers.**
Complete each sentence below by circling the appropriate end mark.

1. Did you know that it's not possible to tickle yourself . (?) !
2. Venus is the Roman goddess of love and beauty (.) ? !
3. The longest word in the English language has 45 letters (.) ? !
4. Take the subway to the 11th Street stop (.) ? (!)
5. What is the most exotic food you've ever sampled . (?) !
6. Watch out for the deer . ? (!)
7. In summer, the surface temperature of the Kalahari Desert is literally hot enough to fry an egg (.) ? (!)
8. Where is Mt. Rushmore located . (?) !
9. Emperor penguins are the largest species of penguin (.) ? !
10. Beta carotene, which is found in carrots, may protect eyesight (.) ? !

57

Identify It
Read the passage below. Use the line following each sentence to identify the sentence type. Write **D** for declarative, **IN** for interrogative, **E** for exclamatory, and **IM** for imperative.

Picture a modern day elephant with smaller ears and 3-foot-long fur. __IM__ This is what the ancient woolly mammoths looked like. __D__ Their long, shaggy fur kept them warm in icy, frigid temperatures. __D__ Their four-inch layer of solid fat helped, too! __E__ One of the reasons that today's elephants have such long, floppy ears is that they help to keep the giant beasts cool in tropical places. __D__ The smaller ear size of woolly mammoths actually helped them conserve heat. __D__

Another difference between elephants and mammoths is tusk size. __D__ The largest elephant tusks measure about 10 feet in length. __D__ The largest mammoth tusks were about 15 feet long! __E__ What was the purpose of such enormous tusks? __IN__ They were most likely used for protection and as a characteristic that attracted females. __D__

Do you know what caused these giants to die out 4,000 years ago? __IN__ Think of how strong they were and how well-suited for surviving freezing weather. __IM__ Unfortunately, there was not enough food for the mammoths to survive the Ice Age. __D__ In addition, they were hunted by early humans for their meat and their fur. __D__ Humans were an even bigger threat than saber toothed cats! __E__

It's fortunate that mammoths lived in such icy places. __D__ Scientists have learned so much from their well-preserved remains. __D__ In fact, they may be able to use the DNA they've found to clone a woolly mammoth some day! __E__

Try It
Write one sentence of each type.

1. Declarative: ______
2. Interrogative: ______
3. Exclamatory: ______
4. Imperative: ______

Answers will vary.

58

An **independent clause** presents a complete thought and can stand alone as a sentence.

Simple sentences are sentences with one independent clause. Simple sentences can have one or more subjects and one or more predicates.
The roosters crowed in unison as the sky lightened. (one subject, one predicate)
Socrates and Plato are important Greek philosophers. (two subjects, one predicate)
Marcel and Naomi *set the table* and *served dinner to their parents.* (two subjects, two predicates)

Compound sentences are sentences with two or more simple sentences, or independent clauses. A compound sentence can be two sentences joined with a comma and a coordinate conjunction. The most common coordinating conjunctions are *and, but, or, yet,* and *so. For* and *nor* can also act as coordinating conjunctions.
The marching band needs to raise money, so band members will sell raffle tickets.

A compound sentence can also be two simple sentences joined by a semicolon.
The marching band needs to raise money; band members will sell raffle tickets.

Identify It
Read each sentence and determine whether it is a simple or compound sentence. On the line at the beginning of the sentence, write **S** for simple or **C** for compound. On the two lines following the sentence, identify the total number of subjects and predicates in each sentence.

__S__ 1. Our three dogs and four cats love hanging out together on the couch. S: __2__ P: __1__
__S__ 2. When you sleep, your heart rate, breathing, and brain activity all slow down. S: __3__ P: __1__
__C__ 3. The *Wizard of Oz* was released in 1930; it became one of the most popular films of all time. S: __2__ P: __2__
__S__ 4. A lioness and her cubs watched a herd of gazelles and several ostriches moving across the savannah. S: __2__ P: __1__
__C__ 5. The Kremlin and the Hermitage Museum are famous Russian landmarks, so they are often crowded with tourists. S: __3__ P: __2__
__S__ 6. Neptune and Uranus are gas giants and orbit farthest from the sun compared to the other planets. S: __2__ P: __1__

59

Rewrite It
Combine each set of simple sentences into a single compound sentence using the conjunction and/or punctuation shown in parentheses.

1. NASA planned to launch the probe last Friday. Due to bad weather, it still hasn't left Earth. (, but)
NASA planned to launch the probe last Friday, but due to bad weather, it still hasn't left Earth.
2. Music is an important part of African culture. Dance is an important part of African culture. Lagos, Nigeria, will be the site of a major international performing arts center. (, so)
Music and dance are important parts of African culture, so Lagos, Nigeria, will be the site of a major international performing arts center.
3. More than a million types of insects have been discovered. About a third of them are species of beetles. (;)
More than a million types of insects have been discovered; about a third of them are species of beetles.
4. Elizabeth might want to become a vet. Elizabeth might want to become a professional dancer. Elizabeth has not made up her mind yet. (;)
Elizabeth might want to become a vet or a professional dancer; she has not made up her mind yet.
5. The Eiffel Tower was built as part of the 1889 World's Fair in Paris, France. For nearly 40 years, it was the tallest structure on Earth. (, and)
The Eiffel Tower was built as part of the 1889 World's Fair in Paris, France, and for nearly 40 years, it was the tallest structure on Earth.
6. Sound waves travel through air at about 1,000 feet per second. Sound waves travel four times faster than that through water. (, but)
Sound waves travel through air at about 1,000 feet per second, but they travel four times faster than that through water.

Try It
Write a few sentences about a recent outing. It could be a trip to the grocery store or a trip to a foreign country. Include a variety of simple and compound sentences in your description.

Answers will vary.

60

Answer Key

A **dependent clause** does not present a complete thought and cannot stand alone as a sentence.

Complex sentences have one independent clause and one or more dependent clauses. The independent and dependent clauses are connected with a subordinate conjunction or a relative pronoun. The dependent clause can be anywhere in the sentence.

Complex sentence (connected with subordinate conjunction):

You can sense sound *because* your inner ear contains an eardrum and tiny bones.

Complex sentence (connected with a relative pronoun):

The Sydney Opera House, *which* was designed by architect Jorn Utzon, is a famous Australian landmark.

The dependent clause can either be the first or second part of the sentence.

After you finish cleaning the fish tank, please put it back in the cupboard.
Please put the fish tank back in the cupboard *after* you finish cleaning it.

Identify It

For each sentence, circle the subordinate conjunction or relative pronoun, and underline the dependent clause.

1. Uncle Ramos spent an hour sifting through the soil (because) <u>we needed worms for fishing</u>.
2. <u>(Until) she turns thirteen</u>, Monique must ride in the backseat of the car.
3. The suspension bridge sways a little bit <u>(whenever) a strong breeze blows across it</u>.
4. <u>(Even though) Dr. Neils is an accomplished chess player</u>, he still loves playing checkers with his niece.
5. Michael Jordan, <u>(who) is well known as one the greatest basketball players of all time</u>, also played professional baseball.
6. <u>(Before) Randall leaves the house each morning</u>, he makes sure the lights are off.
7. The French flag, <u>(which) has three stripes</u>, was designed in the late 1700s.
8. <u>(Unless) you are a feline expert</u>, you might not recognize *ragdoll, Abyssinian*, and *Cornish rex* as popular cat breed names.

61

Complete It

For each unfinished complex sentence, choose a subordinate conjunction from the list and use it to write the missing dependent clause. Do not use the same conjunction more than once.

after	if		
	since	when	whether
before	though	whenever	while

Answers will vary. Possible answers shown.

1. <u>Whenever it storms</u> , the deer seek shelter under the thick brush in the ravine.
2. Captain Spinks was steering the yacht toward a small lagoon <u>while he carefully avoided the dangerous reefs</u> .
3. We plan to drive north to the Arizona Nevada border <u>before we visit the Grand Canyon</u> .
4. <u>After the computer crashed</u> , Jamal rebooted his laptop and crossed his fingers.
5. The polished metal sculptures in the park shine <u>unless it is a cloudy day</u> .
6. <u>Although we didn't finish our unit on Asian history</u> , we learned that the Mongol Empire spread across most of Asia.
7. <u>While he's in California</u> , Han might see Johnny Depp or another famous movie star.
8. The Museum of Fine Arts has been located on Elm Street <u>since it first opened in 1963</u> .
9. In 2012, Park Geunhye became the first woman president of South Korea <u>because most of the citizens voted for her</u> .
10. <u>Although the skull may the most important bone</u> , the femur, or thigh bone, is the largest bone in the human body.

Try It

Write three of your own complex sentences: one that starts with a dependent clause first, one that ends with a dependent clause, and one that contains a relative pronoun.

1. ____________________
2. ____________________
3. ____________________

Answers will vary.

62

An **adjective clause** is a dependent clause that modifies a noun or pronoun. An adjective clause usually follows the word it modifies. The clause begins with a relative pronoun, such as *that, which, who, whom, whose*, or *whoever*.

Grandma Mia, *who lives in Arizona*, will visit us next week.
Comets have tails *that consist of dust and gas*.

An **adverb clause** is a dependent clause that modifies a verb, an adjective, or an adverb. An adverb clause answers the question *How? When? Where? Why?* or *Under what condition?* The first word of an adverb clause is a subordinate conjunction, such as *although, until, once, however, unless, if*, or *while*.

If the space shuttle is going overhead, we can see it with a pair of binoculars.
Most students should do fine on the test *unless they choose not to study*.

A **noun clause** is a dependent clause that acts like a noun.

How you behave at school can affect your grades. (subject)
An abstract painting can be *whatever you want it to be*. (predicate noun)
Maisie will decide *where we go to dinner tonight*. (direct object)
The lead role will be given to *whichever student earns it*. (object of the preposition *to*)

Identify It

Underline the dependent clause in each sentence. On the line, identify the type of clause by writing **Adj** for adjective, **Adv** for adverb, or **N** for noun.

1. <u>Adv</u> <u>Although Venus is the planet closest to Earth</u>, it is very different from Earth.
2. <u>Adj</u> Dinosaurs, <u>which ruled Earth for millions of years</u>, exist today only as fossils.
3. <u>N</u> <u>Whatever you leave in the basket</u> will be donated to the animal shelter.
4. <u>N</u> The community garden was planted in <u>that empty lot located on First Avenue</u>.
5. <u>Adj</u> The monkey <u>that stole Monica's bracelet</u> climbed to the top of the visitors center.
6. <u>Adv</u> <u>If you drive from Halifax to Vancouver</u>, you will be in the car for more than a week.
7. <u>N</u> Phinn tried to describe to his sister <u>what a cello sounds like</u>.

63

Try It

Write a sente

Answers will vary. Possible answers shown.

1. a sentence containing an adjective clause with the relative pronoun *that*
<u>The house that used to be on the corner was moved to another lot two blocks away.</u>
2. a sentence containing an adverb clause with the subordinate conjunction *once*
<u>Once you've finished setting table, please pour drinks.</u>
3. a sentence containing a noun clause with the subordinate conjunction *wherever*
<u>Wherever you can clean will be a big help.</u>
4. a sentence beginning with an adverb clause with the subordinate conjunction *as long as*
<u>As long as you are here, we can go ahead and get started.</u>
5. a sentence containing a noun clause subject with the subordinate conjunction *where*
<u>Where my family vacations each summer has been hit by a hurricane.</u>
6. a sentence containing an adjective clause with the relative pronoun *who*
<u>Uncle Bradford, who lives in Washington D.C., works in the House of Representatives.</u>
7. a sentence containing an adverb clause with the subordinate conjunction *after*
<u>After the rain stopped, we got out of the car and headed for the soccer field.</u>

64

Answer Key

Review: Sentence Types, Simple and Compound Sentences

Read the sentences below. Use the line following each sentence to identify the sentence type. Write **D** for declarative, **IN** for interrogative, **E** for exclamatory, and **IM** for imperative.

1. Bears are not the only mammals that hibernate. D
2. Can you name any other animals that hibernate? IN
3. Chipmunks dig tunnels and crawl underground to spend the coldest parts of winter hibernating. D
4. Snakes, frogs, butterflies, and even a few types of birds hibernate. D
5. What happens when an animal is hibernating? IN
6. Hibernation is a kind of deep sleep; the animal's body temperature drops and its breathing and heart rate slow down greatly. D
7. Some animals hibernate for months! E
8. Search the library or online for more information about hibernation. IM

Identify each sentence below as simple (**S**) or compound (**C**).

1. C A bird might try to grab a lizard by the tail, but a lizard can break off its tail and escape.
2. S Students and teachers interact regularly during classroom time.
3. C An insulator prevents or hinders an electrical current; a conductor enables the current to flow.
4. S The two tallest buildings in the world are the Burj Khalifa and the Petronas Towers.
5. C A forklift carried the pallet of boxes to the back of the truck and raised the load, and then two men emptied the pallet.
6. S The Sydney Opera House was designed to look like ships sailing into the harbor.
7. C Tsetse flies carry a disease called *sleeping sickness*, and they pass along the disease through their bites.
8. S Stars are classified by their temperature and size.

65

Review: Complex Sentences; Adjective, Adverb, and Noun Clauses

Underline the dependent clause in each complex sentence below.

1. After losing its arm to an octopus, the starfish grew a new one.
2. Dr. Weinstein studies pediatric journals because she needs to keep her medical knowledge up to date.
3. Once the helicopter lifts off, the pilot will contact the observation tower.
4. Please take a photo before the rainbow disappears.
5. Although Evelyn Glennie is deaf, she is one of the best drummers in the world.
6. My dad can give us a lift to swim practice, unless you'd rather walk.
7. While Nelson examines the damage, have your father call the insurance company.
8. When everybody gets here, Mr. Langley will begin his lecture.
9. We haven't been able to get across town in less than half an hour since the city closed Harris Boulevard.

Read the sentences below. Circle the adjective clauses, underline the adverb clauses, and underline the noun clauses twice. Some sentences may have more than one clause.

1. What I meant to tell her was that we would be bringing my sister, too.
2. Most residents of the Philippines, who are called *Filipinos* live in the capital of Manila.
3. During the symphony's finale, Patrice got to play a timpani, which is also known as a kettledrum.
4. Between 1861 and 1865, the North and South fought one another in the American Civil War.
5. When you get up, please hand that pitcher of lemonade to Uncle Victor.
6. Although both amphibians and reptiles are cold-blooded animals, what differentiates amphibians in part is that they start life breathing through gills.
7. As light passes through a prism, it becomes separated into different wavelengths.
8. Centipedes, which have poisonous claws around their heads, feed on other insects.

Follow the directions for each item.

1. Write a complex sentence. ______
2. Write a sentence w______
3. Write a compound sentence. ______

Answers will vary.

66

Capitalize the first word of **every sentence**.

Crater Lake, located in southwestern Oregon, is the deepest lake in the U.S.

Capitalize the first word in **direct quotations**.

"*Only one more week until I get my braces off!*" exclaimed Sariya.

Do not capitalize indirect quotations.

Harriet said that the chess club will be holding a yard sale next weekend.

If a continuous sentence in a direct quotation is split and the second half is not a new sentence, do not capitalize it.

"You're going to need a root canal," said Dr. Wan, "as well as two fillings."

If a new sentence begins after the split, then capitalize it as you would any sentence.

"You will have 25 minutes to complete the essay," said Ms. Cruz. "You may begin writing whenever you're ready."

In a **letter**, capitalize the name of the street, the city, the state, and the month in the heading.

528 West Monroe Road
Traverse City, Michigan 49684
September 24, 2014

Capitalize the salutation, or greeting, as well as the name of the person who is receiving the letter. Capitalize the first word of the closing.

Dear Mrs. Grobin, To whom it may concern: Your friend,

Rewrite It

Rewrite each sentence below using correct capitalization.

1. "have you bought any new music lately?" Asked Jackson.
   "Have you bought any new music lately?" asked Jackson.
2. "I want to see my brother's band play on Tuesday night," said Maura, "But I have a test Wednesday morning."
   "I want to see my brother's band play on Tuesday night," said Maura, "but I have a test Wednesday morning."
3. Bashir said His dad likes to listen to vinyl records on an old turntable.
   Bashir said his dad likes to listen to vinyl records on an old turntable.
4. "david, are my CDs in the car?" Asked Mom. "if they are in the car, they might melt."
   "David, are my CDs in the car?" asked Mom. "If they are in the car, they might melt."

67

Proof It

Proofread the following letter for mistakes in capitalization. Underline a lowercase letter three times to make it a capital. m

longview farm
518 bluebell lane
lovettsville, virginia 20180

april 13, 2014

dear ms. weineke,

my name is Meera Danwell, and I believe you know my aunt, Jess Wendt. aunt jess knows how interested I am in farm life, and she suggested I contact you. i would love to have the opportunity to volunteer at Longview Farm this summer. although animals are my main interest, I'd also be happy to help out in the garden, in the house, and with the bees. i don't have any experience specifically with farm animals, but I've always helped to care for my family's two Labrador retrievers and our rabbit. in addition, I volunteer at Purrfect Pets Cat Shelter twice a month. my teachers say that I'm a hard worker and a fast learner. i'm looking forward to learning about farm life firsthand.

thank you for your time. i look forward to hearing from you.

sincerely,
Meera Danwell

Try It

On the lines below, write a short dialogue between two friends discussing summer vacation. Be sure to use capital letters where necessary.

Answers will vary.

68

Answer Key

Proper nouns are specific people, places, and things. Proper nouns are capitalized.
I think that *Ana* is planning to get a haircut after school. (specific person)
The largest city in *Wisconsin* is *Milwaukee*. (specific place)
Mom always buys *Soft Touch* fabric softener. (specific thing)

The titles of books, poems, songs, movies, plays, newspapers, and magazines are proper nouns and are capitalized. In a title, capitalize the first and last words, and capitalize all other words except *a, an,* and *the*. Do not capitalize short prepositions, such as *of, to, in, on,* and so on. Most titles are also underlined or set in italic font in text. Song titles, essays, poems, and other shorter works are placed in quotes.
Nina needs to return *The Skin I'm In* to the library by Friday.
Halle and Ira sang along to the Beatles' "Yellow Submarine."

Titles associated with names are also capitalized, but do not capitalize these titles if they are not directly used with the name.
Before *Dr.* Ames became a *doctor*, he taught biology at the university.

Proof It
Correct the mistakes in capitalization using proofreading marks. Underline a lowercase letter three times to make it a capital. m

1. My cousin, manny, grew up just a couple of blocks from lake erie.
2. I hope you bought creamy naturals peanut butter—it's the only kind my brother will eat.
3. The poem "afternoon on a hill" by edna st. vincent millay is one of my favorites; I memorized it last year.
4. While she was babysitting, Keiko put the twins to sleep by humming "you are my sunshine."
5. kat and todd love to go skiing in breckenridge, colorado.
6. Do you know if mayor peabody will be attending the ribbon-cutting ceremony?
7. Dylan is using *the war to end all wars: world war I* as the main source for his history report.
8. The first book that maggie's book club plans to read is *to kill a mockingbird.*
9. Last week, selma wrote a letter to the editor of the *los angeles times.*
10. arnold schwarzenegger spent two terms in office as the governor of california.

69

Rewrite It
Rewrite each name or title below using correct capitalization.

1. "stopping by woods on a snowy evening" "Stopping by Woods on a Snowy Evening"
2. nelson mandela Nelson Mandela
3. the blue ridge mountains the Blue Ridge Mountains
4. hamburg, germany Hamburg, Germany
5. the president of centerville middle school's 8th grade class the president of Centerville Middle School's 8th grade class
6. the eiffel tower the Eiffel Tower
7. *the firefly letters: a suffragette's journey to cuba* *The Firefly Letters: A Suffragette's Journey to Cuba*
8. dr. alysha johnson Dr. Alysha Johnson
9. the great salt lake the Great Salt Lake
10. *national geographic* *National Geographic*
11. president kennedy President Kennedy
12. *a wrinkle in time* *A Wrinkle in Time*
13. cuyahoga county Cuyahoga County
14. "a dream deferred" by langston hughes "A Dream Deferred" by Langston Hughes

Try It
Answer each of the questions below in a complete sentence. Remember to use correct capitalization.

1. What is the best book you've read in the last year?
2. If you could only listen to one album for the next month, what would it be?
3. You just won a free subscription to any magazine or newspaper. Which one would you choose?
4. What is the name of your city's or town's mayor?
5. If you could travel anywhere, where would you choose to go?
6. What figure from history do you most admire?

Answers will vary.

70

Organizations, departments of government, and sections of the country are all **proper nouns** and all important words are capitalized.

The names of organizations, associations, and businesses are capitalized.
Habitat for Humanity
The Greater Cleveland Arts Council
General Mills, Inc.

Capitalize the names of departments of government.
Bureau of Engraving and Printing
House of Representatives

Directional words that point out particular sections of the country are capitalized. However, words that give directions are not capitalized.
A hurricane affected most of the *Eastern* Seaboard.
The geese flew *south* for the winter.

Historical events and documents, historical time periods, nationalities, languages, and team names are all **proper nouns** as well.
The *Declaration of Independence* marked the beginning of the *Revolutionary War*.
The *Iron Age* lasted from approximately 1000 BC to 400 AD.
Laurie served *French* toast to her friends at camp.
The *Columbus Crew* will play a total of 17 away games this season.

Rewrite It
On the lines, rewrite the proper nouns in boldface so they are capitalized correctly.

1. The **gulf of tonkin resolution** led to an increase of American involvement in the **vietnam war**. Gulf of Tonkin Resolution; Vietnam War
2. The **san diego chargers** play in the **american football conference**. San Diego Chargers; American Football Conference
3. The **rotary club of charlotte** meets each Wednesday in the **south end** neighborhood. Rotary Club of Charlotte; South End
4. Lin is studying the history of the **supreme court**. Supreme Court
5. Uncle Vince joined the **marine corps** and is stationed on the **east coast**. Marine Corps; East Coast
6. The **magna carta** was issued during the **middle ages**. Magna Carta; Middle Ages

71

Proof It
Correct the mistakes in capitalization using proofreading marks. Underline a lowercase letter three times to make it a capital. m Lowercase a letter by making a slash through it. M

Philadelphia, Pennsylvania, is the second largest city on the east coast of the United States. Its name comes from the greek language and means "city of brotherly love." Philadelphia played an important role during the time of Early American History. The Founding Fathers met in Philadelphia to sign the declaration of independence, and the city served as a temporary capital for the United States during the revolutionary war. The continental congresses met in Philadelphia as well to eventually complete and sign the United States constitution.

Philadelphia also has a significant Historical role for african Americans specifically. Even during the time of Slavery, Philadelphia was home to a large free Black community. The african methodist episcopal church was founded in the city by free blacks in the late 1700s. In the 1900s, Philadelphia became a Major Destination during the great migration, in which millions of african Americans left the American south to move north.

Try It
Write one example for each category listed below. Be sure to capitalize each proper noun correctly.

Name of a government department or organization:
Name of a local business:
Name of a charity organization:
Name of a U.S. region:
Name of a historical event:
Name of a historical time period:
Name of a historical document:
Name of a sports team:

Answers will vary.

72

Answer Key

Periods are used at the end of declarative sentences and some imperative sentences.
Mount Fuji emerges ghostlike through the morning fog.
Please wash the teacup by hand.

Question marks are used at the end of interrogative sentences.
Can astronauts send e-mails from space?
How many drops of water are in a milliliter?

Exclamation points are used at the end of exclamatory sentences. They are also used at the end of imperative sentences or interjections that show urgency, strong surprise, or emotion.
The Phillies won the World Series!
Wow! Look at the color of that sunrise!

Identify It
Circle the end mark that correctly completes each sentence.

1. What is the scientific name for an elephant (. **?** !)
2. There's a gorilla loose in the zoo (. ? **!**)
3. How many stars would you rate that movie (. **?** !)
4. Originally, all of Earth's land was connected as a supercontinent called Pangaea (**.** ? !)
5. I am conducting a poll to find out which brand of tissue is most popular (**.** ? !)
6. Please stop writing when you hear the bell (**.** ? !)
7. What I want to know is why all the paintbrushes are still dirty (**.** ? !)
8. Tell me what you thought about Lois Lowry's new novel (**.** ? !)
9. Watch out for that bike (. ? **!**)
10. Continue along this path until you reach the big oak tree (**.** ? !)
11. Who owns most of the world's gold (. **?** !)
12. Which is the tallest species of palm tree (. **?** !)
13. Stop bugging me (. ? **!**)

73

Complete It
Add end marks to the sentences in the passage.

Let's go to the movies_!_ First we buy our tickets, then we grab a treat from the concession stand, and finally we find the perfect seat inside the theater_._ The lights dim, and the show begins_._ But did you ever wonder how the images onscreen appear to move_?_ It's an illusion_!_ They don't really move at all_._ What you see as movement on the screen is really a succession of still images_._ If you slowed the film down, you would see each photograph or drawing appear for a moment before the next one appeared, looking just slightly different from the previous image_._ When all the slightly different images are played back quickly enough, they create the illusion of smooth movement_._

The key to this illusion is persistence of vision_._ What is persistence of vision_?_ When the retina at the back of your eye perceives something, the image lingers for a brief fraction of a second, creating an afterimage_._ When you watch a film, the still images are projected quickly enough that the afterimage of one photograph is still lingering on your retina as the next image is shown_._ You do not perceive the gap between the two images_._ Instead, the change from one image to the next appears fluid_._ Presto_!_ You see what looks like movement on the screen rather than a slide show_._ Pretty cool, isn't it_?_

Try It
Write a paragraph about your favorite film or TV show. Include at least one declarative sentence, one interrogative sentence, and one imperative sentence. Be sure to use appropriate end marks.

Answers will vary.

74

Review: Capitalization of Sentences, Quotations, Names, Titles, Places, and Other Proper Nouns

Proofread each sentence below for capitalization. Lowercase a letter by making a slash through it M, and capitalize a letter by making three lines below it m.

1. The Walker fine art center is located at the corner of First avenue and Stone boulevard.
2. "The solar power plant will come online this saturday," Dr. Nichols explained, "So we need to contact general Rickert at the department of homeland security."
3. The Public School system we are familiar with today in the United States is only about 100 years old.
4. The words of many Western Languages use roots from latin or greek words.
5. The Spring issue of *Manhattan Medical journal* contains an article about working for the National Institutes Of Health.
6. The Moons of Jupiter vary greatly in size, although most are less than 10 Kilometers in diameter.
7. The Appalachian mountains are located in the east, while the Rocky mountains are in the west.
8. Situated on the 53rd floor of wilson oaks tower, the Doctors' offices have a spectacular view of Downtown Atlanta.
9. The assassination of an Archduke of the Hapsburg Empire is considered by most Historians as the event that began world war I.
10. "Which station is showing the Super Bowl this year?" Asked Roshelle. "is it fox or espn?"
11. Many castles were built throughout europe during the middle ages.
12. Jesse Owens's accomplishments at the 1936 summer olympics in berlin, germany, made him an International Celebrity.
13. The official Religion of Israel is judaism.
14. American Astronaut Buzz Aldrin was the second man to walk on the moon.
15. Max told his Friend Henry, "my grandfather was a Pilot for pan am world airways back in the Fifties."

75

Review: Capitalization of Letter Parts, End Marks

Read each letter part below. If it is correct, make a check mark on the line. If it contains an error in capitalization, make an **X** on the line.

1. _✓_ Charlotte, NC 28270
2. _✓_ Sincerely,
3. _✓_ Dear Madam or Sir:
4. _X_ june 12, 2015
5. _X_ dear Mae,
6. _✓_ All the Best,
7. _X_ august 14, 2014
8. _✓_ Yours truly,

Add the appropriate end mark to each sentence below.

1. Are you familiar with the Hindu myth of Garuda_?_
2. Ms. Seely speaks 13 languages_!_
3. Tell me what you think of the museum's new Holocaust exhibit_._
4. I wonder what the first cameras looked like_._
5. Quick, shut that gate before the lamb gets out_!_
6. What I really want to know is the name of the first film that featured a robot_._
7. Is water in the Dead Sea saltier than ocean water_?_
8. The native peoples of a place are called *aboriginals*_._
9. If you were in the orchestra, which instrument would you play_?_
10. Judge Robinson will preside over the court this morning_._
11. Petrochemicals are substances created from petroleum, or crude oil_._
12. Can you believe how quickly this last month went by_?_
13. Name three devices invented by Thomas Edison_._
14. Earth's tectonic plates float atop a layer of molten rock, or magma_._

76

Series commas are used with three or more items listed in a sentence. The items can be words or phrases and are separated by commas.
Salamanders, newts, and frogs are amphibians.
At the Ohio State Fair, we rode on a merry-go-round, a rollercoaster, and a Ferris wheel.

Commas are used to separate the name of a person spoken to from the rest of the sentence. This is called a **direct address**.
When should I make my next appointment, Dr. Reese?
Cesar, you will have the role of narrator in the play.

When **multiple adjectives** describe a noun, they are separated by commas if they are coordinate adjectives.
The dog's wet, matted fur was difficult to comb.
Asia is a vast, diverse continent.

Coordinate adjectives equally modify the noun. If they are coordinate adjectives, you can switch the order without changing the meaning.
The assistant's *agile, experienced* fingers typed about 100 words per minute. (coordinate adjectives because *agile, experienced fingers* and *experienced, agile fingers* both make sense)

Non-coordinate adjectives do not use commas.
Mae and her grandmother completed a *difficult jigsaw* puzzle.
(non-coordinate adjectives because *jigsaw difficult puzzle* does not make sense)

Match It
Read the sentences below. Decide what kind of comma, if any, is needed in each sentence. Write the letter of your answer on the line.

a. series comma — b. direct address comma
c. multiple adjectives comma — d. no comma needed

1. __b__ Mr. Larson could you please set this microscope on the top shelf?
2. __d__ Breyton helped remove the damaged wading pool.
3. __c__ The museum displayed a rusty antique submarine.
4. __a__ Plastic is used in making cars clothing and containers.

77

Proof It
Read the sentences below. Add commas where they are needed. If the sentence is correct as it is, make a check mark on the line.

1. ____ Lewis,be sure to include a self-addressed,stamped envelope.
2. ____ A platypus is an odd creature that has a beak like a duck,a tail like a beaver, and lays eggs like a reptile.
3. ____ Examples of nations in Europe include Liechtenstein,Moldova,and Albania.
4. __✓__ Jupiter's famous Great Red Spot is a giant storm that has lasted for hundreds of years.
5. ____ The website you had trouble viewing is available now,Shawn.
6. ____ Octillion,decillion,and googol are the names of very large numbers.
7. ____ Fresh,clean laundry billowed in a soft summer breeze.
8. __✓__ I left my new laptop computer in the third floor reading room.
9. ____ During the coldest winter days, you should wear that cozy,striped sweater, Manny.
10. ____ On your hike,Raj,you might walk through some sticky spider webs.
11. ____ The Koneyas will visit Los Angeles,San Francisco,Portland,and Seattle.
12. ____ Chewy,garlic-flavored pizza crust is the best, don't you agree,Mom?
13. ____ Earth has four oceans: the Pacific,the Atlantic,the Indian,and the Arctic.
14. ____ A glass of refreshingly cold ice water is the perfect thing on a dry,hot day.
15. ____ Put that dirty measuring cup on the empty,bottom shelf of the dishwasher.

Try It
For each number below, write a sentence that includes the items in parentheses.
1. (series commas) ____
2. (multiple adjectives) ____
3. (series commas) ____
4. (direct address) ____
5. (multiple adjectives and direct address) ____

Answers will vary.

78

Use a comma to **combine two independent clauses** with a coordinate conjunction.
Taylor and Imani held up a car wash sign, *and* Liza directed traffic.

In a complex sentence, **connect a dependent and an independent clause** with a comma and subordinate conjunction.
Although Stephen has a hard time sitting still, he loves to read.

Commas are used when **setting off dialogue** from the rest of the sentence.
"The finalists in the art competition will be announced at 2:00," said Ms. Weiss.
"I'd like the Greek pasta," replied Zachary, "with a side of asparagus."

Complete It
The sentences below are missing commas. Add commas where they are needed using proofreaders' marks ^.

1. George Washington had a lifetime of trouble with his teeth,but he never wore wooden dentures as some myths report.
2. He began having decay and tooth loss in his twenties,which caused him years of pain, embarrassment, and discomfort.
3. Although Washington tried a variety of cleaners, medications, and dentures, nothing really solved his dental problems.
4. When Washington was inaugurated as president,he had only one real tooth left!
5. Washington had several pairs of dentures,but none were very comfortable.
6. Some of his false teeth were crafted of hippopotamus ivory,whereas others were made from human teeth and carved elephant ivory.
7. Because the false teeth were difficult to wear while eating,Washington's diet suffered.
8. For a presidential portrait,Washington once put cotton balls in his mouth to support his lips!
9. Old fashioned dentures stained easily,and they required quite a bit of cleaning.
10. Contemporary researchers performed laser scans of George's teeth,and they found that the dentures were made of gold, lead, ivory, and human,and animal teeth.
11. Throughout his life,Washington was self conscious about smiling.
12. Modern dentures are much more comfortable,but they were long after George Washington's time.

79

Identify It
Read each sentence below. If the use of commas is correct, write **C** on the line. If it is incorrect, write **X** on the line and add commas where they are needed.

1. __C__ "Dad," began Isaac, "I just finished doing a research report on Australia, and I'm practically an expert now."
2. __X__ "You can ask me about it," continued Isaac,"or I can just tell you some of the more interesting things I learned."
3. __X__ "Well," said Mr. Jackson,scratching his head,"I know that Australia is both a country and a continent."
4. __C__ "That's right!" said Isaac. "Australia covers more than three million square miles, but it's the smallest continent."
5. __X__ He added,"Australia's Great Barrier Reef is so massive, it can be seen from space."
6. __X__ "I've heard that there are more sheep than people in Australia and New Zealand," said Mr. Jackson,"but I don't know if that's true."
7. __C__ "Yep," said Isaac, "that is true."
8. __X__ "Some areas are pretty densely populated,but much of Australia is desert," added Isaac.
9. __C__ "If you had to pick the most fascinating thing you learned about Australia, what would it be?" asked Mr. Jackson.
10. __X__ "That's easy," said Isaac. "Animals like the kangaroo, platypus, and koala are unique to Australia,and they aren't found anywhere else in the world."

Try It
Write a short dialogue between two people, being sure to use commas correctly.

Answers will vary.

80

Answer Key

Commas are used in both **personal** and **business letters**.

Personal Letters
Commas appear in four of the five parts of the personal letter.

Heading: 3698 Waltham Rd.
Bismarck, ND 58501
October 3, 2014
Salutation: Dear Crystal,
Body: comma usage in sentences
Closing: Yours truly,

Business Letters
Commas appear in four of the six parts of the business letter.

Heading: 566 Covewood Ct.
Baltimore, MD 21205
January 29, 2014
Inside Address: Ms. Julia Cohen
Redford Musical Conservatory
1311 W. Maple St.
Indianapolis, IN 46077
Body: comma usage in sentences
Closing: Sincerely,

Use a comma to indicate **a pause after an introductory word or phrase.**

No, I won't be able to attend the seminar on Tuesday.
Furthermore, the tombs of pharaohs were filled with treasures to accompany them to the afterlife.
Jumping over the creek, Yusef managed to keep his pants and boots dry.

Complete It
Complete each item below by adding commas where they are needed. If no changes are necessary, make a check mark on the line.

1. _____ First, I'd like you to clean your paintbrushes.
2. _____ In the woods, Kathleen carefully noted the first signs of spring.
3. __✓__ Without her mother's permission, Nola was not permitted to accompany her classmates to the amusement park.
4. _____ Nevertheless, it was still important to inspire confidence in the company's investors.
5. __✓__ Beside the maple tree, clusters of lilies of the valley bloomed.
6. _____ Nearby, an owl called and received an answer in the moonless night.

81

Rewrite It
Rewrite each item below, including commas where they are needed.

1. In spite of the rain we'll still be attending the rally.
In spite of the rain, we'll still be attending the rally.
2. Best wishes
Best wishes,
3. In addition you'll need two cups of oats and half a cup of raisins.
In addition, you'll need two cups of oats and half a cup of raisins.
4. Walking quickly George managed to catch up to the class.
Walking quickly, George managed to catch up to the class.
5. May 5 2010
May 5, 2010
6. Next June Isla will be turning fourteen.
Next June, Isla will be turning fourteen.
7. Once again Antonio has managed to impress us with his memory.
Once again, Antonio has managed to impress us with his memory.
8. Dear Ms. Chun
Dear Ms. Chun,
9. If you are hoping to make the team you should start working out this summer.
If you are hoping to make the team, you should start working out this summer.
10. Austin Texas
Austin, Texas

Try It
On the lines below, write a short letter to a friend or family member about something fun you've done recently. Remember to include commas in all the necessary places.

Answers will vary.

82

Colons have several functions in a sentence.

Colons are used to introduce a series in a sentence. Colons are not needed when the series is preceded by a verb or preposition.

Use the following resources for your report: *books, magazines, or the Internet.*
At the zoo, we *saw a wolf, kangaroo, and three tiger kittens.* (no colon needed)

A colon is sometimes used instead of a comma to set off a clause or to set off a word or phrase for emphasis.

Mr. Hanson reminded the students: *"Do not leave your seats until the bell rings."*
As Darrell approached his front door, he couldn't believe what he saw: *a gift-wrapped box!*

A **semicolon** is a cross between a period and a comma.

Semicolons join two independent clauses when a coordinate conjunction is not used.

The tea was much too hot; I let it cool for a few minutes before taking a sip.

Semicolons are used to separate clauses when the main clause is long and already contains a comma.

When the deer heard us, they darted into the woods, ran just a few yards, and then stopped; but as hard as I looked, I could no longer see them.

Semicolons are used to separate clauses when they are joined by some conjunctive adverbs, such as *consequently, furthermore, however, moreover, nevertheless,* or *therefore.*

After Pilar pulled into the parking space, she realized she had forgotten her purse; consequently, she had to call her sister to ask for a favor.

Identify It
Identify whether a colon or semicolon is needed to correctly complete each sentence. Circle the correct punctuation.

1. (**(:)** ;) The following animals are often found in rain forests ___ toucans, leafcutter ants, and tree frogs.
2. (: **(;)**) Although they were allies during World War II, the Soviet Union and the United States soon grew distrustful of each other ___ the result was a Cold War lasting for decades.
3. (: **(;)**) Renewable resources used today include wind, solar, and water power ___ but most electricity is still created through nuclear power or by burning fossil fuels.
4. (**(:)** ;) Light travels amazingly fast ___ 299,792,458 meters per second!
5. (**(:)** ;) Andrew explained to his mother ___ "Even if I get there by nine, most of the seats will be taken."

83

Proof It
In the sentences below, colons and semicolons are missing or used incorrectly. Correct each sentence by adding, replacing, or deleting colons and semicolons as needed.

= deletes punctuation
= inserts punctuation

1. Electrical generators contain the following parts; a coil of wire, magnets, and carbon brushes. (; replaced with :)
2. If you see a white cloud billowing from the top of a nuclear power plant, it is not smoke; it is steam. (: inserted after smoke)
3. Batteries produce DC, or direct current, electricity; whereas the electricity you get from a plug is AC, or alternate current, electricity. (; replaced with ,)
4. Both nuclear power plants and coal-burning power plants produce electricity by heating water to create steam that turns a generator; however, each produces a different kind of pollution. (; inserted after generator)
5. The electrical power grid consists of electrical energy produced by: nuclear power, fossil fuels, wind turbines, and hydroelectric dams. (: deleted)
6. The chain reactions inside a nuclear reactor release a huge amount of heat, therefore, the reactor is housed inside a thick, concrete container. (, replaced with ;)
7. For centuries, wind power has been used to move boats, to grind corn, or to pump water; but its use for generating electricity is much more recent.
8. Fossil fuels, nuclear energy, wind, water, and sunlight can all be used to create electricity; however, fossil fuels and nuclear energy are nonrenewable resources.
9. Although sunlight is a renewable resource, solar panels utilize a nonrenewable resource: silicon.
10. Wind farms need to be located in windy places, such as mountaintops, coastlines, or treeless plains; but dozens, or even hundreds, of wind turbines in these places might create a kind of visual pollution.

Try It
On the lines below, write your own sentences containing colons or semicolons. Write two sentences that use a colon and two sentences that use one or more semicolons.

1.
2.
3.
4.

Answers will vary.

84

Answer Key

85

Quotation marks are used to show the exact words of a speaker. The quotation marks are placed before and after the exact words.

"Let's look for a game to play," said Cho. "I think this rain is going to last all afternoon."

Quotation marks are also used when a direct quotation contains another direct quotation.

"Mom said, *'Ask Branson to help you pick up the yard,'"* Jaden told his brother.

Note that single quotation marks are used to set off the inside quotation. Single quotes express what Mom said. Double quotes express what Jaden said.

Quotation marks are used with some titles. Quotation marks are used with the titles of short stories, poems, songs, and articles in magazines and newspapers.

Emily's favorite song on Kelly Clarkson's album *Stronger* is *"Mr. Know It All."*

If a title is quoted within a direct quotation, then single quotation marks are used.

"Please read *'The Lottery'* over the weekend so we can discuss it in class on Monday," said Ms. Shin.

Complete It

Add double or single quotation marks where they are needed in each sentence.

1. "Have you ever read the poem 'Jabberwocky' by Lewis Carroll?" asked Aiden.
2. Ms. Yates explained to the class, "I was told by Principal Lincoln, 'Your students will receive the credit they deserve.'"
3. Noah's essay was titled "Harris Jr. High: Clean and Green."
4. "When we were at breakfast," said Rae, "my brother said his favorite Edgar Allan Poe story is 'The Pit and the Pendulum.'"
5. "It's break time!" yelled the foreman. "And remember what Mr. Powers said: 'Everyone must be back to work by 12:30.'"
6. O. Henry's "The Gift of the Magi" is one of the most famous short stories of all time.
7. After Ms. Hanna recited "A Narrow Fellow in the Grass," she said, "That poem was written by Emily Dickinson."
8. In his list of sources, Liam included "A New Bike for a New Millennium," an article he found in the June 2000 issue of *Outdoor Magazine*.
9. "In celebration of Arbor Day," Emma announced, "I will be reading the poem 'Trees.'"
10. "Aunt Victoria said, 'Please bring a side dish or a dessert,'" Louis reminded his mother.

86

Try It

Two classmates (you choose their names) are discussing a reading assignment. Their teacher (you choose his or her name) has told them to choose one of these poems, read it, and write a report: "On This Wondrous Sea" by Emily Dickinson, "A Noiseless, Patient Spider" by Walt Whitman, or "Eldorado" by Edgar Allan Poe. Use the lines below to write a short dialogue between the classmates as they discuss which poem each will choose. Include at least one quotation within a quotation in your dialogue, and be sure to punctuate the dialogue correctly.

Answers will vary.

87

When you are working on a computer, use **italics** for the titles of books, plays, movies, television series, magazines, and newspapers. If you are writing by hand, **underline** these titles.

Last Saturday, my friends and I watched *Ferris Bueller's Day Off.* (movie)
The Washington Post carried an ad for the senator's reelection. (newspaper)
The Atlanta Community Theater is presenting *Death of a Salesman.* (play)

Identify It

Underline the title or titles in each sentence that should be italicized.

1. Director Steven Spielberg attended the premiere of <u>Jurassic Park</u>.
2. Kayla enjoyed reading the novel <u>Holes</u> more than seeing the film they made of it.
3. Several nights a week, Vince and his family watch reruns of the TV show <u>Home Improvement</u>.
4. Although <u>The Lion, the Witch, and the Wardrobe</u> was the first book C. S. Lewis wrote in the Narnia series, the events in <u>The Magician's Nephew</u> take place at an earlier time.
5. We canceled our subscription to <u>Time Magazine</u> because most of the same articles are available online.
6. Winston Churchill earned the Nobel Prize in Literature for his nonfiction book <u>The Second World War</u>.
7. "The Beach Boys' best album is <u>Pet Sounds</u>," Chris insisted.
8. Cameron's stomach felt queasy with nerves as he waited to audition for the lead role in <u>Bye Bye Birdie</u>.
9. The season premiere of <u>The Voice</u> airs next Thursday at 8 PM.
10. I found a copy of <u>The World Almanac for Kids 2014</u> at the library.
11. Joseph Campbell's classic book <u>The Hero with a Thousand Faces</u> was assigned as part of our unit on mythology.
12. <u>The San Francisco Chronicle</u> published an essay written by our history teacher, Mr. Sampson.
13. The latest episode of <u>Glee</u> featured music by the Beatles.
14. I used an article about polar bears from the June 2012 issue of <u>National Geographic</u> as a source for my report.

88

Try It

Write a few sentences answering each set of questions. Be sure to use complete sentences.

1. What is the most popular book among your friends or classmates? Have you read the book? If not, do you plan to?

   Answers will vary.

2. What is the last movie you saw? Write a sentence comparing it to another movie you liked better.

   Answers will vary.

3. What books, magazines, or newspapers have you used as resources for school projects or reports? Include a brief description of the report or project.

   Answers will vary.

4. What TV show have others encouraged you to watch? What TV shows have you recommended to others?

   Answers will vary.

5. Who is your favorite author? Which of his or her books have you read? Which book did you like most? Which did you like least?

   Answers will vary.

Answer Key

Apostrophes are used in contractions to form possessives.

Apostrophes take the place of the omitted letters in contractions.
have not = haven't   she will = she'll

Possessives show possession, or ownership. To form the possessive of a singular noun, add an apostrophe and an *s*. This rule applies even if the noun already ends in *s*.
The flower**'s** petals were pale yellow.   I borrowed Ross**'s** CD.

To form the possessive of plural nouns ending in *s*, add an apostrophe. If the plural noun does not end in *s*, add both the apostrophe and an *s*.
The naturalists' tour of the new nature center was very informative.
The men**'s** glee club will be performing on Saturday night.

Match It
Read each sentence below. From the box, choose the type of apostrophe that is used and write the letter of your choice on the line.

a. contraction	b. singular possessive
c. plural possessive ending in *s*	d. plural possessive not ending in *s*

1. b Carlita's new journal
2. d the people's reaction
3. b the professor's last class
4. c the Boy Scouts' campout
5. a you're
6. c the coaches' meeting
7. b Darius's math homework
8. a couldn't
9. c the chickadees' nest
10. b the tree trunk's bark
11. d the geese's feathers
12. d the children's umbrellas

89

Proof It
In the sentences below, add the apostrophes where they are needed using this proofreading mark ↓̌ . Delete unnecessary apostrophes ℊ.

1. The archeologists' expedition was led by Professor Abdul Naasir.
2. King Tut's tomb was found in Egypts' Valley of the Kings.
3. An archaeologist named Howard Carter found a step under some workmens' huts.
4. Pharaohs' tombs were often a place for thieves to find amazing riches.
5. Tutankhamun's tomb held over 5,000 objects because it had remained undisturbed by robbers.
6. The king's canopic chest held his organs.
7. The mummy's coffin was made of solid gold.
8. It is'nt easy to imagine how the massive pyramids could've been built without the use of modern-day machinery.
9. Newspapers' reports that there was a curse on the tomb of Tutankhamun were purely rumor.
10. The Nile River's location in northeast Africa contributed to the development of the Ancient Egyptians' advanced civilization.
11. It's estimated that the Pyramid of Khufu is constructed of blocks weighing almost six million tons!
12. The British Museums' website on Ancient Egypt is filled with interesting facts and isn't difficult to navigate.

Try It
Write a sentence for each of the various types of apostrophes.

1. contraction
2. singular possessive
3. plural possessive ending in *s*
4. plural possessive not ending in *s*

Answers will vary.

90

Hyphens are used in compound modifiers only when the modifier precedes the word it modifies. Hyphens are not used for compound modifiers with adverbs ending in *-ly*.
Jiang's *well-written* paper received an A. I knew it would be *well written*.
The *gently snoring* child rolled over in her sleep.

Use hyphens in some compound nouns. You will need to check a dictionary to be sure which compound nouns need hyphens.
Mom has a very close relationship with her *mother-in-law*, my grandmother.

Hyphens are used between compound numbers from twenty-one through ninety-nine.
Julian needs to read another *forty-two* entries in the short fiction contest.

Dashes indicate a sudden break or a change in thought.
Aunt Jeanine—*she's a doctor*—will be visiting next month.

Parentheses show supplementary, or additional, material or set off phrases in a stronger way than commas.
We plan to go to the barbecue *(hosted by the Boy Scouts)* next weekend.

Ellipses can be used to indicate an omission, or words that have been left out.
The hearing will be at noon . . . at the courthouse downtown.

An ellipsis can also be used to indicate a pause in a sentence.
"I'm not really sure what to say . . . but I am sorry."

Complete It
Add hyphens where they are needed in the phrases below. If no hyphens are needed, make a check mark on the line.

1. ____ a close‸up photograph
2. ____ twenty‸four chapters
3. ✓ a brightly lit room
4. ____ the last get‸together
5. ____ a life‸size statue
6. ____ sixty‸five students
7. ✓ a teacher who is well known
8. ✓ a patiently waiting dog
9. ____ a long‸distance race
10. ____ the worn‸out jeans

91

Rewrite It
Each sente[...]ses. Rewrite each sentence u[...] be more than one correct answer for s[...]

Answers may vary. Possible answers shown.

1. My neighbor he lives in the blue house has six cats.
My neighbor (he lives in the blue house) has six cats.
2. Simone is participating in the spelling bee this weekend and she plans to win.
Simone is participating in the spelling bee this weekend—and she plans to win.
3. Audrey downloaded her photos she just got a digital camera and started to edit them. **Audrey downloaded her photos—she just got a digital camera—and started to edit them.**
4. Mr. Toshi just turned forty four.
Mr. Toshi just turned forty-four.
5. Ian thought and thought he thought some more but couldn't think of an excuse.
Ian thought . . . and thought . . . he thought some more but couldn't think of an excuse.
6. Daniel babysits for a set of well behaved twins.
Daniel babysits for a set of well-behaved twins.
7. Traveling to Rochester to see Grandma even though it's a long trip is always the best part of summer.
Traveling to Rochester to see Grandma (even though it's a long trip) is always the best part of summer.
8. After you've mixed the batter make sure the oven is preheated you can fill up the muffin cups.
After you've mixed the batter—make sure the oven is preheated—you can fill up the muffin cups.
9. The high today should be between seventy five and seventy eight degrees.
The high today should be between seventy-five and seventy-eight degrees.
10. We should go now unless you'd like me to pick you up later.
We should go now . . . unless you'd like me to pick you up later.

92

Review: Commas, Colons, and Semicolons

Add commas where they are needed in each item below.

1. We can make the muffins if you have ripe bananas, buttermilk, blueberries, flour, sugar, and eggs.
2. "I woke up this morning to the sound of birds chirping," said Aunt Sadie, "so I'm pretty sure that spring is on its way."
3. Your truly,
   Becca Stanich
4. "Kyra, if you want to make it to cheerleading practice on time," said Mrs. Bell, "we need to get going in 15 minutes."
5. 1452 Maple Grove Ln.
   Tulsa, OK 74102
6. Eating an apple each day can boost your immune system, and it can also help prevent tooth decay.
7. Rohit, have you taken the recycling out to the curb yet?
8. At first, Dr. Ortiz wasn't certain how to interpret the results of the experiment.
9. The rusty, ancient car has been parked in our neighbor's driveway for over a year.
10. Monika has packed T-shirts, shorts, sundresses, and two pairs of shoes.
11. The sleek, silky baby otter searched for its mother as the thick gray clouds gathered on the horizon.
12. Hillary Clinton was the First Lady during Bill Clinton's presidency, but she is also a politician in her own right.
13. Despite the unexpected storm, the plane was still scheduled to land on time.
14. Maurice's dad is returning from his deployment in Iraq tomorrow, and the whole family will be there to welcome him home.

Each sentence below is missing a colon or a semicolon. Circle the missing punctuation mark in parentheses.

1. The following items are not allowed in the auditorium (; (:)) food, beverages, cell phones, and cameras.
2. There was a sign posted on the studio door ((;) :) it said that classes were canceled.
3. Katrina grew to dislike her own name ((;) :) it never failed to remind her of the hurricane.
4. The daily lunch special includes the following (; (:)) half a sandwich, a cup of soup, an apple, and a fountain drink.

93

Review: Quotation Marks, Using Italics and Underlining, Apostrophes, Hyphens, Dashes, Parentheses, Ellipses

Rewrite each sentence below to add quotation marks or apostrophes where they are needed. Two sentences also contain words that need to be underlined when you rewrite the sentences.

1. In spite of last nights loss, said Coach Trammel, I have a good feeling about next weeks game.
   "In spite of last night's loss," said Coach Trammel, "I have a good feeling about next week's game."
2. I think that the movie Oz: The Great and Powerful is a prequel to Frank L. Baums novels about Oz, commented Eva.
   "I think that the movie Oz: The Great and Powerful is a prequel to Frank L. Baum's novels about Oz," commented Eva.
3. Why arent you doing your presentation on the Salem witch trials? asked Nates sister.
   "Why aren't you doing your presentation on the Salem witch trials?" asked Nate's sister.
4. If youll be going on the field trip to Gaston County History Museum on Friday, announced Ms. Mahmood, please bring your lunch with you.
   "If you'll be going on the field trip to Gaston County History Museum on Friday," announced Ms. Mahmood, "please bring your lunch with you."
5. On Saturday, Rubens cousin is going to a performance of the play The King and I.
   On Saturday, Ruben's cousin is going to a performance of the play The King and I.

Add hyphens where they are needed in each item below.

1. twenty-four roses
2. a one-way street
3. chocolate-covered strawberries
4. a mid-August birthday
5. the well-loved professor
6. five-year-old sister

Add the missing ... There may be more than one ...

Answers may vary. Possible answers shown.

1. Reed's brother (he goes to school in Vermont) is coming home for summer.
2. Tilly looked for hours and hours — she just didn't know what else to do.
3. The theme for Andrea's birthday party — she turns 13 on May 15th — is the Eighties.
4. The weeds are taking over the garden ... but at least we're still getting a decent harvest.

94

The **root** of a word is the main part of the word. It tells the main meaning, and other word parts add to the main meaning.

The root *spect* means "look" or "see."
The word *inspect* means "to look closely or carefully."
The word *spectacle* means "something interesting to look at."

If an unfamiliar word contains a familiar root, knowing the meaning of the root can give you a clue to the meaning of the unfamiliar word.

Most roots in the English language come from the Latin or Greek languages.

Latin Root Examples	Greek Root Examples
audi means "hear"	*bio* means "life"
dict means "say"	*chrono* means "time"
mis means "send"	*geo* means "earth"
port means "carry"	*graph* means "write"
sens and *sent* mean "feel"	*phon* means "sound"
vid or *vis* mean "see"	*photo* means "light"

Identify It

Review the exam... d in the words below. On the li... contains the same root. Use a dictionary if yo...

Answers will vary. Possible answers shown.

1. synchronize chronology
2. invisible visor
3. respectful inspection
4. photosynthesis photography
5. graphically telegraph
6. prediction dictionary
7. autobiography biology
8. geothermal geography
9. transmission missile
10. auditory audition
11. insensitive sensation
12. telephone phonics
13. deportation portable
14. resentful sentimental

95

Complete ... Fill in the ... below. Use a dictionary if you need help.

Some answers may vary. Possible answers shown.

Root	Meaning	Example
prim	"first"	primitive
spher	"ball"	hemisphere
dia	"across"	diameter
bene	"good"	beneficial
magn	"great"	magnify
levi	"light"	levity
grav	"heavy"	gravity
script	"write"	inscription
pos	"put"	position
retro	"back"	retrospect
rupt	"break"	disrupt
auto	"self"	automatic
ped	"foot"	centipede
giga	"billion"	gigabyte
cogn	"to know"	recognize
astr	"star"	astrology
vac	"empty"	evacuate
duc	"make"	produce

Try It

Choose four roots from the list above. Think of a word other than the one shown for each root and use it in a sentence. Write your sentences on the lines below.

1. root: ________ sentence: ________
2. root: ________ sentence: ________
3. root: ________ sentence: ________
4. root: ________ sentence: ________

Answers will vary.

96

Prefixes and suffixes change the meanings of root and base words. A **prefix** is a word part added to the beginning of a root or base word. For example, the prefix *pre-* means "before," so *precut* means "cut **before**."

Some common prefixes and their meanings are listed below.

in-, im-, ir-, il- = "not"	irregular, impolite, illiterate
re- = "again"	refreeze
dis- = "not, opposite of"	disconnect
non- = "not"	nonslip
over- = "too much"	overcook
mis- = "wrongly"	miscalculate
pre- = "before"	precut
inter- = "between, among"	intercoastal

Rewrite It

Add a prefix fr[illegible] ...rd on the first line. If nece[illegible] ...e prefix and base word form an accepted Engli[illegible] ...n, use the new word in a sentence.

Answers may vary. Possible answers shown.

1. understand misunderstand
   Sometimes I misunderstand my uncle because he has a heavy accent.
2. state interstate
   We'll take the interstate because it is much faster.
3. order preorder
   Preorder your books now and receive a special discount.
4. organized disorganized
   Your folders are so disorganized, I don't understand how you find anything.
5. applied reapplied
   I reapplied for the class again this semester.
6. perfect imperfect
   Don't worry if the stitch is a little imperfect; no one will notice.
7. issue nonissue
   Your hairstyle is a nonissue; we're more interested in your work experience.
8. excited overexcited
   Now, don't get overexcited, but we may get to go backstage!

97

A **suffix** is a word part added to the end of a root or base word. Sometimes, the spelling of the root or base word changes when a suffix is added. For example, the suffix *-ness* means "state or condition of." *Happiness* means "**the state or condition of** being happy." Note that the final *-y* in *happy* changes to *i* before adding the suffix.

Some common suffixes and their meanings are listed below.

-ful, -y = "characterized by or tending to"	playful, chilly
-ly = "characteristic of"	angrily
-er, -or, -ist = "one who" or "person connected with"	dreamer, cellist
-ion, -tion, -ation, -ition = "act or process"	animation
-ic = "having characteristics of"	allergic
-less = "without"	harmless
-en = "made of" or "to make"	brighten
-ment = "act or process"	fulfillment
-ness, -ity = "state or condition of"	stubbornness, infinity

Complete It

Complete each sentence below by adding one of the suffixes listed above to the root word in boldface. Then, underline the suffix. Use a dictionary if you need help.

1. A stove covered in **grime** is grimy.
2. If you make something **light**er you lighten it.
3. An **athlete** can be described as someone who is athletic.
4. A gift that has **meaning** to you is meaningful.
5. Someone who **climbs** is a climber.
6. If you don't have a **penny**, you are penniless.
7. A doctor who studies **paleontology** is called a paleontologist.
8. Placement is the process of putting something in a specific **place**.
9. Graduation is the process of **graduat**ing from school.
10. Someone who works in **realty** is a realtor.
11. A **grumpy** person is in a state of grumpiness.
12. If you are very **thirsty** as you drink water, you drink it thirstily.

98

Adding a suffix to a base word, or changing an existing suffix, often changes the word's part of speech. For example, *generous* is an adjective. When the suffix *-ity* is added to *generous*, the word *generosity* is formed, which is a noun meaning "the state of being generous."

Identify It

On the first line, identify the part of speech of the word shown. Then, add the suffix and write the new word on the second line, followed by the part of speech of the new word. The first problem has been done as an example.

1. adjective happy + -ness = happiness noun
2. verb run + er = runner noun
3. noun stress + ful = stressful adjective
4. noun or verb limit + less = limitless adjective
5. verb animate + tion = animation noun
6. adjective purposeful + ly = purposefully adverb
7. verb squeak + y = squeaky adjective
8. noun violin + ist = violinist noun
9. adjective moist + en = moisten verb
10. verb govern + ment = government noun

Try It

On each line below, write a sentence that includes a word with the prefix or suffix indicated.

Answers will vary.

1. the suffix *-ic*
2. the prefix *dis-*
3. the prefix *inter-*
4. the suffix *-y*
5. the prefix *in-*
6. the suffix *-ful*

99

Solve It

Read each definition below. Fill in the correct space in the crossword puzzle with a word that begins with a prefix or ends in a suffix and matches the definition.

Across
2 not sane
4 state or condition of being sweet
6 one who directs
7 without hair
8 to calculate wrongly

Down
1 to wrongly file
3 the act or process of entertaining
4 to make straight

Across
2 insane
4 sweetness
6 director
7 hairless
8 miscalculate

Down
1 misfile
3 entertainment
4 straighten

100

Answer Key

Double negatives occur when two negative words are used in the same sentence. Negative words include *not, no, never, neither, nobody, nowhere, nothing, barely, hardly, scarcely,* and contractions containing the word *not.* Avoid using double negatives—they are grammatically incorrect.

Negative: Ava and Emma *couldn't* see any stars because of the clouds.
Double Negative: Ava and Emma *couldn't* see *no* stars because of the clouds.

To correct a double negative, you can delete one of the negative words or replace it with an affirmative, or positive, word. Affirmative words are the opposite of negative words. Examples include *some, somewhere, someone, anyone, any,* and *always.*

Double Negative: *No one* did *nothing* to fix the broken chair in the hall.
Possible correction: *No one* did *anything* to fix the broken chair in the hall.

Identify It

Underline the word or words in parentheses that best complete each sentence below.

1. The doors are still locked, so nobody (is, isn't) sitting in the waiting room yet.
2. The horses won't eat (no, any) feed until Mr. Yates fills the food trough.
3. I could barely hear (nothing, anything) because I was seated at the back of the auditorium.
4. Uncle Joshua (will, won't) never finish repairing your car at the rate he's going.
5. The turtle won't (ever, never) stick its head out of its shell if you're too loud.
6. Ms. Henks won't accept (no, any) papers that are turned in after Friday.
7. The bus is hardly (never, ever) late arriving to pick up students from school.
8. Justin couldn't remember (no one, anyone) ever cleaning out the bottom drawer of the desk.
9. Grandma's been sewing for two hours, but she still hasn't finished mending (none, any) of the socks.
10. Despite several announcements that taxes would be reduced, the governor (has, hasn't) still not followed through on his promise.
11. We scarcely (never, ever) visit this restaurant anymore.
12. Months after leaving the Dust Bowl of Oklahoma, the Judsons still hadn't found (no, any) suitable place to settle.
13. Please don't allow (anyone, no one) to enter the living room while I wrap presents.
14. Because of heavy snowfall, no trucks (could, couldn't) reach the delivery dock.

101

Rewrite It

Each sentence [...] the sentences to eliminate the double ne[...] more than one correct answer for each item.

Answers may vary. Possible answers shown.

1. We couldn't get none of the sheep into the barn before the storm hit.
   We couldn't get any of the sheep into the barn before the storm hit.
2. Carl seldom never plays chess, but when he does, he usually wins.
   Carl seldom ever plays chess, but when he does, he usually wins.
3. Marty wouldn't give nobody a turn riding his new skateboard.
   Marty wouldn't give anybody a turn riding his new skateboard.
4. Ms. Reynolds didn't want to hear nobody complaining about the due dates for our reports. Ms. Reynolds didn't want to hear anybody complaining about the due dates for our reports.
5. If it keeps raining like this, we will not be going nowhere this weekend.
   If it keeps raining like this, we will not be going anywhere this weekend.
6. Don't nobody come near this stove while it's hot.
   Nobody come near this stove while it's hot.
7. Drew didn't find none of the books he needed at the library.
   Drew found none of the books he needed at the library.
8. The Lewis twins can't hardly wait for the next *Star Wars* movie to be released.
   The Lewis twins can hardly wait for the next *Star Wars* movie to be released.

Try It

Write three sentences using double negatives. Trade papers with a friend and correct each other's errors.

1.
2.
3.

Answers will vary.

102

Synonyms are words that have the same, or almost the same, meaning. Using synonyms can help you avoid repeating words and can make your writing more interesting. A thesaurus, either in book form or online, is a good source for finding synonyms.

empty/vacant   inspect/examine   casual/informal   brief/concise

Antonyms are words that have opposite meanings. A thesaurus, either in book form or online, is a good source for finding antonyms.

blunt/sharp   likely/unlikely   bold/timid   frequent/seldom

Match It

Read each set of words below. Circle the two words in each set that are synonyms.

1. renew (reliable) (dependable) unreliable
2. (mock) (ridicule) lodge comfort
3. (faithful) preserve (loyal) lonely
4. relative (negotiate) rejoice (bargain)
5. (residence) community singular (dwelling)
6. (subject) column (topic) explanation
7. assert divide (nestle) (snuggle)
8. (putrid) (rotten) fresh mysterious

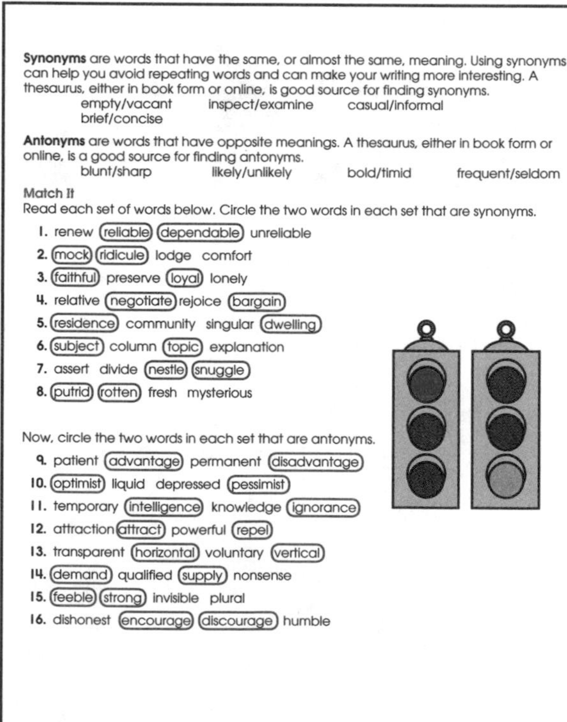

Now, circle the two words in each set that are antonyms.

9. patient (advantage) permanent (disadvantage)
10. (optimist) liquid depressed (pessimist)
11. temporary (intelligence) knowledge (ignorance)
12. attraction (attract) powerful (repel)
13. transparent (horizontal) voluntary (vertical)
14. (demand) qualified (supply) nonsense
15. (feeble) (strong) invisible plural
16. dishonest (encourage) (discourage) humble

103

Identify It

Read each sentence below. The letter in parentheses will tell you whether to look in the box for a synonym or antonym for the boldface word. Write your answer on the line.

outstanding	weaken	progress	observant	irregular
reimbursed	fertile	cheerful	unprofitable	attractive

1. (S) irregular — The temperatures this month have been **erratic**, so we won't plant the seeds quite yet.
2. (A) weaken — The builder advised that we **fortify** the porch before we build the addition.
3. (S) attractive — Grandma says that the first time she saw my grandpa, she wondered, "Who on Earth is that **comely** boy?"
4. (A) outstanding — The review said that the food at Tacos-to-Go is only **mediocre**.
5. (A) unprofitable — Fatima has come up with an idea for a summer job that we hope will be very **lucrative**.
6. (S) reimbursed — My dad will be **compensated** for the time he spends editing the proposal.
7. (A) progress — I'm hoping that Jonathan doesn't **revert** to some of his old behaviors.
8. (A) fertile — The **barren** fields have not produced a harvest in years.
9. (S) observant — Part of the reason Leah is such a good writer is that she is very **perceptive**.
10. (A) cheerful — The **dour** expression on Viktor's face told me that he was in a difficult mood.

Find It

Use a dictio[...] the following synonyms or antonyms. [...] more than one correct answer.

Answers may vary. Possible answers shown.

1. an antonym for *descend* ascend
2. a synonym for *animosity* hatred
3. a synonym for *rebuttal* reply
4. an antonym for *vacant* full
5. an antonym for *expulsion* acceptance
6. a synonym for *improbable* unlikely
7. an antonym for *immense* microscopic
8. a synonym for *illegible* unreadable

104

Answer Key

An **analogy** is a comparison between two pairs of words. To complete an analogy, figure out how the pairs of words are related.

Attract is to *repel* as *conceal* is to *reveal*.
Attract is the opposite of *repel*, just as *conceal* is the opposite of *reveal*.

Pedal is to *bicycle* as *row* is to *canoe*.
You pedal a bicycle to move it, just as you row a canoe to move it.

Zipper is to *jacket* as *lead* is to *pencil*.
A zipper is part of a jacket, just as lead is part of a pencil.

Analogies are often presented without using the phrase *is to* and the word *as*. Instead, colons are used in place of *is to*, and two colons are used in place of *as* to separate the pairs being compared.

Horse is to *hoarse* as *road* is to *rode*.
horse : hoarse : : road : rode

Solve It
To solve each analogy below, unscramble the word in parentheses and write it on the line.

1. *Goose* is to geese as *mouse* is to *mice*. (esege)
2. *Russia* is to country as *Paris* is to *city*. (rycntou)
3. *Five* is to *twenty-five* as twelve is to *one hundred forty-four*. (lvtewe)
4. *Satisfied* is to *unsatisfied* as write is to *rewrite*. (iewtr)
5. *Book* is to *read* as *ruler* is to measure. (eerasmu)
6. *Dance* is to *tango* as song is to *lullaby*. (gsno)
7. *Blender* is to kitchen as *computer* is to *office*. (thckein)
8. *Pack* is to wolves as *school* is to *fish*. (sloevw)
9. Pen is to *letter* as *keyboard* is to *e-mail*. (npe)
10. *Doe* is to *deer* as sow is to *pig*. (wso)
11. *Hola* is to *Spanish* as hello is to *English*. (lhewlo)
12. *Inch* is to *yard* as centimeter is to *meter*. (etceetimrn)

105

Complete It
Circle the letter of the word that best completes each analogy.

1. Skin : ________ : : crust : Earth.
   a. wheat (b.) apple c. nose d. moon
2. Bean : legume : : ________ : crustacean.
   a. chili b. shark c. peanut (d.) shrimp
3. Beef : cow : : ________ : pig.
   (a.) pork b. calf c. barnyard d. pen
4. ________ : yarn : : pulp : paper.
   a. knit b. draw (c.) wool d. cotton
5. Was : were : : ________ : dreamed.
   (a.) dream b. dreaming c. is d. am
6. Apple : McIntosh : : tree : ________.
   a. orange (b.) sycamore c. seed d. climb
7. Sandals : summer : : ________ : winter.
   a. flip-flops (b.) mittens c. sundress d. high heels
8. ________ : amazing : : acknowledge : respond.
   a. expect b. unusual c. respectful (d.) extraordinary
9. Mad : ________ : : happy : overjoyed.
   (a.) furious b. exhausted c. confused d. suspect
10. Sixty-three : thirty-six : : ________ : eighty-two.
    a. twenty-six b. fifteen (c.) twenty-eight d. eighty-eight

Try It
Follow the directions to write your own analogies.

1. Write an analogy in which the words are homographs.
2. Write an analogy that shows a part-to-whole relationship.
3. Write an analogy that shows a ... relationship.
4. Write an analogy that shows an object-use relationship.
5. Write an analogy in which the words are antonyms.

Answers will vary.

106

Review: Word Roots, Prefixes and Suffixes, Negatives and Double Negatives
For each suffix or prefix, locate its meaning in the box. Write the meaning on the first line, and then write an example of a word that uses the prefix or suffix on the second line.

wrongly	made of or to make	too much	state or condition of
one who	not or opposite of	without	having characteristics of

1. -or one who — director
2. over- too much — overeat
3. -en made of or to make — brighten
4. -ness state or condition of — goofiness
5. mis- wrongly — misunderstand
6. -less without — joyless
7. -ic having characteristics of — athletic
8. non- not or opposite of — nonspecific

Each sentence below contains a root or base word with a familiar prefix or suffix. Underline the root or base word, and circle the familiar prefix or suffix. (Each root or base word, prefix, and suffix was used in a previous lesson.)

1. The grav(ity) of the situation became clear as the judge entered the courtroom.
2. The crew anticipates that construct(ion) on the stadium will be completed next month.
3. In spite of the (dis)rupt(ion) the alarm caused, the students returned to the exam in just a few minutes.
4. Davis has inherited his mom's optimist(ic) outlook on life.
5. We were horrified to find that the car was unrecogniz(able) after the accident.
6. The weather station's (pre)dict(ion) for Saturday was right on target.
7. Amina's love for photograph(y) began when she was still a teenager.
8. It is quite common for people to (mis)pronounce my last name.

Underline the word or words in parentheses that best complete each sentence below.

1. Despite a lengthy e-mail correspondence last year, Brady hardly (never, ever) writes to his pen pal anymore.
2. The builder won't do (anything, nothing) until she's had a chance to speak with the architect.
3. Dante and Ava won't eat (none, any) of the foods at the potluck until they know what ingredients have been used.
4. Because the side streets had not been plowed yet, the buses couldn't go (nowhere, anywhere).

107

Review: Synonyms and Antonyms, Analogies
Read each word pair. Write **A** on the line if the words are antonyms, and write **S** on the line if the words are synonyms

1. S brief concise
2. A disgruntled pleased
3. S smug satisfied
4. S pertinent relevant
5. A approached departed
6. S necessary required
7. A captivity freedom
8. S endow grant
9. A majority minority
10. A positive negative
11. S previous former
12. A victory defeat
13. A plentiful scarce
14. S crooked askew
15. A artificial natural
16. S ominous sinister
17. S pollute contaminate
18. A qualified unqualified
19. A poverty wealth
20. S surly grumpy

Circle the word in parentheses that best completes each analogy.

1. *Reptile* is to (*vertebrate*, (*snake*)) as *mammal* is to *dolphin*.
2. *Clause* is to *claws* as *vain* is to ((*vein*), *cat*).
3. *Past* is to ((*present*), *memory*) as *peace* is to *war*.
4. *Pane* is to *window* as (*climb*, (*rung*)) is to *ladder*.
5. (*Artist*, (*Mozart*)) is to *compose* as *Monet* is to *paint*.
6. *Word* is to *dictionary* as *bristle* is to ((*brush*), *page*).
7. *Happy* is to *happiness* as ((*curious*), *sadness*) is to *curiosity*.
8. (*Classroom*, (*Principal*)) is to *school* as *surgeon* is to *hospital*.
9. *Hurricane* is to *ocean* as *tornado* is to (*cloud*, (*land*)).
10. *Potter* is to *clay* as (*sculpture*, (*writer*)) is to *words*.
11. *Dublin* is to ((*Ireland*), *city*) as *Berlin* is to *Germany*.
12. *Leap* is to *bound* as *walk* is to ((*stroll*), *swim*).

108

Homophones are words that sound the same but have different spellings and different meanings. There are hundreds of homophones in the English language.

pain - ache or soreness
pane - one section of glass in a window

gilt - covered in a thin layer of gold
guilt - remorse or regret

berries - small fruit
buries - places below ground

If you are unsure about which homophone to use, look up the meanings in a dictionary.

Complete It

Each sentence is followed by a pair of homophones in parentheses. Complete the sentence by choosing the correct homophone and writing it on the line.

1. During the avalanche, a **boulder** rolled downhill and came to rest in the middle of the highway. (bolder, boulder)
2. Rapunzel tossed her long **locks** out the window when she heard the prince's call. (lox, locks)
3. According to geological time, we live in the Holocene **epoch**. (epoch, epic)
4. Aaron Burr and Alexander Hamilton fought a **duel** in 1804. (dual, duel)
5. Grandpa Taylor told me he was **wracked** with guilt about forgetting my birthday. (wracked, racked)
6. Seventeen trapped **miners** were rescued yesterday in Australia. (minors, miners)
7. Chef Alexis **kneaded** the pizza dough for nearly ten minutes before rolling it out. (kneaded, needed)
8. Pa attached a harness to the **yoke** encircling the oxen's necks. (yoke, yolk)
9. **Adolescence** is generally considered the time period between puberty and adulthood. (Adolescents, Adolescence)
10. **Their** gym clothes were left in the locker overnight. (They're, Their)
11. After school today, **we're** going to pick up your father and head to the dentist. (were, we're)
12. Underneath the bark, the rotten wood was **teeming** with beetles and other insects. (teeming, teaming)
13. On January 12, President Romero will step down and **cede** power to her successor. (seed, cede)
14. After hiking in his new boots, Andrew's right **heel** ached from a blister. (heal, heel)
15. The **reign** of King Louis XVI ended with the French Revolution. (rein, reign)

109

Proof It

Each sentence below contains at least one error in homophone usage, and some sentences contain two errors. Use proofreading marks to correct the mistakes.

ℯ - deletes letters, words, punctuation
^ - inserts letters, words, punctuation

1. Library patrons are not ~~aloud~~ **allowed** to ~~raze~~ **raise** their voices, because the noise may disturb others.
2. Louisa ~~rapped~~ **wrapped** a gift in colorful paper and placed a big green bow on top.
3. Please ~~ewes~~ **use** the backdoor ~~win~~ **when** you deliver the refrigerator.
4. Marvin found himself counting down each ~~our~~ **hour** until he would have ~~too~~ **to** take the stage for his recital.
5. As costs rise in the future due to inflation, the impact of the new tax will ~~lesson~~ **lessen**.
6. We ~~red~~ **read** in the newspaper that an anime festival would be coming to the city.
7. A ~~not~~ **knot** in the rope keeps it from slipping through the ~~whole~~ **hole** in the board.
8. We ~~new~~ **knew** earlier in the year that we ~~wood~~ **would** be traveling to Minnesota.
9. The ~~cent~~ **scent** of fresh flowers drifted in through the open window.
10. Some old jars are left down in the ~~seller~~ **cellar**, along with a ~~pare~~ **pair** of windows from the barn.
11. Officer Ruiz let his patrol car ~~idol~~ **idle** by the curb as he went inside to investigate.
12. The flowers have ~~groan~~ **grown** ~~sew~~ **so** much taller since you added some fertilizer.

Try It

Write sentences for each pair of homophones. Be sure to use the correct meaning of the homophone in your sentence. Use a dictionary if you need help.

1. **dessert:** ______
   desert: ______
2. **taught:** ______
   taut: ______
3. **serial:** ______
   cereal: ______
4. **medal:** ______
   meddle: ______

Answers will vary.

110

Multiple-meaning words, or **homographs**, are words that are spelled the same but have different meanings. They may also sometimes have different pronunciations.

The word *refuse* can mean "trash or garbage," or it can mean "deny or reject."

The empty lot was littered with *refuse*, including broken bottles and an old mattress.
I *refuse* to believe that you read all of *War and Peace* in a single night.

Solve It

Read each pair of definitions below. Think of the multiple-meaning word that fits both definitions and write it on the lines. Then, take the first letters of the words and place them, in order, onto the lines at the end to answer the question.

1. a legal agreement; to become shorter
   c o n t r a c t
2. part of a minute; after first
   s e c o n d
3. a soft metal; have others following you
   l e a d
4. a place to come in; fill with delight or wonder
   e n t r a n c e
5. turned; an cut or other injury
   w o u n d
6. make angry; a substance burned to create a pleasant odor
   i n c e n s e
7. topic or course of study; a person who lives under the rule of a king
   s u b j e c t

What famous author wrote: "Humility is not thinking less of yourself, it's thinking of yourself less."

C. S. L e w i s

111

Rewrite It

Read each s[...] nt meaning for the underline[...]

Answers will vary. Possible answers shown.

1. My grandmother has dozens of old *Reader's Digest* magazines stored in a closet.
   I like to relax after lunch so my food can digest properly.
2. The recipe called for half a teaspoon of almond extract to be added last.
   The dentist will extract my wisdom teeth on Friday.
3. "The kids at school were upset to learn that the arts program would lose funding," said Jamal.
   Lexie bumped into the tray and upset all the glasses.
4. When teenagers rebel, it's often to show their independence.
   James Dean was considered a rebel in the 1950s.
5. After evening the boards, Sandy glued them together.
   Let's go out to eat this evening.
6. The detective took the suspect into custody and prepared to question him.
   I suspect that my mother will be home soon.
7. "That pink is too strong for this room," said Ms. Ling. "Let's try a softer shade."
   Isabelle will come along with us to the flower shop, too.
8. Bella lit a match and touched the flame to the wads of paper underneath the twigs.
   The soccer match will begin at two o'clock sharp.
9. With his baton held high, Maestro Kubelik prepared to conduct the orchestra.
   Your conduct at the store today was less than ideal.
10. First the waiters will clear the tables, and then they will serve dessert.
    It is clear to me that you want to learn computer programming.

Try It

Choose your own multiple-meaning word and use each of its meanings in a different sentence.

Multiple-meaning word: ______

Meaning #1: ______

Meaning #2: ______

Answers will vary.

112

A word's **denotation** is its actual, literal meaning. It is the meaning you would find if you looked the word up in a dictionary.

A word's **connotation** is the meaning associated with the word. The connotation may be more emotional, or tied to an idea or feeling about the word. Connotations can be positive, negative, or neutral.

For example, the words *aroma, smell,* and *stink* are all synonyms with approximately the same denotation, or actual, meaning: "odor." The connotation of these words, however, is different. *Aroma* has a positive connotation—it brings to mind the odor of baking bread or other good foods cooking. *Smell* is neutral because it can have a positive or negative connotation depending on how it is used. *Stink* has a negative connotation because it is almost always used to describe things that smell bad.

Complete It

Each row in the [...] t connotations. The first row is c[...] ppropriate words. Use a th[...]

Answers may vary. Possible answers shown.

Positive	Neutral	Negative
prudence	caution	paranoia
laid-back	relaxed	lazy
home	house	hovel
amusing	funny	ridiculous
encouraging	interested	nosy
rustic	old	dilapidated
ornate	elaborate	fussy
frugal	less expensive	cheap

113

Rewrite It

Rewrite each sentence below, replacing the underlined word with a word that has a similar denotation but different connotation. Use a thesaurus or dictionary if you need help. Then, identify the connotation of the new word by writing **P** for positive or **N** for negative on the short line. Leave the line blank if the connotation is neutral.

1. Rudy collects old newspapers and stores them in his attic.
   Rudy hoards old newspapers and stores them in his attic. N
2. Energetic children raced around the rec center, chasing each other and making a lot of noise. Wild children raced around the rec center, chasing each other and making a lot of noise. N
3. My sister has a unique way of riding her bike.
   My sister has a bizarre way of riding her bike. N
4. Lucas's flimsy model ship barely made it to school in one piece.
   Lucas's fragile model ship barely made it to school in one piece. P
5. A youthful group of teens laughed and whispered throughout the performance.
   An immature group of teens laughed and whispered throughout the performance. N
6. Shawn's reckless behavior during the game resulted in a penalty.
   Shawn's risky behavior during the game resulted in a penalty. N
7. The miserly owner seldom ever gave his employees bonuses or raises.
   The frugal owner seldom ever gave his employees bonuses or raises. P
8. Ms. Sanchez was surprised at seeing Lauren in such a casual outfit.
   Ms. Sanchez was surprised at seeing Lauren in such a sloppy outfit. N

Try It

Write a sentence for each word below. The words in each pair have similar denotations but different connotations.

1. fussy
   detailed
2. stare
   glower
3. calculated
   thoughtful

Answers will vary.

114

A **simile** is a figure of speech that compares two things using the words *like* or *as*.

The skin on my great-grandad's hands was like *the rough bark of an ancient tree.*
The fireflies in the jar were as bright as *tiny fallen stars.*

A **metaphor** is a figure of speech that compares two unlike things that are similar in some way.

The sound of the whirring fan was a lullaby that quickly put me to sleep.
The cheery yellow daffodils were a sign announcing "Spring is here!"

Personification is a figure of speech that gives human characteristics to something that is not human.

The blank computer screen *stared reproachfully* at Luke, *wondering* when he would begin his paper.

Identify It

Read each sentence below. Circle a boldface letter to indicate whether the sentence contains a metaphor, simile, or personification.

1. S M **[P]** When Paco lit the fire, the flames quickly and greedily ate the dry leaves.
2. **[S]** M P Tears ran down Grace's face, leaving shiny tracks like snails on the move.
3. S **[M]** P Dread was a mountain that loomed over Tanya.
4. **[S]** M P The baby's hair was as soft as a dandelion puff.
5. **[S]** M P Murphy's heart hung like a heavy steel weight in his chest.
6. S **[M]** P After the ice storm, the trees glittered with thousands of crystal ornaments.
7. **[S]** M P Fat snowflakes drifted to the ground like small parachutes.
8. S M **[P]** The balloon drifted higher and higher, teasing the boy who jumped for its string.
9. **[S]** M P The icy wind cut through the layers Esther wore like a freshly sharpened knife.
10. S **[M]** P The hurtful words Dominic had spoken were a wall between his mother and him.
11. S **[M]** P The stitches on Mark's leg were tiny railroad tracks leading to his ankle.
12. S M **[P]** The clock ticked impatiently, urging Toshi to hurry up.

115

Rewrite It

Rewrite each [...] n to make the writing more c[...] be of figure of speech at lea[...]

Answers will vary. Possible answers shown.

1. Brandon worried about his upcoming math test.
   Brandon's upcoming math test was a monster lurking around the corner.
2. The mug shattered on the floor.
   The mug shattered on the floor like a bomb exploding.
3. A flock of starlings flew into the maple tree.
   A flock of starlings flew into the maple tree like arrows.
4. Myla's dog scurried under the couch when she heard the thunder.
   Myla's dog scurried under the couch when she heard the thunder, and the dark space embraced and relaxed her.
5. The plane left a white trail behind it in the sky.
   The plane left a white trail behind it in the sky, like a chalk mark drawn across blue slate.
6. The giraffe nibbled at the leaves of the tree.
   The giraffe nibbled at the leaves of the tree, its tongue a snake wrapping around each piece of green.
7. The morning glory vine twined around the mailbox post.
   The morning glory vine danced in circles up the mailbox post.
8. Connor flipped on the stereo and covered his ears as music blasted from the speakers.
   Connor flipped on the stereo and covered his ears as the music blaring from the speakers assaulted him.
9. Through the open window, I could hear the waves washing up on the beach.
   Through the open window, I could hear the waves washing up on the beach, steady as a clock.
10. Peter and Phong jumped as high as they could on the trampoline.
    Peter and Phong jumped as high as they could on the trampoline, like a pair of acrobats performing in a circus.

116

Answer Key

Verbal irony is when a statement's literal meaning is different from, or even opposite of, its intended meaning.

When Beth saw her favorite teapot lying in pieces on the floor, she said, "Oh, great. I was hoping that would happen." (Beth is saying the opposite of what she means.)

A **pun** is a humorous play on words. Puns are often based on similar-sounding words or multiple-meaning words.

Vladimir Putin never slows down; he's always *Russian*. (*Russian* is used instead of *rushing*.)

"Where does a spy go at bedtime?" Rani asked. "Undercover!"(*Undercover* refers to both "in disguise" and "under the covers in bed.")

Hyperbole is exaggerating for effect. The exaggeration is extreme and obvious, so it is not meant to be taken seriously.

By the time we got to the theater, the ticket line was a hundred miles long, so we decided to leave.

Identify It

Identify each example below with **I** for irony, **P** for pun, or **H** for hyperbole.

1. I My brother left the door wide open when he came home, so I told him, "Thanks for airing out the front hall. Mom will really appreciate it."
2. H This song is so hard. It'll be years before I learn all the notes!
3. P I've been to the dentist plenty of times; I know the drill.
4. H Look at that sandwich. There must be a million ants crawling on it.
5. P The ringing bell tolled us it was time to leave.
6. I As Louis looked out at the pouring rain, he said, "It's just a lovely day, isn't it?"
7. P It was foggy this morning, but I woke up late and mist it.
8. H Today was so cold, I saw a penguin wearing a parka.
9. I Matthew handed the comic back to his younger brother and said, "Nothing makes me feel as grown-up as reading books with pictures."
10. H We must have walked a thousand miles to get to this side of the airport!

117

Try It

Use the descrip[tions] ... verbal irony. **Answers will vary. Possible answers shown.**

1. A classm[ate disturbs] you while you are studying. What do you say to him or her?
   verbal irony: Thanks for being so helpful!
2. You visit the observation deck on the top floor of the tallest skyscraper in the city. What do you say as you look out the windows?
   hyperbole: I think I can see for a million miles!
3. You visit the grocery store on the night before Thanksgiving. It is as crowded as you've ever seen it. What do you say?
   hyperbole: We had to wait in line for hours to pay!
4. You see a bicyclist weaving dangerously through the cars in a traffic jam. What do you say about it?
   verbal irony: That sure is a safe way to travel!
5. You arrive to class several minutes late. What do you say to the teacher if you're trying to be funny?
   verbal irony: It's a good thing I got here early!
6. You've just completed a very difficult exam. How do you describe it?
   hyperbole: Einstein couldn't have passed that test!

Write the word that completes each pun.

1. Turtles talk on shell phones.
2. Fish are smart because they live in schools.
3. Wolves like cards because they come in packs.
4. Don't try to use that broken pencil; it's pointless.
5. You can't beat a hard-boiled egg for breakfast.
6. A golfer wore two pairs of pants to the course just in case he got a hole in one.

118

Review: Homophones, Multiple-Meaning Words

Read each definition. Choose the correct homophone from the box, and write it on the line beside the definition.

lightning	they're	mustered	mustard	fourth
ceiling	forth	sealing	their	lightening

1. ceiling the top of an enclosed room
2. lightening making something less dark
3. forth onward or outward from a place or time
4. mustered assembled or gathered
5. mustard spicy yellow or brown sauce
6. their a plural possessive pronoun
7. lightning bright electrical discharge, usually from a cloud
8. fourth after third
9. sealing closing tightly
10. they're contraction formed from *they* and *are*

Read each sent[ence] ... meaning for the underlined w[ord]. **Answers will vary. Possible answers shown.**

1. Hank's library card was invalid because it had expired over the summer.
   Uncle Joseph is an invalid and must live in a nursing home.
2. I'm avoiding Rachel today, because I refuse to subject myself to her rudeness.
   Please identify the main subject of the essay.
3. Judge Unger ruled that a 5-year sentence would be excessive for minor vandalism.
   What end mark belongs at the end of this sentence?
4. Please conduct yourself with grace and humility when you meet the Queen.
   Your conduct this evening was superb.
5. Mr. Jenkins showed us several slides from his vacation to Europe during the 1970s.
   The metal slides at the park are being replaced with plastic ones.
6. Hydrogen is listed first on the periodic table of elements.
   You mother brought the flowers sitting on the table.
7. "I'll be with you in a minute, Mr. Fields," said Daisy.
   Even a minute scratch can affect the quality of a DVD.
8. Dr. Munson placed a cold compress on Eliza's bruised ankle.
   Compress the paper between these boards to remove as much water as possible.

119

Review: Conno[tations and Denotations]

Write a sentenc[e] ... [b]y adding whether the w[ord] ... has a positive, neutral, or negative connotation. **Answers will vary. Possible answers shown.**

1. **odd** I thought Lindsey was acting a bit odd tonight, didn't you?
   neutral
2. **pride** Abby's pride kept her from apologizing.
   negative
3. **wild** The zoo has an exhibit of wild birds from Madagascar.
   neutral
4. **immature** Saplings are immature trees.
   neutral

Each sentence below contains a simile, a metaphor, or personification. Underline each figure of speech, and write **S**, **M**, or **P** on the line to tell what type of figure of speech it is.

1. The flag on top of the fort waved invitingly, announcing a warm, sheltered place for us to spend the evening. P
2. The old photo album was a time machine carrying us back to more youthful days. M
3. As the wrecking ball drew back for a final swing, the last wall of the abandoned factory bravely awaited its fate. P
4. Like metal balls bouncing around inside a pinball machine, the squirrels chased each other in zigzag patterns across the lawn. S
5. The red sun sank in the west, a ship carrying the final moments of the day out of sight beyond the horizon. M
6. The field of wildflowers stretched before us like an ocean of green littered with confetti. S

Identify each example below with **I** for irony, **P** for pun, or **H** for hyperbole.

1. After working all afternoon in the scorching heat, Matthew exclaimed, "I'm so hot, you could fry an egg on my head!" H
2. When Emma's little sister asked her to tell the story of *Goldilocks and the Three Bears*, Emma replied, "I bear-ly remember how it goes!" P
3. Paul noticed there were two dozen pies on the dessert table at the potluck, so he remarked, "Gee, do you think we have enough pie?" I
4. At the little kids' tea party, Louisa pointed to her teddy bear and said, "He doesn't want any food. He's stuffed." P

120